The COOK'S GARDEN

RADISH
BEET

The COOK'S GARDEN

For cooks who garden and gardeners who cook

Mary Browne, Helen Leach & Nancy Tichborne

REED

To our parents, Peggy and Harvey Keedwell,
who kindled our enthusiasm for gardening.

Published by Reed Books, a division of Reed Publishing (NZ) Ltd, 39 Rawene Rd, Birkenhead, Auckland. Associated companies, branches and representatives throughout the world.

ISBN 0 7900 02019

First published 1980
Reprinted 1981, 1982 (twice), 1983, 1985, 1987, 1990, 1993, 1996

Printed in Hong Kong

Contents

Acknowledgements

Many relatives and friends have contributed to the production of this book by filling in the gaps in our knowledge and experience, donating produce for drawing and cooking, typing and proofreading the manuscript and caring for the smaller members of our families at crucial times. Nancy would like to extend special thanks to Jan Whaley, Prue Townsend, Mandy Stock, Murray Linton C.B.E. and Bryan Tichborne, all of Rotorua. Mary is especially grateful to Mike Browne, Elsie Browne and Wendy Holt for their help, and to her friends in Christchurch who contributed ideas and recipes. Rex Davis and Harvey Keedwell of Akaroa have given us the benefit of their many years of vegetable-growing experience and in Dunedin Jill Hamel, Jenny Cave and Bernard and Thelma Leach have provided invaluable information and support.

We are also grateful to the writers and illustrators of the many gardening and cookery books which have inspired us over the years. We would particularly like to mention Tui Flower and Alison Holst, who have done so much for New Zealand cooking in recent years, and Margaret Costa and Elizabeth David, our favourite English cookbook authors. Some of the gardening works which proved most useful are listed at the end of this book.

Finally we should like to thank the following seed and plant suppliers for providing seed catalogues, brochures and stock lists:

Watkins Seeds Ltd. P.O. Box 468, New Plymouth

Arthur Yates and Co. Ltd. P.O. Box 1109, Auckland 1

F. Cooper Ltd. P.O. Box 12347, Penrose, Auckland

C.J. Law Ltd. P.O. Box 47-076, Auckland 1

Parva Plants. R.D. Tauranga

M.E.B.
H.M.L.
N.M.T.

Preface

The idea for this book sprang from a casual remark made in 1977 at a family reunion in Rotorua. The conversation turned so frequently to the subject of growing and cooking vegetables that a suggestion that we should collaborate on a gardener's cook book (or a cook's gardening book) seemed quite logical. Each of us could utilise our own special field of interest: Mary wanted an excuse to sort over many recipes that she had tried and modified to suit local varieties. She also saw an opportunity to try out some of her own recipes on an unusually co-operative family who were keen to act as guinea pigs for the cause. Nancy saw a chance to illustrate her conception of the ideal back garden — productive, attractive and orientated to family living. In the course of preparing landscape designs for her clients, she had felt a growing need for an integrated approach which would involve vegetable gardens as well. Helen regarded the assembling of horticultural notes as an opportunity to learn more about modern gardening practices; she had just finished writing a thesis on prehistoric horticulture in New Zealand.

In the final product, these divisions of interest have been largely maintained, although each of us has contributed material to Mary's recipe sections and Helen's gardening notes. Nancy was solely responsible for the drawings.

Mary Browne
Nancy Tichborne
Helen Leach
30 June 1978

ABBREVIATIONS AND NOTES

Abbreviations

tb —tablespoon
dsp—dessertspoon
tsp —teaspoon
c —cup
ml —millilitre
g —gram
kg —kilogram
cm —centimetre
mm—millimetre
°C —degrees Celsius

degrees Celsius (°C) (to nearest 10°C)		degrees Fahrenheit (°F)
140	—	275
150	—	300
160	—	325
180	—	350
190	—	375
200	—	400
220	—	425
230	—	450

Measurements All measures should be level.
N.Z. standard kitchen measures have been used for all the recipes.
1 cup (c) holds 250 ml
1 tablespoon (tb) holds 15 ml
1 dessertspoon (dsp) holds 10 ml
1 teaspoon (tsp) holds 5 ml

Equivalents (to the nearest 5 grams)

Grams		Ounces
30	—	1
55	—	2
85	—	3
100	—	3½
115	—	4
140	—	5
170	—	6
200	—	7
225	—	8
285	—	10
340	—	12
400	—	14
455	—	16 (1 pound)

Herbs

Quantities given are for fresh herbs. If you are using dried herbs, halve the quantity specified.

Stock

Although homemade stocks are best, instant stock powders and cubes have their place providing they are used with care. Excessive saltiness is the main problem. Do not add salt to any recipe containing an instant stock until you have tasted it.

Grated cheese

Cheese goes well with so many vegetables that we find it convenient to have a supply of grated cheese always on hand. Either grate dry tasty cheddar and store it in a jar in the refrigerator or buy commercially-packed grated Parmesan cheese. Parmesan cheese is very tasty and only a small amount is needed to flavour a recipe.

Sealing pickles and relishes

Cellophane covers, although ideal for jam, are not satisfactory for relishes or pickles. The vinegar tends to evaporate and the contents become dry and shrunken. Save jars with plastic or laquered metal self-sealing lids which provide airtight storage.

The setting point of jam or jelly

1. Using a sugar thermometer:
   Most jams will set at a temperature of 104°C (220°F) though sometimes a degree higher may give better results.
2. Saucer test:
   Spoon a little jam on to a saucer and leave to cool for a minute or two. If it wrinkles when pushed with a finger it is ready.
   We combine both these tests to determine the setting point.

Introduction

Cooks and gardeners

This book is written for cooks who want to garden and gardeners who want to cook. In this century it has become common practice for husbands and fathers to grow vegetables for wives and mothers to cook. You might remember your own father or grandfather proudly washing his carrots under the garden tap before presenting them at the back door. But this division of labour between the sexes is not as old as you might think. In many traditional societies of Oceania, Asia, America and Africa, women both grew vegetables and cooked them because their husbands and male relatives were often far from home engaged in fishing, hunting or the gathering of raw materials. Women, as the bearers and rearers of small children, could not be so mobile. In prehistoric New Zealand the heavy work of felling trees and cutting down burnt scrub in spring was performed by men before the main fishing began. Day-to-day weeding in the summer was women's work. Everyone participated in the harvest.

Today there are signs of greater flexibility in the division of labour, and we know of many men who are quite at home in the kitchen and an equal number of women who grow all the vegetables needed by their families. Just who should garden and who should cook must be left up to the individual members of each household who may make their decision on the basis of personal interests, physical limitations, career requirements or family responsibilities. We are not trying to urge busy mothers out into the vegetable garden or tired businessmen into the kitchen. What we have in mind is improving the lines of communication between cooks and gardeners, making it easier for each to switch roles or take on both and making the backyard vegetable garden, like the kitchen, more of a focal point of family life.

There are good, practical reasons for improving this dialogue between cooks and gardeners. Many wives find themselves working late on the eve of their summer holidays shelling peas or slicing beans for freezing because their husbands planted too many rows at the wrong time of the year. Many husbands will have watched a beautiful summer cabbage go limp and grey in the vegetable box because the rest of the family wanted lettuce and tomatoes after a hot day on the beach. With a little more co-operation the garden could be planned to supply small amounts of "greens" at frequent intervals to avoid wastage, and large amounts for freezing when there are lots of helpers and sufficient time for processing. The tendency to grow vegetables like kohlrabi to tennis-ball size when they taste much better at golf-ball size would disappear if the cook played a more active role in the harvest and the

THE IDEAL BACK GARDEN

The ideal vegetable garden slopes gently towards the afternoon sun. Plots 1, 2 and 3 are designed for crop rotation. These plots are 2·4 m × 5 m. Flowering perennials and annuals are also included for beauty and for picking: marguerites, golden rod, agapanthus, iris, bergenia, red hot pokers, geraniums in pots, lavender and French marigolds. Below the crabapple are spring bulbs and variegated periwinkle.

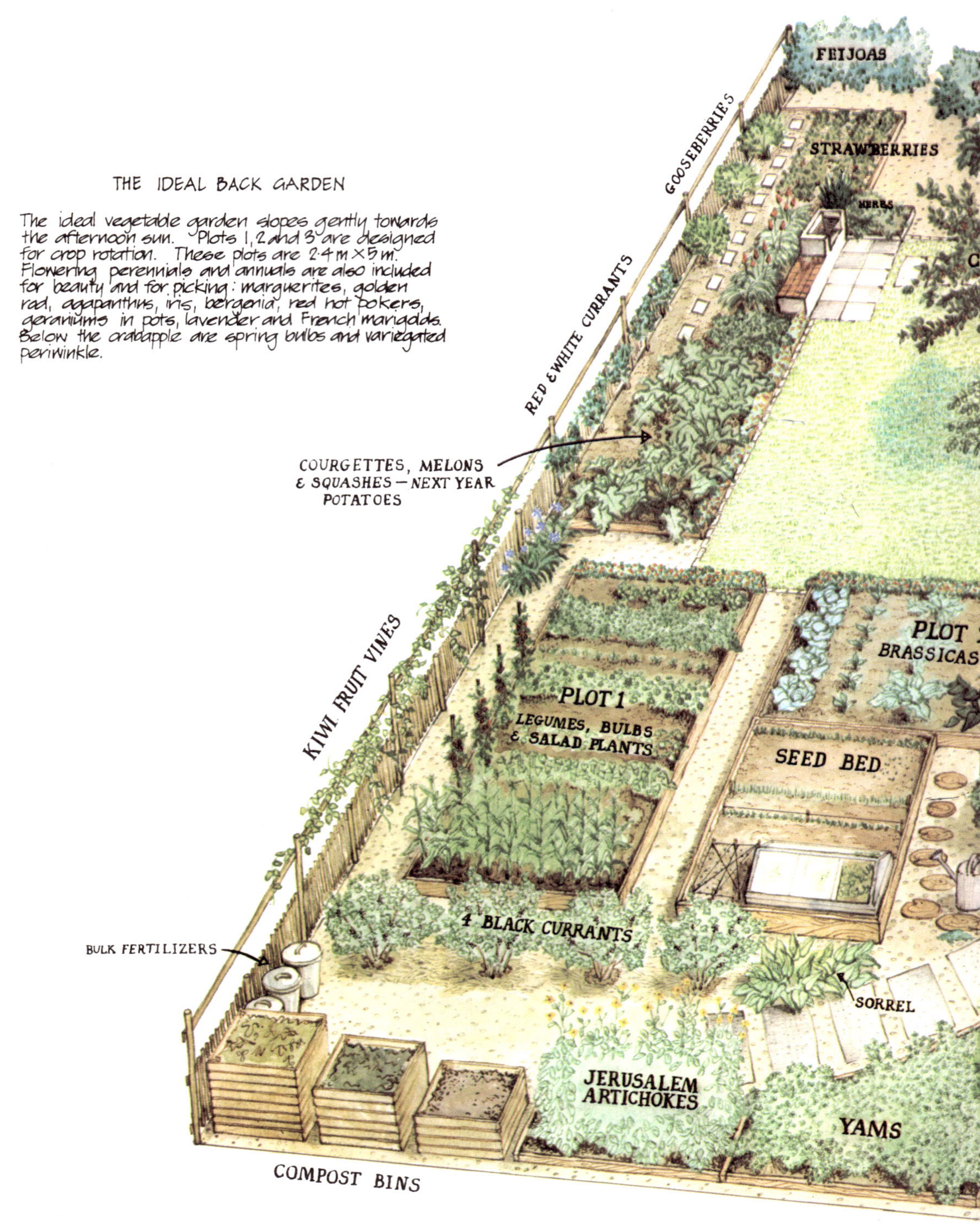

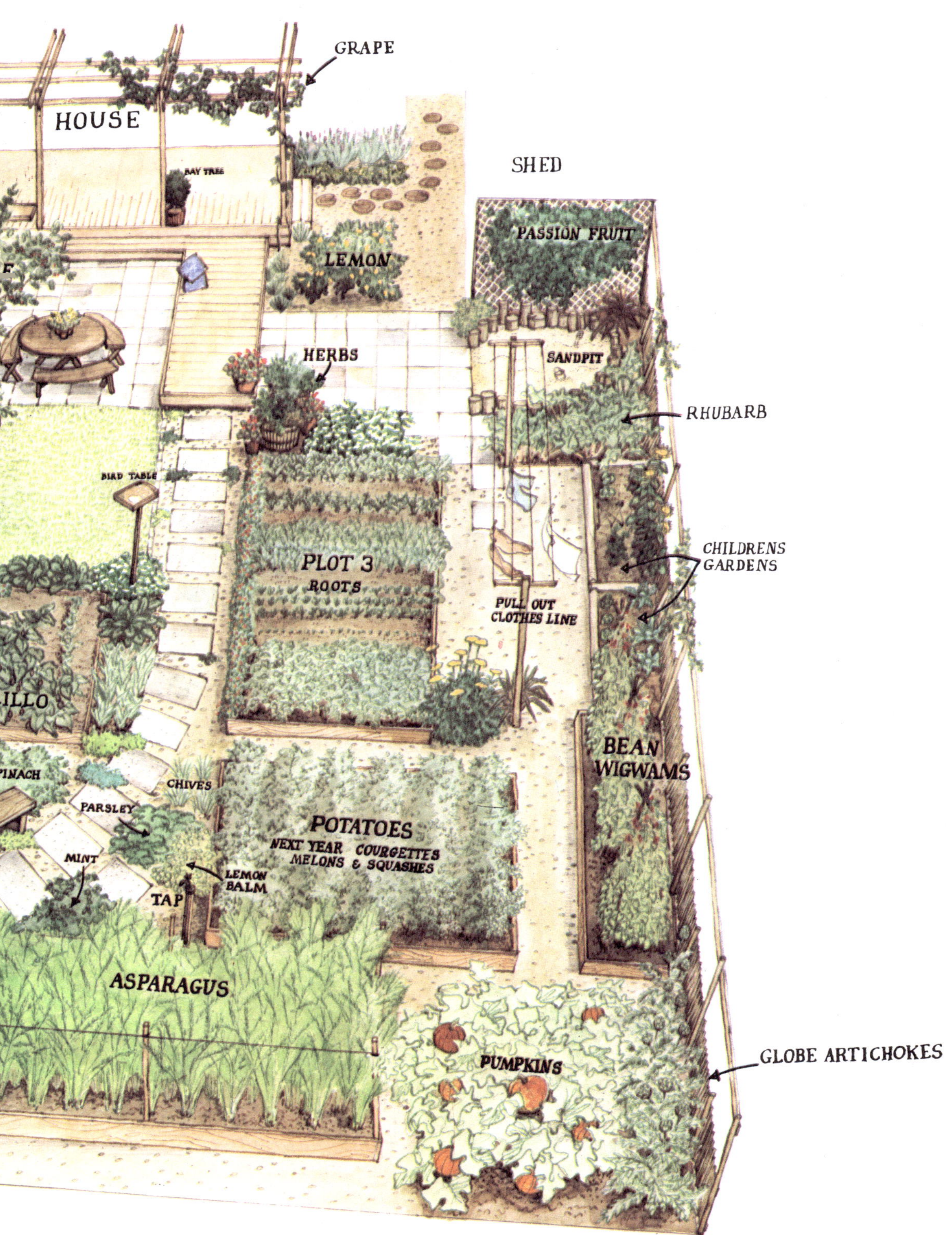
GRAPE
HOUSE
SHED
PASSION FRUIT
LEMON
HERBS
SANDPIT
RHUBARB
BIRD TABLE
PLOT 3
ROOTS
PULL OUT
CLOTHES LINE
CHILDRENS
GARDENS
CHIVES
PARSLEY
BEAN
WIGWAMS
POTATOES
NEXT YEAR COURGETTES
MELONS & SQUASHES
MINT
LEMON
BALM
TAP
ASPARAGUS
PUMPKINS
GLOBE ARTICHOKES

gardener kept comments on his produce at the meal table in the right perspective.

Costs and benefits

Sellers of seeds, sprays and garden chemicals emphasise the cheapness of home-grown vegetables in their springtime advertisements. But they don't include the gardener's time, nor the cost of the petrol used in carting fertilizer. We know of some gardeners who travel 50 or 60 km for a few "cheap" bales of straw or mushroom compost, and we often spend several hours a week weeding and thinning out in springtime. A more realistic accounting of home gardening costs might therefore show market produce in a better light. But should one include labour costs when the weeding is done on a quiet spring evening with the smell of wallflowers and viburnum in the air? Should one count petrol costs when the children thoroughly enjoyed their outing in the country and everyone helped to shovel compost on to the trailer?

Writers of vegetable gardening books often stress the superior flavour of home-grown vegetables and the wider range of varieties. Those advocating strict organic gardening warn us, too, of the unknown long-term effects of selective weed killers and chemicals used in weeding, spraying, storing and processing produce. "Survival" and "subsistence" gardening books talk of preserving horticultural skills in expectation of the collapse of urban life and our complex technology, necessitating a return to a simpler economy. Depending on your particular philosophy, one or more of these reasons may be your motivation for growing your own vegetables.

Our philosophy of gardening encompasses all these factors but builds them on a foundation which is rather less explicit. We believe growing and eating your own vegetables is a satisfying experience, and it is good for you. The various stages of preparing the ground, caring for the plants and harvesting involve physical exertion which keeps the body trim and fit. Why play squash when you can grow and eat one? Gardening is an acknowledged therapy for taut minds and tense muscles and it is often cited by centenarians as a contributing factor to longevity. Horticulture has been practised by mankind for more than 8000 years and is at least as ancient as animal husbandry and cereal cropping. Some of our feelings of pleasure and satisfaction with what we grow could therefore emanate from an almost instinctive level. Just as the process of evolution has endowed us with pleasurable sensations when we perform vital activities such as eating and procreating, perhaps the satisfaction we feel when we cultivate the soil reflects the evolutionary value of gardening.

Time and space

At one time the traditional quarter-acre garden could supply nearly all the vegetable and small fruit requirements of a five-to-six-member family, and allow for crop rotation and green manuring, (both methods of maintaining fertility and productiveness). But there is an increasing trend for larger gardens to be divided and sold, to reduce maintenance time.

In new areas urban pressures have reduced garden sizes even further, resulting in a complete change in the proportions of lawn, flower garden and vegetable garden. Lawns have shrunk to little squares around clothes lines with narrow flower borders along their edges. Front gardens have become havens for pebbles, heaths and conifers, and vegetable gardens have withdrawn to an unwanted corner up against the back fence.

If people with small gardens want to continue their traditional cultivating interests they need to integrate their flower garden, vegetable garden and outdoor living areas. Why should the most productive garden of all, the vegetable plot, be hidden from view and located as far away from the kitchen as possible? Just as kitchens are often the true heart and hub of a house where the family gathers for meals and conversation, the "open-plan" vegetable garden can easily become a delightful place in which to relax, cook and eat.

PART 1

Getting started with vegetable gardening

The ideal back garden

When we were children we spent many hours drawing and describing imaginary islands on which we placed romantic castles, farms, forests and treasure coves. Perhaps the adult version of the island is the ideal garden or small farm holding, now appearing as elaborate and detailed drawings in many books and articles on self-sufficiency. We have presented our ideal garden as a source of visual inspiration and not as a model or plan of a real garden to be copied by our readers. For in reality, failures in vegetable gardening go hand and hand with successes. A good season for dwarf beans may be a bad one for beetroot. Not only do growing seasons differ in the amount and distribution of dry sunny spells, but also in the behaviour of pests and diseases which attack crops. So don't judge your gardening efforts against this plan, nor against the coloured photographs of lush vegetable plots which appear in glossy magazines. Even cameras lie when recording real gardens, for the camera position is invariably chosen to avoid untidy corners or unthrifty plants and the magnification is never sufficient to reveal colonies of aphids or fat green caterpillars.

The real test of a vegetable garden is how well it produces from season to season and from year to year. This productivity cannot be captured in a single illustration or a carefully selected photograph. The true purpose of a garden drawing is to remind us that the garden is a functioning whole in which ground is prepared, seed sown, plants fed, watered and harvested and waste products returned to the soil.

The ideal climate and location

Our ideal back garden is set in a mild but temperate zone where there is a well defined winter, when growth slows right down for two to three months and a series of light frosts knock back garden pests and diseases. It is a zone where carrots, parsnips and cabbages can be left in the ground over winter to be harvested as required, without fear of the plants bolting to seed or rotting. In this location, the growing season for tender plants stretches over at least six months (when monthly mean temperatures average over 15°C), so that ridge cucumbers, outdoor tomatoes, sweet corn and sweet potatoes can be grown with reasonable success every year.

The garden slopes gently towards the afternoon sun. This orientation avoids rapid thawing of frost on plants, which may rupture the leaf cells. The gentle slope contributes to good drainage. Shelter from cold winter winds is supplied by a hedge which is separated from the garden beds by a wide path to prevent the hedge roots robbing the garden of moisture and nutrients. On the sunny side of the garden, summer breezes are tempered by an open-boarded fence lined with small-fruit bushes such as gooseberries and blackcurrants. At the bottom of the garden allowance is made for cold air to drain out of the plot instead of accumulating in a frost pocket. No tall trees can be found within 15 m of the vegetable garden for the majority of vegetables are sun-lovers and gross feeders, needing far more nourishment than flowers and ornamental shrubs. In competition with tree roots, vegetables are usually the losers.

The ideal soil

The soil of the ideal garden is a fertile loam derived from geologically recent deposits, either volcanic or alluvial in origin. This means that it is well endowed with the necessary elements, is easy to work because of the amount of sand or ash mixed with the silt and clay particles and yet retains adequate moisture for steady plant growth in summer. It warms up reasonably quickly in spring to allow for the sowing of mid summer crops such as peas, beans and lettuces. In addition it has deep topsoil (30-50 cm), which provides the essential vegetable nutrients, making it ideal for root crops such as carrots and parsnips.

The pH of this topsoil is between six and seven, which means it is slightly acid, a condition which most vegetables prefer. Where members of the cabbage family are planted as well as peas and beetroot, the soil has been lightly limed bringing the pH level closer to neutral. As light applications of lime wash out of the topsoil, especially in winter, this area becomes suitable after one or two seasons for plants which prefer more acid conditions (like strawberries and potatoes).

Compost, fertilizers and manure

If soil, sunshine and water are the essential elements for gardens in general, compost (a homemade supply of decayed organic matter) is the essential ingredient of a productive vegetable garden. When you consider how little of the flower garden or shrubbery is ever removed compared with the vegetable garden, it is not surprising that so much more nourishment must be returned to the vegetable plot. Just think of the quantity of potatoes, pumpkins, cabbages and onions that can be harvested from one back yard in a single season. Although 75-95 per cent is water, dry matter composed of elements such as potassium, phosphorus, calcium and nitrogen must constitute many kilos of the total harvest. If this is not restored productivity inevitably declines.

One method of returning these elements to the soil is to purchase concentrated fertilizers such as superphosphate, sulphate of ammonia, nitrate of soda and sulphate of potash. If correctly applied these can rapidly increase the yield of a particular crop, but if they are used as the sole source of nutrients, the soil structure deteriorates by compaction and cultivation to a point where the plant roots are so constricted that they can no longer utilise the fertilizer. An open, friable soil structure is maintained by regular additions of humus or decayed vegetable matter. Humus can be "imported" into the vegetable garden in the form of sacks of leaves, seaweed, old sawdust or bales of straw. These materials can be rotted down on vacant plots or applied as a mulch around growing plants, or they may be decomposed in compost bins. We prefer to rot fresh organic matter in compost bins, because if the rotting process takes place in the garden it "borrows" nitrogen which would otherwise be available for growing plants.

The compost bins illustrated in the ideal garden consist of three stacks of square frames placed side by side. In the tallest, layers of soft annual weeds and grass clippings (not docks, dandelions, oxalis or couch) are interspersed with kitchen waste such as peelings, banana skins and tea leaves, and with blood and bone and animal dung which speed up the rotting process and convert the various materials into humus.

As the heap is built up decomposition spreads up through the middle. After six weeks (or two to three months in winter) the contents of this bin are forked into the centre bin and any undecomposed portions are moved into the centre of the pile. When the heat dies down this now smaller pile can be shovelled into the third bin for future use in the garden. Meanwhile, the process can begin again in the first bin. The rich, black, finished compost can be spread around plants as a fertilizing mulch or laid at the bottom of a trench into which celery or leeks are planted. In late autumn it can be strewn over the surface of roughly-dug ground to be broken up and washed into the topsoil during winter rains. Many gardeners have found that if this type of compost is made with liberal quantities of animal dung (for example, several sacks of poultry droppings a year) no artificial inorganic fertilizers need to be used. It is almost impossible to apply too much compost to a vegetable plot, so the dangers of burning tender plants with an overdose of nitrate of soda can be completely avoided.

Green manuring is another method of increasing the humus in the soil. This is only possible in a large garden where plots are empty for three to four months at a time. Lupin, mustard or oat seeds are sprinkled on the surface, raked in, watered and allowed to grow to a point just before seed heads are formed. The crop is then dug under and left to rot for at least six weeks before vegetables are grown in the same spot. Except for leguminous green crops, such as lupin, which increase the available nitrogen in the soil, green manuring does not add

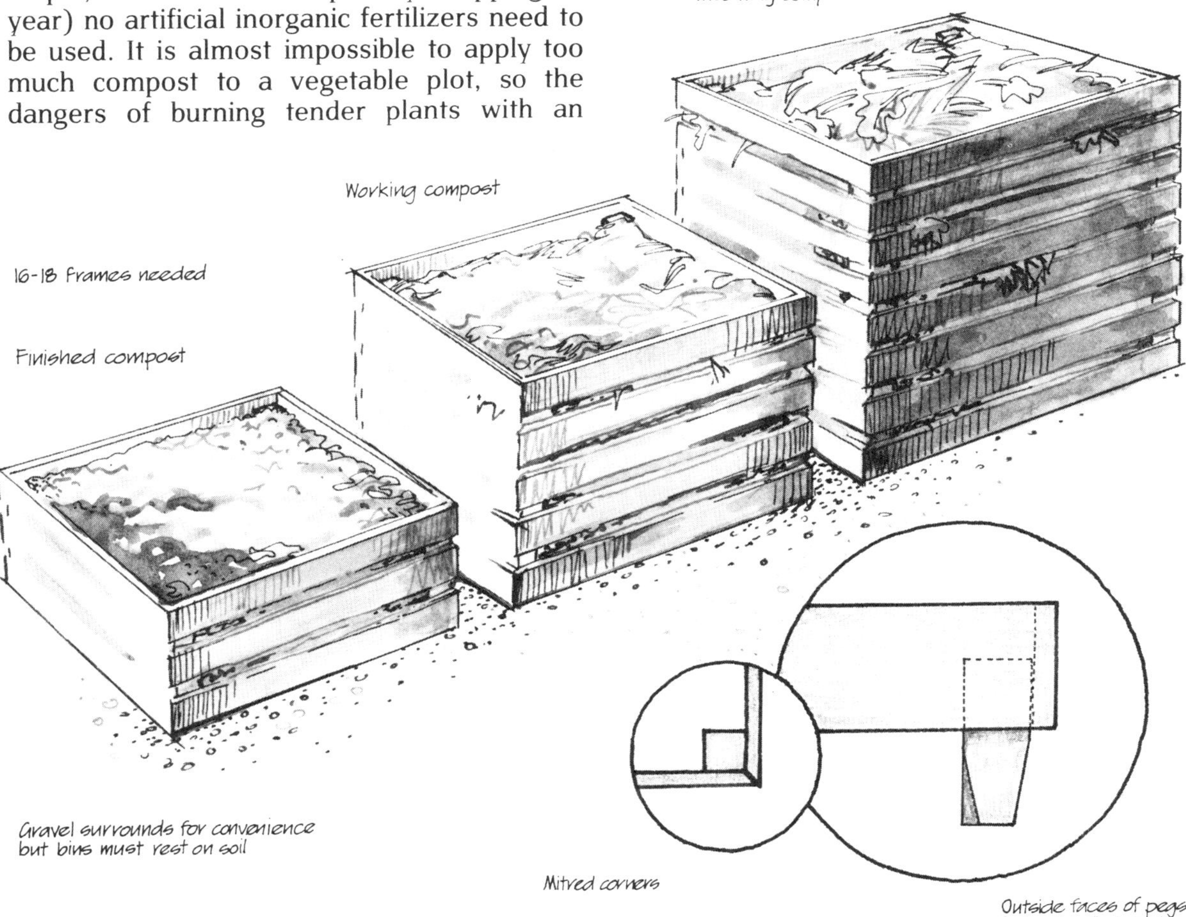

Another composting method

30cm x 5cm x ·36cm timber box reinforced at the corners. Lever frames up with iron rods as required

to the nutrients. But it is an excellent source of humus and in high-rainfall areas it prevents compaction of the surface of empty plots.

Animal manures such as crushed sheep dags, stable litter and poultry droppings can also be dug directly into the soil, but if these are fresh allow a period of six weeks before sowing and planting. If you need to use the ground immediately, bury the manure in trenches or holes well beneath the seedlings or young plants, so that their tender roots are not "burnt" by contact with the decomposing dung.

Where to obtain organic matter for composting and mulching

Baled straw (pea, barley, etc. must not have been sprayed with selective weed killers)	Farms and some agricultural merchants
Spoiled hay	Farms
Hay-stack bottoms	Farms
Mushroom compost	Mushroom farms
Straw and dung	By-product of pastoral shows
Spent hops	Breweries

Commercial bulk fertilizer can be stored outside in metal or plastic rubbish bins with tight pressing lids

Another type of compost heap (wire netting and posts)

Sawdust (must not be from tanalised wood)	Saw-mills
Coffee grounds, cocoa husks	Food processors
Blood and bone, dried blood	Garden shops and farmers' supplies
Crushed dags	Wool stores
Sheep manure	Farms and some agricultural merchants
Chicken manure	Poultry farms
Horse manure	Stables and pony shows
Other manures (pig, cow)	Farms. Also watch your local paper for advertisements
Seaweed and lakeweed	Beaches

In many areas service organisations sell and deliver some of these materials as a means of fund-raising.

Raising seed

Some hardy root vegetables such as carrots, parsnips and turnips so resent disturbance to their roots that they are always sown directly in the open garden. In the ideal garden this poses no problems. As the ground warms up in spring, the soil is forked over and raked to a fine tilth (a texture almost like breadcrumbs mixed with coarse wholemeal flour). A V-shaped depression is made in this soft, moist soil with the back of a rake and the seed is sprinkled thinly along the row. A shallow layer of soil is raked over the seed and the ground is firmed with the front of the rake. After 7 to 21 days, depending on the type of vegetable, the seed germinates and seed leaves push their way through the moist soil. When the first true leaves appear (which allow you to distinguish with certainty between the weeds and the vegetables), the plants are watered thoroughly and thinned to the appropriate distance apart.

Certain large-seeded vegetables such as peas, dwarf beans and broad beans are also sown directly into the garden. Instead of a V-shaped hollow, a flat-bottomed trench about 20-25 cm wide and 10 cm deep is made with a draw hoe and the seeds are scattered over the bottom, so that the plants will be 3-5 cm apart. The soil is drawn over the seed and no thinning is required after germination.

To obtain an early start for plants which like a long growing season it is customary to sow their seed in boxes or in a specially-prepared seed bed located in a sheltered part of the garden. Extra warmth is obtained in cooler areas by placing a mini-glasshouse over this bed or even a permanent cold frame. The soil in

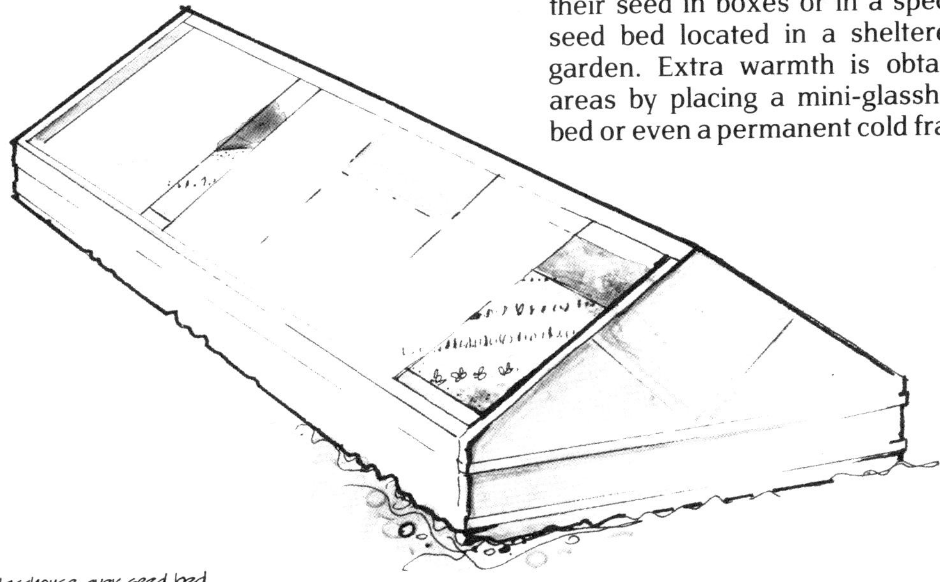

Mini glasshouse over seed bed

the seed bed is a fertile loam into which compost, blood and bone and a little lime and superphosphate was worked during the previous autumn. Just before sowing, a 3-4 cm layer of peat mixed with an equal quantity of sand is scuffled into the surface of the bed and watered thoroughly. When the ground has warmed up under the glass or polythene-covered frame, the seed can be sown in short drills about 12 cm apart and lightly covered with the peat and sand mixture. Ideally, the sand should be river sand, but beach sand from which the salt has been washed or weathered is also suitable.

Cabbages, cauliflowers, brussels sprouts and broccoli are commonly raised in seed beds as well as celery, leeks, lettuces and silver beet. Of course these can be bought as plants from garden shops and nurseries but only one or two varieties of each vegetable may be offered. After germination in the seed bed, the plants are thinned to 5-8 cm apart. Growth is usually rapid in a well situated seed bed and after a few weeks the plants can be set out in their permanent positions in the garden. Short, stocky plants transplant much better than tall, spindly ones which have been left in the seed bed too long. If a mini-glasshouse has been used over the seed bed remove the panes progressively until the plants are fully hardened off.

Rules for transplanting

1. Choose a cloudy day or cool evening.
2. Prepare planting holes in advance.
3. Don't leave roots exposed any longer than necessary.
4. Lift with plenty of soil attached to the roots.
5. When in position lightly firm the soil around the base of the plants.
6. Water well to wash soil particles into close contact with roots.

Another method of raising plants if small quantities are required for planting at intervals through spring and summer is to use small plastic containers filled with a homemade seed mix (see recipe) or a commercially-prepared product. The seed is scattered on the surface and lightly covered with the mix. After watering, the whole container is inserted into a large plastic bag and left in a warm sheltered place until the seed germinates. In early spring this

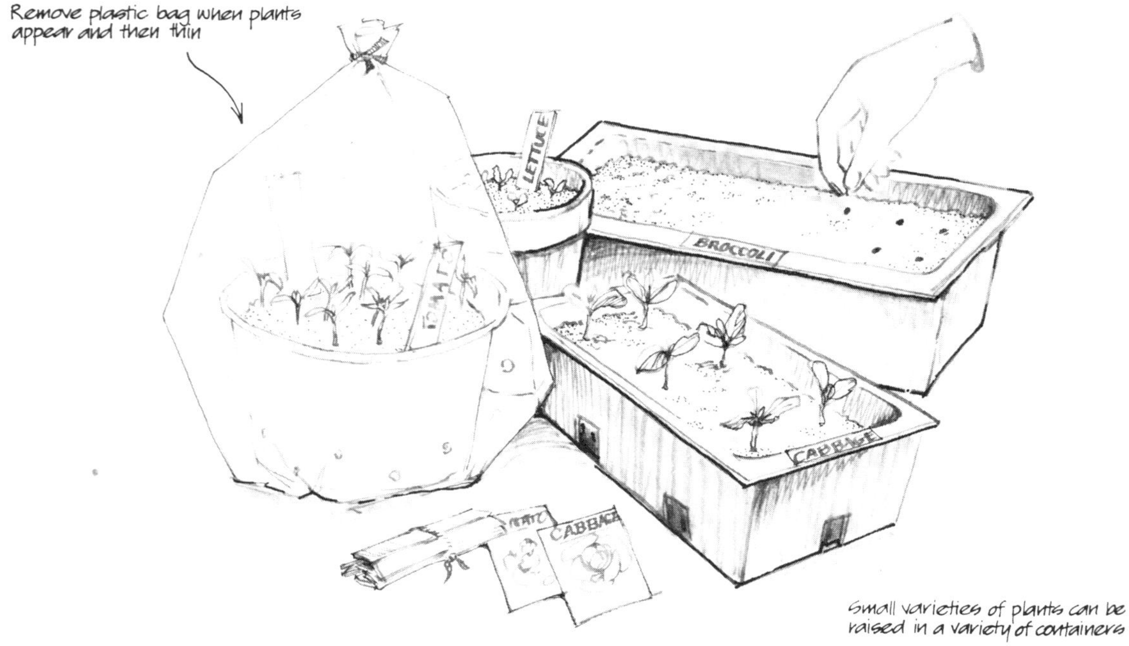
Remove plastic bag when plants appear and then thin
LETTUCE
BROCCOLI
CABBAGE
CABBAGE
Small varieties of plants can be raised in a variety of containers

can be a sunny window sill but later in the season the boxes should be placed in dappled shade. When the plants appear, the plastic bag is removed and the seedlings are thinned out to 5 cm apart and hardened off. Plants in containers need more watering than those in the seed bed, but this operation is easily performed by lowering the whole container into a large basin or baby's bath partly filled with water.

RECIPE FOR HOMEMADE SEED-RAISING MIX

N.B. (Not always as reliable as a sterilized commercial mix)

Using a 2 gallon bucket (approximately 9 litre):
½ bucket loam (as weed-free as possible)
¼ bucket moist peat or leaf mould
¼ bucket coarse sand (river sand preferable)
1 tsp lime (omit if washed sea sand is used)
1 dsp superphosphate

Thoroughly mix loam, peat or leaf mould and sand on a sheet of thick plastic. Sprinkle lime and superphosphate over heap and mix again. Pour back into the bucket. Sieve on to the plastic sheet and then pour into seedboxes.

A small group of tender plants resent root disturbance but cannot be sown in the open ground in early spring. For these, individual containers made from peat can be purchased from garden shops. They include "Jiffy" pots which are a compressed peat and fertilizer pellet wrapped in a nylon net. When soaked in water they expand to a height of 4-5 cm. Two or three seeds of tomatoes, sweet peppers or lettuces can be pushed into each one with a toothpick. After germination takes place the best plant is selected and the rest discarded. When hardened off like other container-grown plants, they are planted in the garden, pot and all. "Jiffy" pots are too small for larger seeds such as pumpkin, which produce vigorous roots. These are best planted in taller peat pots filled with your own seed mix. Once again the whole container is planted in the ground and the roots have no difficulty breaking through the peat walls. Take care to have the top edge of the pot just below the surface of the soil. If left sticking up it acts as blotting paper, evaporating water which would otherwise be used by the plant.

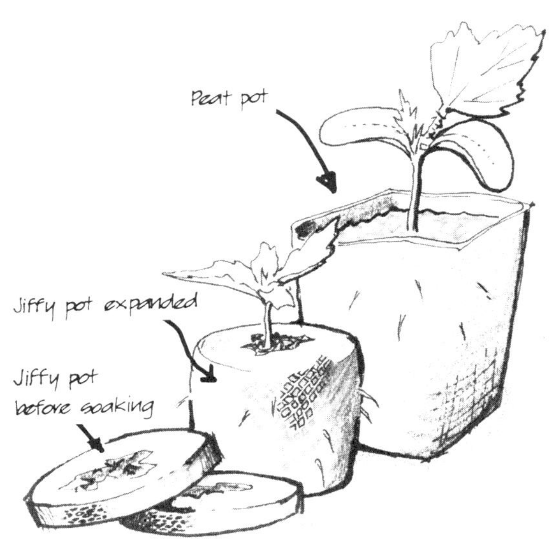

Just when seed should be sown and what varieties should be chosen varies considerably between regions. The best advice we can give you is to go for walks around your neighbourhood on weekends and spring evenings when keen gardeners are busy in their plots. Most will be delighted to tell you what peas they grow and when they plant early potatoes, for example. Some areas have gardening guides published in the form of a calendar or appearing as a weekly article in the newspaper. There may be a regular garden session on local radio. Remember to keep a garden notebook or diary, so that you can judge the performance of your crops according to varieties and improve your planting times as you gain experience.

Growing on to maturity

All vegetables respond to a deeply-dug soil into which finely broken-down compost is dug every year. If intensive gardening is practised (that is when there is never any vacant ground and two or three crops are produced from the same area in the space of a year), it is advisable to add some extra fertilizer when the ground is being prepared for each crop. The basic ingredients in the table below include two organic manures — blood and bone and dried blood — and three inorganic fertilizers — superphosphate, sulphate of ammonia and sulphate of potash. All are readily available from garden shops or farmers' supply merchants.

FERTILIZER RECIPES

General (complete) fertilizers

by volume

Either	8 parts blood and bone 1 part sulphate of potash
Or	2½ parts sulphate of ammonia 5 parts superphosphate 1 part sulphate of potash
Or	1 part sulphate of ammonia 5 parts blood and bone 2 parts superphosphate 1 part sulphate of potash

Apply 1 cup per square metre when preparing ground. Give later side dressings of liquid manure, dried blood or blood and bone for crops whose leaves are eaten.

Tomato/pepper/eggplant fertilizer

by volume

2 parts dried blood
1 part sulphate of ammonia
4 parts superphosphate
3 parts sulphate of potash

Apply ½ cup per square metre when preparing ground. When fruit is filling out apply side dressings of 1-2 teaspoons every fortnight.

Many gardening books stress the importance of crop rotation. If the vegetable plot is large enough, rotation is a sound practice as it helps to prevent a build-up of pests and diseases in the soil and makes economical use of plant foods. The general rule of rotation is that after compost and bulky manures have been dug in, legumes, and bulb and salad crops are grown, followed by brassicas (cabbages, cauliflowers, etc.) and then root crops. The last two groups are supplied with fertilizer and extra lime if needed. In small, intensively-cultivated gardens this rule often conflicts with factors of season and crop height. A row of broad beans, for example, will shade an entire plot if grown along the sunny side. So each year this should be planted towards the back of the garden. These broad beans may need to be followed by tall peas, another legume, before flower-of-spring cabbages are planted out in late autumn. Strictly speaking, peas should be grown where a root crop such as early beetroot has just been cultivated but their height may cause shading of onions, dwarf beans or other members of their group. In a small garden the principle of rotation must therefore be rewritten as a simple rule: don't grow the same crop in the same ground in successive plantings.

In the ideal garden the vegetables' water requirements are met by regular showers (preferably at night), and the humus in the ground stores water for hot, dry days. But even with regular rainfall some plants crop better if given a boost at particular stages of development. Runner beans set extra-heavy crops if the ground around their roots is thoroughly

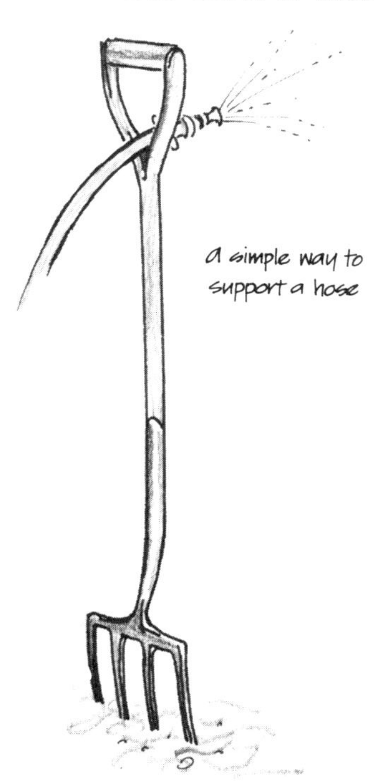
a simple way to
support a hose

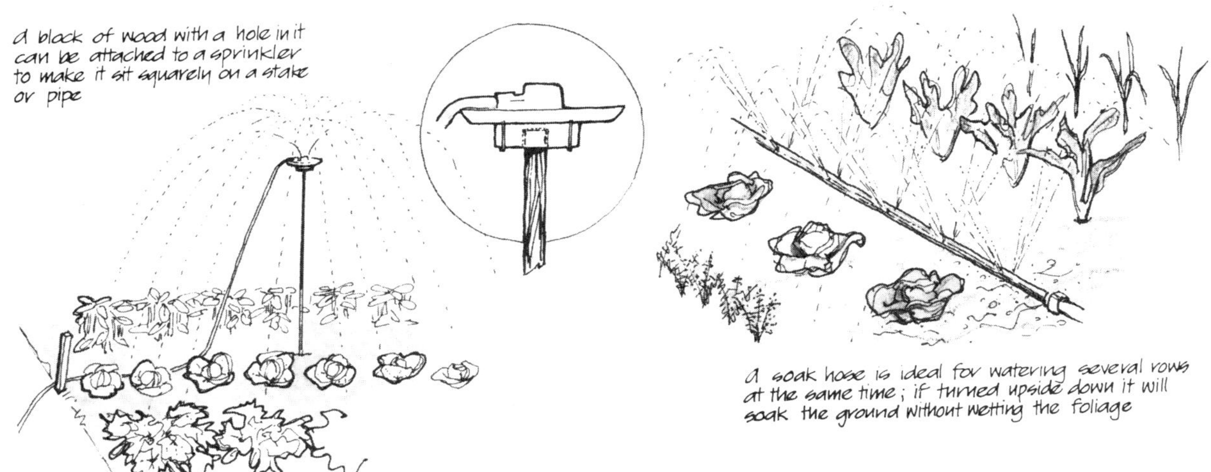

soaked at flowering time. Carrots need most water at their seedling stage and just before harvest. In general, a thorough soaking once or twice a week (depending on soil type) is better than superficial watering every day. Plants that thrive in warm conditions (such as tomatoes or peppers) should be watered in the morning before a hot day, since evening watering cools a plant and its surrounding soil by several degrees. Cool weather plants such as lettuces thrive on evening watering.

A block of wood with a hole in it can be attached to a sprinkler to make it sit squarely on a stake or pipe
A soak hose is ideal for watering several rows at the same time; if turned upside down it will soak the ground without wetting the foliage

A major cause of moisture loss in vegetable gardens is weeds, and control of these is as important as regular watering. Shallow cultivation between rows using a sharp push hoe is a good task for a hot day for if the weeds' roots are severed just below the surface the plant dies from desiccation. This sort of hoeing should be frequent, because a plant that has reached the stage of setting seed will have its sun-ripened seed scattered widely by the hoe. The loose surface soil that is created by frequent SHALLOW hoeing helps to lessen moisture loss from the firmer ground beneath; thus the practice promotes a type of dry mulch.

Modern market gardeners control weeds in many types of crops with selective weedkillers which are applied before or after the emergence of seedlings. Although some of these herbicides are sold in garden shops, they are not likely to appeal to any home gardener with lingering doubts about their long-term effects. It is also important that they are applied extremely accurately. Even a small overdose will kill the crop as well as the weeds. Hormone weedkillers have no place anywhere near a vegetable garden because certain vegetables — tomatoes and beans in particular — literally keel over from a slight whiff of the chemical. Non-selective herbicides of the paraquat type kill any vegetation with which they come in contact by desiccation. It is claimed that these herbicides are inactivated as soon as they encounter particles of clay. They may not cause any further harm to plants but containers of concentrated paraquat stored in the gardener's home are a potential danger to animals and children.

The less-than-ideal back garden(er)

So far, the ideal back gardener has been a shadowy figure in the background, cheerfully performing all the various tasks of digging, hoeing and harvesting. From our own experience we can surmise that this phantom figure has a strong back, well-muscled arms and strong flexible knees. He or she has few other demands on his or her spare time in spring and early summer, and can spend several whole Saturdays in the garden at this time of the year. The family pets have been exceptionally well trained to keep off the garden and the children are quite content to play hopscotch rather than cricket.

Of course this is an unlikely situation because the urge to grow vegetables is usually strongest in young couples with little money, a big mortgage and two or three exuberant young children. At this time of their lives they may be fit, but they are chronically busy and are usually looking after toddlers from dawn to dusk. As children grow up parents may have more time to garden, but are physically less capable as each year goes by. Slipped discs and displaced knee cartilages are major handicaps for a gardener. Even pregnancy amounts to a temporary disability and makes tasks like hand weeding and deep digging extremely difficult.

Raised beds

One solution for gardeners who experience trouble in bending or kneeling is to grow plants in raised beds. These may be square plots arranged in a grid or long, parallel strips separated by paths. Whatever pattern is used, the centres of individual beds must always be within easy reach for weeding and hoeing. The edges of the beds can be made from a variety of materials from railway sleepers to concrete blocks. When the soil is added, it should be a friable loam mixed with plenty of compost and care should be taken not to incorporate any perennial weeds as they are very difficult to eradicate. Raised beds are also advisable where gardens are waterlogged in winter and spring. In this case, coarse sand or gravel can be added to the soil in the beds to improve drainage.

"No-digging" techniques

Gardeners who cannot dig or fork their ground should experiment with mulch-gardening techniques. These create a new, friable topsoil, extremely rich in humus in which salad crops, potatoes, strawberries and most surface-rooting vegetables flourish.

The selected plot should first be cleared of vegetation or covered with several thicknesses of newspaper. On this surface spoiled hay or stack-bottom hay is piled loosely to a depth of 20-30 cm. Other bulky organic matter such as seaweed, autumn leaves or old sawdust may be incorporated, together with blood and bone and superphosphate sprinkled over the layers like a dusting of flour. If straw rather than hay is used as the primary mulching material, extra fertilizer or, preferably, animal manure should be added. The mass is left open to the weather for two to three months. After this time the bottom is dark, moist and full of worms.

Potatoes make an excellent first crop. The dry surface hay is simply pulled back and the seed potatoes placed in the blackened hay beneath. As the hay decomposes in the first season, other crops can be planted including broad beans and pumpkins. Cabbage and silver beet plants can be placed in small hollows in the mulch which should be filled with good soil to help them establish roots quickly. Each year a new layer of hay is applied to suppress weeds and keep the crops clean. After several seasons a thick new topsoil will have formed and worms will have thoroughly mixed the underlying layers. Even long-rooted vegetables such as parsnips can then be grown successfully.

This technique is best suited to light sandy or gravelly soils. On heavy clays we have found that the underlying humus is very slow to warm up in spring and that worm action is concentrated within the mulch layer for several seasons, delaying the planting of deep-rooting crops. In one location slugs and wire-worms were troublesome. However, the method is ideal for a large potato and pumpkin patch which can be virtually left alone between planting and harvesting.

Mulching

Mulching to suppress weeds and to conserve moisture is a rather different procedure. The mulch may be organic (sawdust, clean straw, lawn clippings or food processing wastes) or inorganic (black plastic, clean gravel or stones). If its primary purpose is to conserve moisture in summer it is usually applied after the ground warms up in spring, but before it dries out. It is most important to choose a mulch which is coarser in texture than the underlying soil. American experiments have shown that if the space between the particles of mulch is greater than that of the pores of the soil beneath, the mulch will act as a one-way valve, letting water into the soil and retaining it. If the space is less, water will be sucked out of the ground into the mulch and then evaporated by the sun.

Organic mulches serve several purposes: suppressing weeds, conserving moisture and eventually adding to the humus content of the topsoil. In clay soils they are dug into the ground in late autumn when no longer required as a mulch. Although black plastic cannot improve the soil, it compensates by warming it up significantly in early spring. Before the strip of ground is covered it should be shaped into a smooth, low ridge and well watered. After the covered area has had a few days of sunshine, plants are inserted into slits cut in the plastic. The method is most suitable for spring cropping because if the ground dries out beneath the plastic during the summer it is difficult to restore it to a moist condition.

Difficult clay soils

Gardening on difficult soils, especially clays and sands, has been the subject of several recent books. These invariably recommend regular heavy applications of compost and an initial heavy dose of lime (one cup per square metre). During the early stages of improving clay soils it was found that special attention to the ground immediately beneath each plant or seed row is also worthwhile. For example, instead of laboriously breaking up clay clods over the whole cabbage plot, dig holes for each plant roughly 30 cm across and deep and fill with your best soil mixed with compost, fertilizer and one tablespoon of lime. Instead of working up a fine tilth over the entire root crop area, dig a shallow trench under each row, seiving the soil that comes out. The next step is to mix the seived soil with compost and fertilizer and return most of this to the trench. The narrow seed bed is now ready for sowing and the remaining portion of sievings is used to cover the seed.

Windy gardens

Exposed gardens also pose problems. Windbreaks of hardy shrub varieties such as phebalium need to be established quickly. Flax makes a fast-growing hedge, especially if sheltered initially by bales of straw. Strong open-slatted fences also make good windbreaks. Transplanting in a windy garden can be much assisted by the use of tin collars. Pet food tins (of 450 g size) with tops and bottoms removed are very suitable. They are pushed about 3-4 cm into the ground around the young plants and left in position for one to two weeks. The plants are partly shaded from the hot sun, cannot be damaged by wind and are protected from slugs. Tins are particularly suitable for brassica plants, which can be permanently stunted by unfavourable conditions during transplanting.

Mini-glasshouses also supply much needed shelter in exposed gardens, and are much more stable than traditional cloches. Gardeners with windy plots can take some consolation from the fact that winged aphids cannot undertake colonizing flights when wind speeds exceed 2½-3½ knots. This also reduces the incidence of virus diseases commonly spread by aphids.

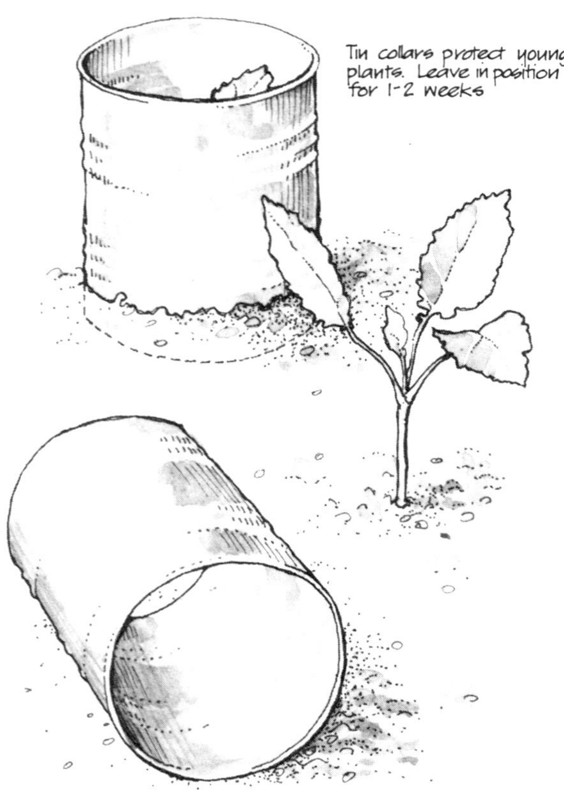

Tin collars protect young plants. Leave in position for 1-2 weeks

Lack of space

Whole books are devoted to gardening in a restricted area, and many techniques have been devised to save space. These include growing climbing vegetables over sheds and boundary fences and inter-planting quick-maturing plants between those which are grown slowly in the ground for several months. Catch cropping involves sowing or planting a quick maturing crop in ground which is intended for a later main crop. Spinach, silver beet and radishes can be grown as catch crops. Don't forget that if a good supply of compost is added to replace lost humus, ground vacated by one crop can be planted immediately with another. Depending on the vegetable, additional fertilizer may be needed.

Boxes and large pots filled with good soil can be located wherever sun is available. Plants such as tomatoes, peppers, cucumbers and courgettes do particularly well in containers. In the vegetable plot, dwarf varieties can be grown in order to cut down the space between the rows. Vegetable plots need not look out of place in the front garden, especially those planted with parsley, carrots, ruby-coloured silver beets, lettuces and scarlet runner beans. Herbs can be grown in boxes on the kitchen window sill and bean sprouts raised on the kitchen bench. Some vegetables will tolerate partial shade, in particular Jerusalem artichokes, American cress, summer lettuces, silver beet and New Zealand spinach.

Valuable vegetables for small gardens

Unobtainable commercially	Kohlrabi, golden beetroot, salsify, celeriac, New Zealand spinach

Expensive especially in early part of season	Tomatoes, courgettes, spinach, celery, French beans, peas
When freshness is vital	Lettuces, radishes, baby carrots, cauliflowers, sweet corn, peas, silver beet
Indispensable	Silver beet, leeks, rhubarb, runner beans

Lack of time

One solution to this problem for those with plenty of space is to mechanise basic gardening operations. Rotary hoes which break in new ground (provided it is not heavy clay), mix in fertilizer and compost, mound up potatoes and cultivate between rows are available in sizes which can be handled by both men and women. For this approach the plot should be large and rectangular with long rows and no permanent internal paths or stepping stones. Space between rows must always be sufficient for the rotary hoe to pass through when slicing up weeds.

A large deep freeze is vital to the success of mechanised home gardening as so much time is saved by harvesting and processing in bulk. This means that instead of growing cauliflowers and broccoli for succession, or worrying about spinach bolting in hot weather, the whole crop is grown for gathering at one time when it is in peak condition. Of course the kitchen must be equipped for bulk freezing and ideally the whole family should be available to lend a hand. Co-operation between the cook and the gardener is most important so that harvesting takes place at a convenient time.

Garden pests

There can be no dispute that if plants are growing in conditions which supply their requirements of sunshine, moisture and soil nutrients, they seldom suffer debilitating diseases or insect attacks. This may be why some

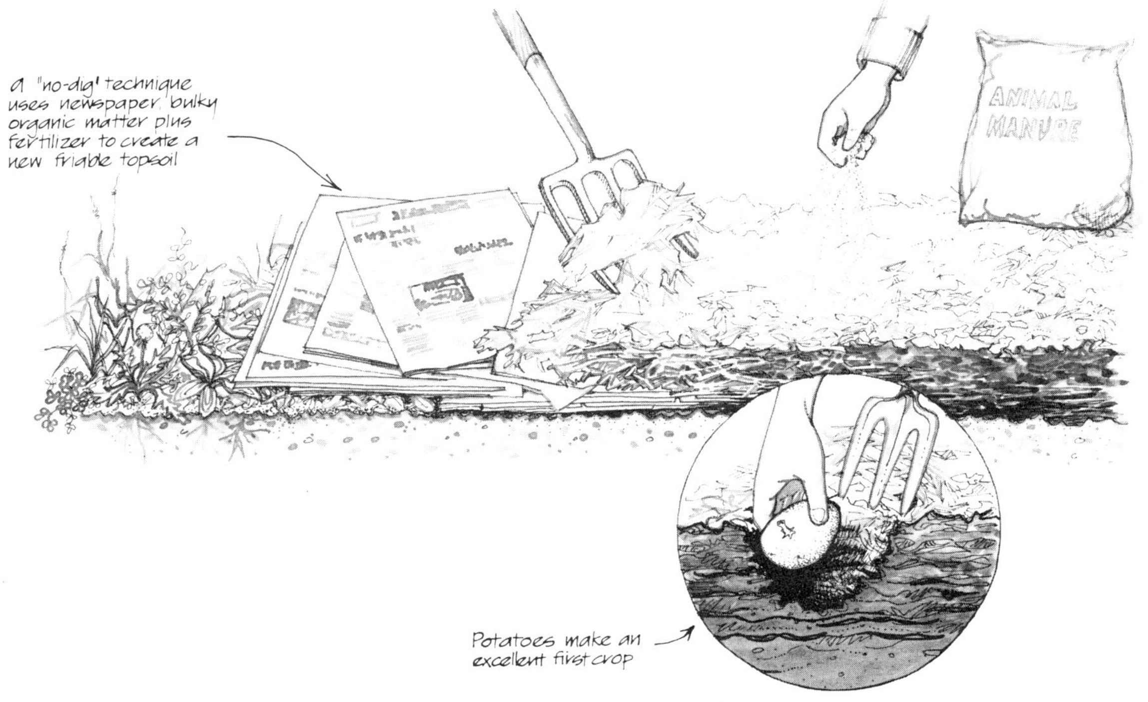
a 'no-dig' technique uses newspaper, bulky organic matter plus fertilizer to create a new friable topsoil
ANIMAL MANURE
Potatoes make an excellent first crop

enthusiastic organic gardeners are able to claim great success with certain old-fashioned remedies which scientists declare to be useless. Organic gardens are usually so rich in humus that the healthy plants growing in them successfully resist most pests and diseases.

Animal pests are a rather different matter. Small animals (such as opossums) may actually prefer organic gardens because of the tender, lush vegetation. Shooting or trapping them may be illegal or ill-advised in particular areas but they can be effectively discouraged by extensive use of bird nets, which don't need elaborate frames, and by liberal applications of blood and bone and dag manure. Apparently they dislike products which give off ammonia.

Cats come into conflict with gardeners by scratching in seed beds and sleeping in mini-glasshouses. Damage may be avoided by covering newly-sown rows with netting or wire-mesh screens, and by leaving an area of soft, dry dirt in a handy part of the garden for the cat to use as a toilet. Leave a few bales of dry straw in a strategic shady place close to seed beds. The presence of a snoozing cat might discourage birds from eating young pea shoots or scratching up young plants in their search for worms. We feed sparrows regularly in spring to curb their appetites for polyanthus flowers and pea shoots. Blackbirds and thrushes are a rather different matter for they eat slugs as well as worms. The tin collars described earlier offer good protection to young plants without discouraging blackbirds.

If conditions do become unfavourable in a garden, usually as a result of climatic extremes, certain fungus diseases can spread quickly, ruining many susceptible plants. Bordeaux mixture or copper oxychloride sprays are old-fashioned but safe to use and are usually effective as a preventative. When warm dry weather occurs in spring, aphid colonies quickly appear on rose shoots and the soft buds of many flowers. This is the time to take preventative measures in the vegetable garden by applying pyrethrum and rotenone (Derris Dust) (two relatively safe contact insecticides) to young plants about once a week. Garden shops stock many more powerful products but the DDT "affair" makes us unwilling to trust claims that the organo-phosphate and systemic insecticides and fungicides are perfectly safe for long-term use. We consider the cook-gardener's peace of mind to be more important than any case of rust on beans or caterpillars on cabbages.

PART 2

Growing and cooking individual vegetables

Artichokes

(1) GLOBE ARTICHOKES
(Cynara scolymus)

Varieties
Globe artichokes have been described as superthistles, growing 1.2-1.3 m high and bearing large flower heads above rather striking grey leaves. They need a lot of room (1.2 x 1.2 m) so some gardeners with little space grow them in the flower garden. A family of four could grow four to six plants. Seed of the green variety is available but there is a considerable variation in the quality of artichokes grown from seed. You might need to raise ten or more plants to maturity and select out a few with really fleshy buds. Globe artichokes are usually propagated by suckers and by this means the superior strains (often those with purplish buds) can be perpetuated. They have fewer scales on the flower bud and these have very thick succulent bases. The purple artichoke is ready a few weeks after the green variety.

Cultivation
Globe artichokes are never successful on heavy, cold soils which are waterlogged in winter, nor do they tolerate hard frosts. A medium, friable loam deeply cultivated and enriched with several buckets of old animal manure and rotted seaweed is considered ideal. The ground must never dry out, especially where young suckers have been planted. They prefer cool summer conditions or partial shade in warm districts.

The usual planting time is spring when four to five suckers are detached from the parent plant when about 20 cm long. They should have a portion of the old stock attached, as well as a good growth of roots emerging just below the leaf stems. Set them at least 1 m apart in prepared ground, trim back the leaves to reduce water loss and keep very well watered. Depending on their size and growing conditions, they may produce edible buds in their first year towards the end of the growing season. The next year they will be in full production with buds ready in mid summer.

Adult plants crop well for up to five years if they are given a heavy annual and late winter dose of animal manure or a general fertilizer. Every year they will send up a group of suckers. These should be reduced to four to five per plant and used to replenish your artichoke patch (as well as your neighbour's).

Aphids may be troublesome, especially in dry weather, but the plants should not be sprayed with any poisonous insecticide if the buds are forming. Instead use pyrethrum or a strong jet spray from the hose.

Harvesting
Cooks who like very large heads to work with may remove the lateral flower buds around the

main heads when they reach the size of an egg. These small buds can be fried, pickled or eaten raw. Later the main heads are cut from the plant while still tight but beginning to spread at the base. Harvest before the scales develop hard brown tips. Wash your hands well after handling the stems as artichoke juice is extremely bitter.

In the kitchen

Slice away any bottom stalk and snip off the points of the leaves with scissors. Wash thoroughly. Cook in a large saucepan of boiling salted water for 25-45 minutes until a leaf comes away easily when pulled. Lift out with a perforated spoon.

Serve hot with melted butter or hollandaise sauce (see page 208). Serve cold with vinaigrette (see page 209) or herb-flavoured mayonnaise (see page 209).

Using your fingers, pull away leaves one by one, dip in dressing and nibble each tender, light green base. Use a small fork to remove the inedible choke. Add a little dressing to the remaining heart and eat it with a fork.

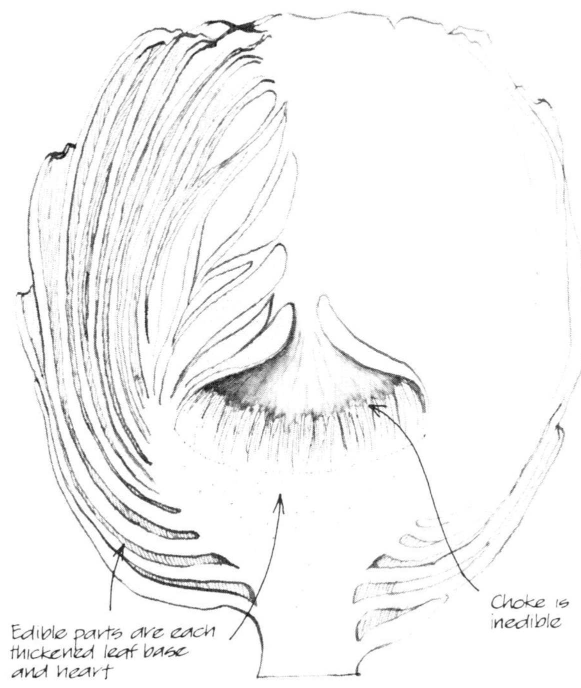
Choke is inedible
Edible parts are each thickened leaf base and heart

(2) JERUSALEM ARTICHOKES

(Helianthus tuberosus)

Varieties

Jerusalem artichokes were eaten and probably first cultivated by North American Indians. Tubers which were sent to Europe in the early seventeenth century aroused considerable interest, for they bore some resemblance to potatoes, tasted a little like globe artichokes and when they flowered (in warm areas) they looked like sunflowers. In fact, they belong to the same genus as the sunflower. They have not become popular as a vegetable partly because some strains are knobbly and liable to discolour when cooked. Soon after their introduction, an even greater drawback was discovered. Some people experienced indigestion and wind after eating them. To some extent this can be overcome by eating toast at the same time. The only way to discover an allergy to artichokes is by trying them. If they agree with you they make a welcome and tasty addition to winter meals. Named varieties are not sold in some countries so take care to obtain the best quality tubers, through a friend or garden club. They should be of even size and free from knobbliness and deep eyes.

Cultivation

For Jerusalem artichokes, a separate bed should be prepared and moderately fertilized with a general mixture. It should be well drained but not necessarily placed in full sunlight. Wood ash and compost, dug into the bed, enhance the quality of the tubers. Plant the tubers 8-12 cm deep and 35-40 cm apart in early spring. As they grow, stake and tie them and keep them weeded.

In autumn the 2-3 m high stalks will bear small sunflowers. Some gardeners recommend removing the buds before they open in case the quality of the tuber is affected.

Harvesting

About four to six weeks after the buds appear, the tubers can be dug as required. Avoid lifting too many at a time as they do not keep well out of the ground. In late winter, dig up the remainder (every single tuber) and replant the best tubers in a new bed or in the same spot, freshly manured.

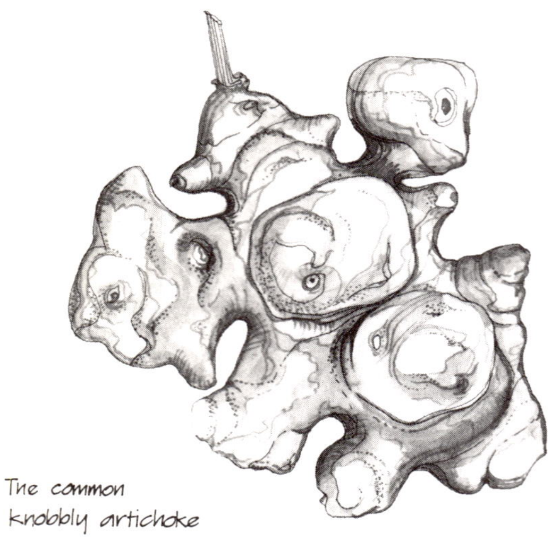

The common knobbly artichoke

In the kitchen

The importance of growing a less knobbly variety becomes obvious when preparing artichokes. We have grown two varieties. One produces red-skinned, almost smooth tubers which are easy to prepare. The other type has pale-skinned, knobbly tubers which are difficult and time consuming to clean and result in excessive wastage when peeling.

Allow 200-300 g for each serving. Scrub tubers thoroughly. Cut off any knobs which make cleaning too difficult. Cook in boiling, salted water until tender. Be careful not to overcook. Drain and peel immediately by rubbing off the skins under cold running water.

Return to the saucepan and reheat gently with melted butter, seasoning, chopped parsley and a squeeze of lemon juice. They may also be served with béchamel sauce (see page 208).

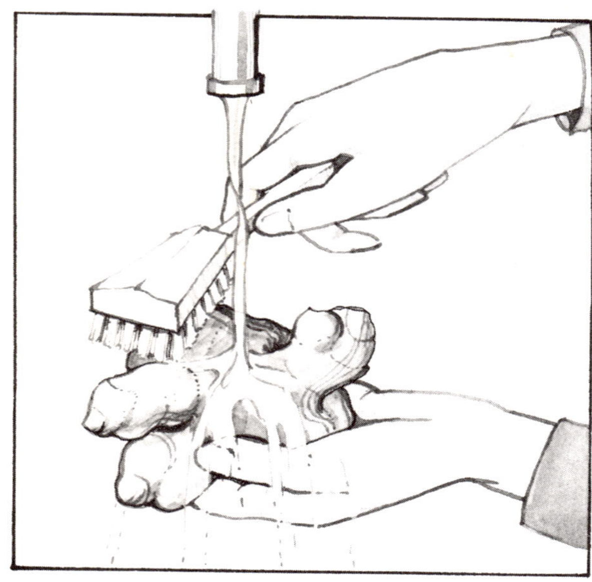

Scrub tubers thoroughly

ARTICHOKE PURÉE

Serves 6

1.4 kg artichokes
2 tb cream
2 tb butter
1 egg yolk
freshly-ground black pepper
salt to taste
2 tb chopped parsley

Cook, drain and peel artichokes. Put through a fine sieve. Return purée to rinsed-out saucepan. Add cream, butter, egg yolk and seasoning. Beat well. Cook gently, stirring constantly until thick and heated through. Serve garnished with chopped parsley.

ARTICHOKES AU GRATIN

Serves 4-6

800 g artichokes

Sauce:

2 tb butter
2 tb flour
1½ c milk
½ tsp salt
freshly-ground black pepper
100 g grated Cheddar cheese
2 tb grated Parmesan cheese

Cook, drain and peel artichokes. Slice them into a greased ovenproof dish.

To make sauce, melt butter in a saucepan, add flour and cook for 1 minute. Gradually pour in milk, stirring until sauce is thick and boiling. Add seasoning and half the grated Cheddar and Parmesan cheese. Pour over the artichokes. Sprinkle with remaining cheese. Bake at 200°C for 10-15 minutes until heated through and golden brown.

Variation: add a few lightly-sautéed mushrooms to the artichokes before covering with the sauce.

ARTICHOKE SOUP

Serves 6

500 g artichokes
2 tb butter
1 small onion, chopped
600 ml chicken stock
½ c cream or top milk
salt and pepper to taste
2 tb chopped parsley

Cook scrubbed artichokes in boiling, salted water until almost tender. Drain and peel. Slice. Melt butter in a large saucepan. Sauté the onion until soft. Add artichoke slices and cook gently for 3 minutes. Add stock and simmer until artichoke is very soft. Put through a blender or fine sieve. Return to saucepan, add cream and seasoning and reheat gently. Serve with chopped parsley sprinkled on top.

Variation: add a half-litre jar of preserved tomatoes and the grated rind of half an orange with the stock and continue to follow recipe. Add juice of half an orange and the cream before reheating. Omit parsley.

Asparagus

(*Asparagus officinalis*)

Varieties

This long-lived, hardy perennial can be called a luxury vegetable as it gives so little return for the time spent on it and the space it occupies. However, a dedicated asparagus lover will go to great lengths to create an enriched, permanent bed which will result in several dozen large, succulent spears once a year.

Five varieties are commonly grown. Connover Colossal is well known for its thick stalks. Connistor and Mary Washington have proved popular, but California 500, an improved Mary Washington type, is recommended for new beds. Brooks F.1 Hybrid produces spears earlier than the others. The seeds of these last two new varieties are now obtainable from most specialist seed merchants.

Cultivation

Spring-sown seeds grow into quite strong plants in one season but most impatient asparagus lovers buy one-year-old crowns. Preparing the permanent home in a raised bed makes it easier to incorporate rich compost and manure with the existing topsoil; it also provides perfect drainage. The summer foliage is large and floppy so it is wise to tie back the outer stalks for tidiness. A good way to do this is by extending the pegs at the corners of the raised bed to a height of 60-70 cm. Strong twine can then be tied from corner to corner. Depending on the size of your bed, you may need an extra stake in the middle of each long side. Dig the ground very deeply, forking in at the bottom well-rotted manure and as much compost as you can spare. Add about one bucket of compost per square metre several weeks before planting. Just before the crowns are set out in early spring, dress the bed with a general fertilizer — about a half a cup per square metre.

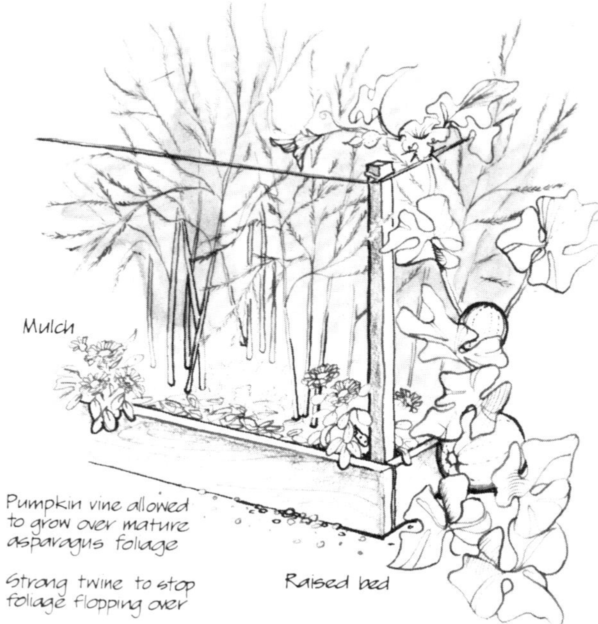

Dig a trench 30 cm deep and 30 cm wide with 60 cm between trenches. Place the crowns 45 cm apart on slight mounds at the bottom, spreading the long spidery roots evenly around. Cover immediately with soil, making sure that 15-20 cm of soil covers the top of each crown. Make sure the roots of the crown do not dry out at any time prior to planting.

Weed carefully so as not to disturb roots. Dress the bed with compost in autumn, and every spring apply a general fertilizer — half a cup per square metre. Cut back foliage when it turns yellow in the autumn and compost it.

A minimum of 25 plants will be needed for an average-sized family.

Perennial weeds must never be allowed to take over, but if you obtain a mature bed that has been neglected it is possible to solve the problem by mulching very thickly with any organic matter, leaving this in position for six to eight months and then raking it off. The roots of the perennial weeds grow into the mulch and both mulch and perennial roots can be removed together.

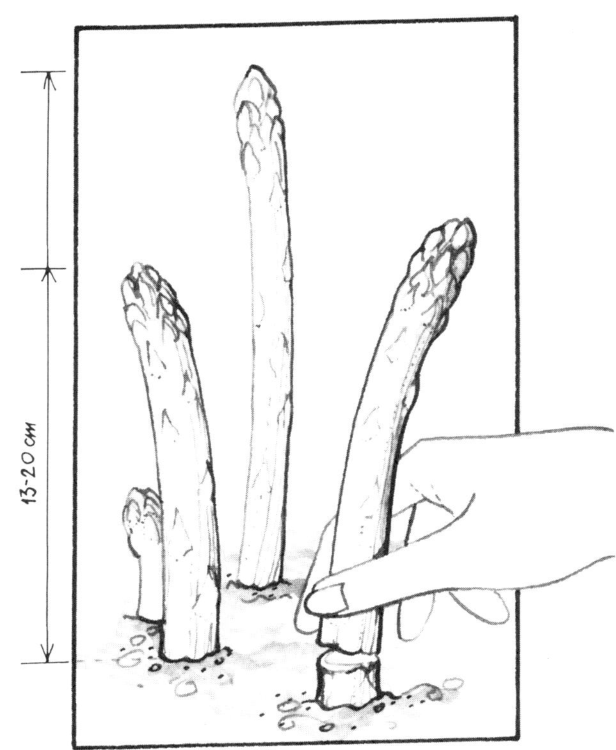

Snap off spears as low as possible

Harvesting

Try very hard not to cut the spears for the first two years after planting. During the third year cut for no more than two weeks, and in the fourth year the cutting period should not exceed four weeks. In subsequent years cut for six to ten weeks, depending on the vigour of the bed. The appearance of thin stems indicates that you have been overcutting and/or underfeeding the plants.

Asparagus need not be cut below the surface as many books suggest but snapped off as low as the spears will break. This means you are picking only the tender part.

In the kitchen

Wash asparagus well. Cut off any woody ends. If the stalks have tough scales scrape them with a sharp knife, working downwards from just below the head.

For best results, asparagus should be cooked with the stalks in boiling, salted water and the tips in steam. An asparagus cooker is the answer but as these are rare, we have compromised with the following methods:

1. Tie the spears in bundles with string and stand upright in boiling water in a deep saucepan. The water should come three-quarters of the way up the stalks. Support the bundle with crumpled aluminium foil if necessary. Cook with the lid on.
2. Very young asparagus spears can be stood in a preserving jar of 1 litre capacity. Almost fill the jar with boiling water. Cover with perforated aluminium foil and stand the jar in a saucepan half filled with boiling water. The cooking time will be 30-45 minutes.

Properly-cooked asparagus should be neither crunchy nor limp but easy to pierce with the tip of a sharp knife. The colour should be a bright green. Drain and serve immediately.

You will need about 200 g of asparagus for each serving. The flavour of home-grown asparagus is so good that we prefer to use it as

Cooking asparagus in a jar

a separate course. Serve simply with butter, salt and freshly-ground black pepper or hollandaise sauce (see page 208). Make the sauce and keep it warm while the asparagus is cooking. Serve the cooked spears on individual plates with a little sauce poured over each portion.

ASPARAGUS WITH BUTTER SAUCE

Serves 4

A simple way of serving your prize spears.

800 g asparagus
150 g butter
2 tb lemon juice
2 tb finely-chopped parsley

While the asparagus is cooking, melt the butter in a saucepan. Add the lemon juice and parsley. Serve the hot asparagus seasoned with salt and freshly-ground black pepper. The sauce may be poured over the spears before taking the individual plates to the table. Alternatively, serve the sauce in a bowl to be used as a dip at the table.

To serve asparagus cold: You will need 200 g of fresh asparagus per serving. Cook according to general method. Drain well and allow to cool. Serve with vinaigrette dressing (see page 209) or homemade mayonnaise (see page 204).

The next three recipes are useful for making a small harvest of spears go further.

ASPARAGUS WITH SCRAMBLED EGGS

Serves 3

6 eggs
2 tb cream or top milk
salt and pepper to taste
12 asparagus spears, cooked
2 tb butter
2 tb grated Parmesan cheese
hot buttered toast

Beat eggs, cream and seasoning together until just mixed. Cut the asparagus into 2 cm slices. Melt the butter in a heavy-based frying pan. Add the asparagus pieces and cook gently for 1 minute. Pour in the egg mixture and cook over low heat, stirring constantly until the mixture begins to set. Remove from the heat and add the cheese. The residual heat in the pan will complete the setting of the eggs. Serve with triangles of hot, buttered toast.

ASPARAGUS AND MACARONI

Serves 4

250 g macaroni
250 g fresh or frozen asparagus
250 ml creamy milk
salt and pepper to taste
2 eggs
½ c grated Cheddar cheese
2 tb grated Parmesan cheese
1 tb butter

Cook the macaroni in boiling, salted water until just tender. Drain in a colander. Cut the asparagus into 2 cm slices and cook in boiling, salted water until barely tender. Drain. Pour the creamy milk into a large saucepan, add the asparagus and seasoning and heat through. Remove from the heat. Add the well-drained macaroni, lightly-beaten eggs and grated Cheddar cheese. Pour the mixture into a well-buttered ovenproof dish. Sprinkle with the Parmesan cheese and dot with butter. Bake at 200°C for 15-20 minutes until the mixture is set and the top golden.

ASPARAGUS PANCAKES

Serves 6

Basic pancake batter — makes 12 pancakes

115 g flour
pinch salt
1 egg
1 egg yolk
250 ml milk
1 tb melted butter

Sift the flour and salt into a bowl. Make a well in the centre, add the egg and yolk and begin to add the milk slowly, stirring all the time. When half of the milk has been used, stir in the melted butter and beat well until smooth. Add the remaining milk and combine thoroughly. The batter should have the consistency of thin cream; if too thick, add a little extra milk. Pour into a jug and leave for 30 minutes before using.

To cook pancakes: the ideal pancake pan is about 15 cm in diameter and made from cast iron. Wipe out the pan before putting over moderate heat. When hot pour in a few drops of oil. Pour in sufficient batter just to coat the bottom (the thinner the better). Cook until the underneath is golden brown. Flip or turn over with a fish slice. Cook for about 10 seconds on the second side. Turn pancakes out on to a teatowel on a rack. Stack them on top of each other. Cover with the towel until cool.

Pancakes can be made fresh on the day required or made a couple of days in advance and stored in a plastic bag in the refrigerator. They can also be frozen. When freezing, place a layer of greaseproof paper between the pancakes and seal inside a plastic bag.

Filling:

24 cooked asparagus spears

Sauce:

2 tb butter
2 tb flour
1 c milk
¼ tsp salt
½ c grated tasty Cheddar cheese
2 tb grated Parmesan cheese for the topping

Melt the butter in a small saucepan, add the flour and cook for 1 minute. Gradually add the milk, stirring constantly until the sauce thickens and boils. Remove from the heat. Add the salt and grated Cheddar cheese. Stir until smooth.

Method: roll up 2 spears in each pancake. Arrange side by side in a shallow oven-proof dish. Pour the sauce over the pancakes. Sprinkle with the Parmesan cheese. Heat through in the oven at 190°C for 15-20 minutes until the cheese is bubbly and golden.

Freezing

Asparagus deteriorates quickly after harvesting so speed with processing is important.

Sort into thin, medium and thick spears. Each pile should be blanched separately — 2 minutes for thin, 3 minutes for medium and 4 minutes for thick spears. Cool quickly and pack in plastic boxes so that the delicate tips are not damaged. To use: thaw long enough to separate spears, before cooking in boiling, salted water.

Beans

(1) DWARF FRENCH BEANS
(Phaseolus vulgaris)

Varieties
Many of the old names like Canadian Wonder have disappeared from seed catalogues because plant breeders have been concentrating on producing stringless, dwarf beans which are resistant to various virus and root infections. At present, one can choose from five green-podded, stringless types and three yellow-podded butter beans. Top Crop, Seminole and Tendergreen are erect, green-podded varieties which are disease resistant and carry heavy crops of 15-16 cm-long cylindrical pods. Green Crop grows about 45 cm high and bears flat pods, 18 cm long. Where very hot summers are experienced, it is usually sown as an early or late crop as the pods do not set in hot, dry weather. Butter beans include Cherokee Wax and Pencil Pod Black Wax, which bear 15 cm-long yellow pods. Cherokee Wax grows about 40 cm high and is disease resistant. Golden Wax is also described as "rustproof".

Cultivation
Green and butter beans are not only killed by light frosts, but die if their roots are waterlogged for 12 hours. They must therefore be planted in warm soil of open texture. (Germination is suppressed in cold, wet soils and in temperatures below 15°C.) The soil should be a good loam into which compost and animal manure was dug the previous autumn. Use a dusting of lime in early spring, if this has not been added to the ground in the previous two years.

In addition to organic manure, some gardeners apply a complete fertilizer (see page 8) or just superphosphate, Because young beans are susceptible to "burning" by inorganic fertilizer, apply half the quantity three weeks before planting and the rest just before flowering.

The spacing between plants depends on the richness of the soil. The more nutrients available, the bigger the plants will be and the greater the chance of overcrowding. Thus, gardening books recommend spaces between individual seedlings varying from 5-15 cm. The bean rows may be single lines 30 cm apart or double-row strips 20 cm wide, with 45-75 cm between strips. The latter are more convenient in a windy garden where the beans may need the support of twiggy branches or strings. Whatever system is chosen, the seeds should be planted 3-6 cm deep, not too deep to be waterlogged in spring and not too shallow to dry out in summer. Where both problems are experienced, use cloches to warm the ground in spring and then try the deeper sowing position.

Dry soil around the roots at flowering time usually results in a failure to set pods. A good way of avoiding this trouble, without water-logging the ground, is to run a perforated soak hose (upside down) between the rows to moisten the soil but leave the foliage dry and free from mildew.

Fortunately these fussy beans don't usually suffer severely from insect attacks. If caterpillars appear, dust with Derris. Treat aphids with pyrethrum. Slugs occasionally attack young beans and they can be trapped under flower pots placed beside the rows. Regular hoeing between rows, removal of weeds and keeping the garden edges well trimmed also deters slugs. Yellow leaves may be visible in the young plant. This is not a disease but a reaction to cold, wet weather.

Harvesting

Once the seeds within the pods become rounded and full size, flowering in dwarf beans ceases, so aim to start picking beans when about two-thirds grown. Never let the seeds develop beyond slight bulges on the outside of the pod. A common test is to bend the pods. If they snap apart with a clean break they are ready to be harvested. Using a knife or your thumbnail, cut the pod just before the stem connection, leaving the little hard nub on the plant. This saves time in the kitchen as the beans can be placed straight on to the chopping board and sliced. To keep the bushes in production for several weeks, pick every four to seven days. Succession sowing every two to three weeks prolongs the harvest period, or you may prefer to grow a large quantity for simultaneous harvesting and freezing.

Sever the bean with your thumb nail, leaving the little hard nub on the plant

(2) CLIMBING BEANS (Phaseolus vulgaris and Phaseolus coccineus)

The climbing varieties of French beans are particularly suited to warm areas where they can produce three times the crop from the same area as the dwarf varieties. Like the dwarfs, they are annuals and they suffer from the same diseases. The Mangere Pole variety has been developed in New Zealand for its resistance to rust. It has shiny pods, which are also a characteristic of the Shiny Fardenlosa variety. A purple-podded variety used to be popular but in the United States it is regarded as very susceptible to rust. Occasionally listed are climbing butter beans.

Runner beans are perennials and at the end of autumn when the foliage has dried off, the rootstock is often left in the ground to produce a new plant in spring. These reach the harvest stage two to three weeks earlier than runner beans sown from seed. Runner beans are grown in preference to French climbing beans in cooler regions, because they set more pods in unfavourable weather and because very hot weather inhibits setting. But they are no hardier than French beans in frosty conditions or if the soil is wet and cold. Few varieties are available and there has been a tendency for seedsmen to concentrate on very long podded types, sometimes 65 cm long, with names like Goliath, Empire State and Mammoth Long Pod. Keen gardeners with many years' experience may have their own favourite from which they save the seed. Try to obtain a vigorous and hardy black-seeded type, as opposed to the varieties with purple and black mottled seed.

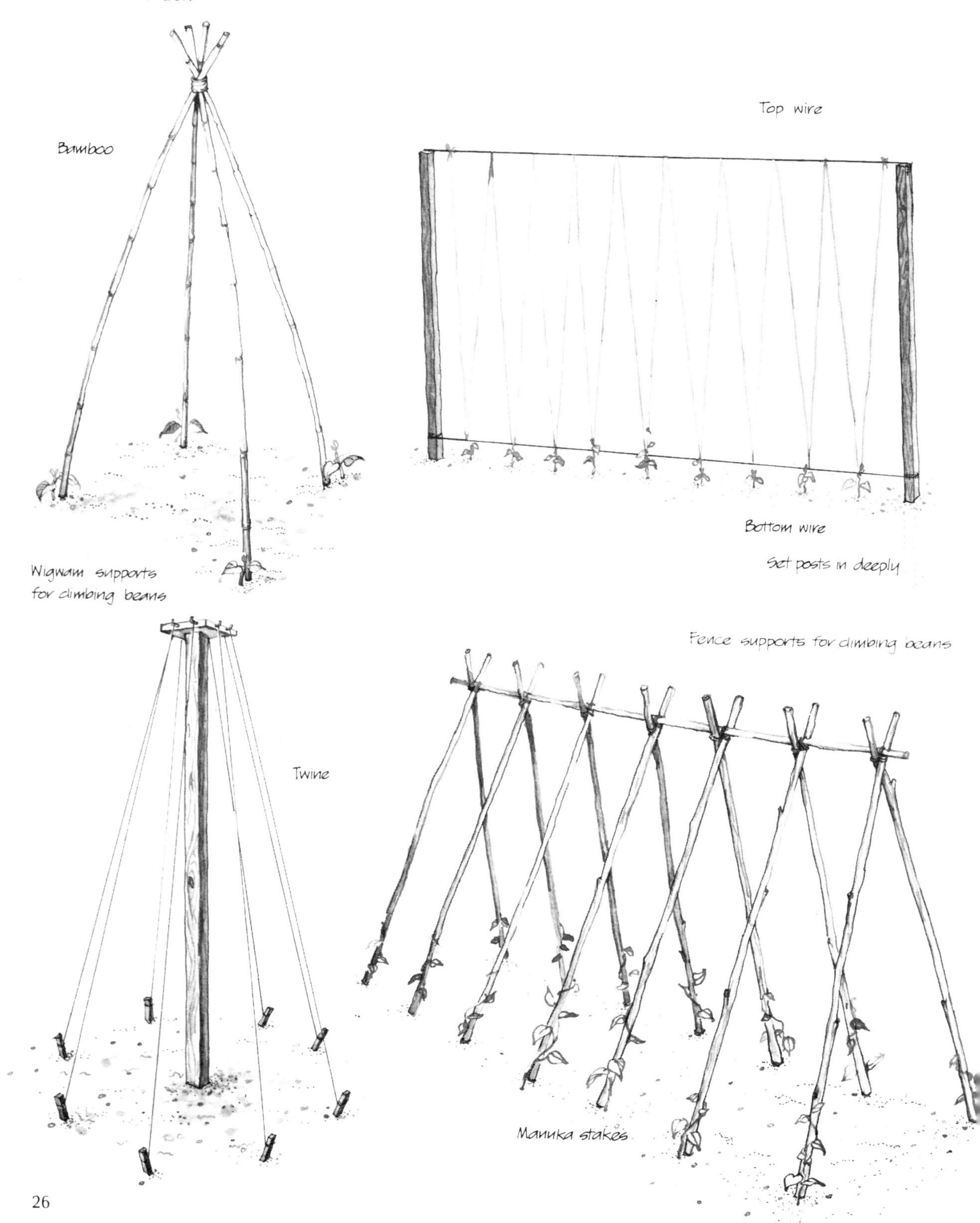
Bamboo
Wigwam supports
for climbing beans
Top wire
Bottom wire
Set posts in deeply
Fence supports for climbing beans
Twine
Manuka stakes

Cultivation

Climbing bean enthusiasts prepare the bed in autumn by digging out a 40 cm-wide trench, filling it with liberal quantities of compost and animal manure and replacing the topsoil. Some even line the trench with newspapers to hold moisture for summer needs. The seeds are planted about 5 cm deep and the final spacing between plants should be 15-30 cm. Alternatively, seeds can be sown in peat pots under glass and transplanted when fully hardened off.

It is advisable to have the main framework of supports in position before planting time. Much ingenuity has gone into the design of bean frames but there are basically two types: the fence and the circle. Circular arrangements include stout, central posts with strings radiating outwards, and wigwams of three to four poles, 2.5 m long and set into the ground 50-60 cm deep. Fences can have heavy, braced posts at each end with two wires running between them and strings tied vertically for the beans to climb. Alternatively, they can consist of a double row of arched stakes with a horizontal stake lashed firmly at the top of each pair of uprights. Long stakes can be placed leaning against an existing fence or wall. Avoid plastic-covered vertical strings or wires as the beans have difficulty climbing them.

Plenty of moisture must be available to the beans at flowering time, so a mulch of compost is often applied after a thorough watering. When the plant reaches the top of the frame the leading shoots are usually pinched out. Blue flowers like borage, planted nearby, attract bees to the area and promote pollination.

Harvesting

An English gardening book states that if picked regularly before the seeds fill out, pods from a 3 m row will feed a family of four for at least two months, allowing two pickings per week. In some countries longer cropping is possible if the plants are well supplied with nutrients. Liquid manure is often recommended.

In the kitchen

This section applies to dwarf and climbing French beans and runner beans.

Rinse beans and if you didn't snip the ends off in the garden, do it now. Remove strings from runner beans with a potato peeler. Leave beans whole or slice, according to type and recipe.

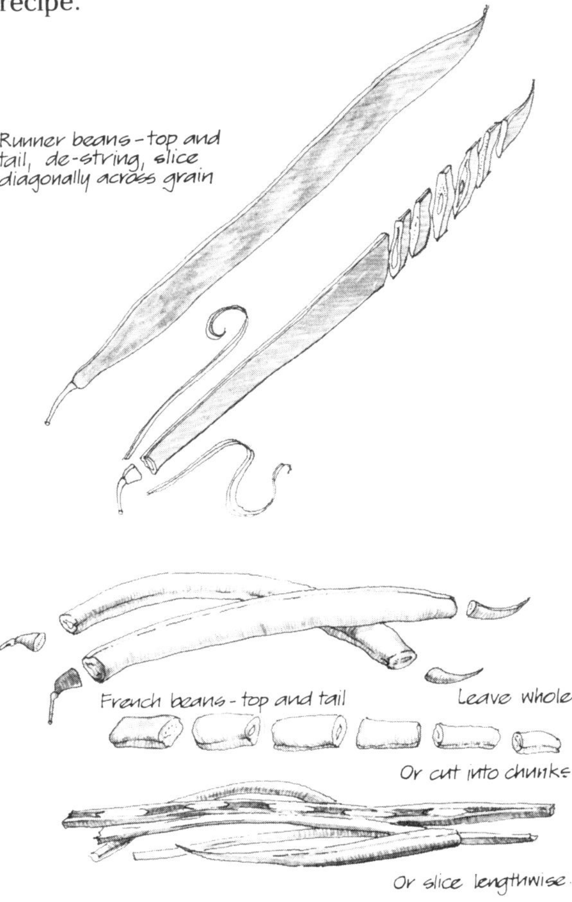
Runner beans - top and tail, de-string, slice diagonally across grain
French beans - top and tail
Leave whole
Or cut into chunks
Or slice lengthwise

Cook beans in boiling, salted water until just tender but still bright green and slightly crisp. Serve simply with butter, freshly-ground pepper and salt. Add finely chopped herbs to taste — basil, chives, tarragon, savory or parsley. Pesto sauce (see page 99) or herb butter (see page 107) are also delicious accompaniments. For a special dinner you may like to add small pieces of crisp, fried bacon or blanched, slivered almonds fried in butter until golden.

SPICED GREEN BEANS
Serves 6

500 g French or runner beans
½ tsp salt
2 tb cider or wine vinegar
1 tsp sugar
1 clove garlic (cut in half)
1 bay leaf
2 tb butter
¼ tsp allspice

Cut French beans lengthwise. Cut runner beans diagonally into 1 cm slices. Cook in boiling, salted water until just tender. Drain. Add the remaining ingredients and heat gently for 3 minutes. Remove garlic and bay leaf. Serve hot or cold.

GREEN BEANS À L'ESPAGNOLE
Serves 6

500 g French or runner beans
1 red pepper
1 tb cooking oil
1 tb butter
1 clove garlic, finely chopped
2 tb chopped parsley
salt and pepper to taste

Prepare beans according to type. Cook in boiling, salted water until just tender. Drain. Remove stalk and seeds from the red pepper. Dice flesh finely. Sauté pepper, garlic and parsley in the oil and butter in a medium-sized frying pan for 5 minutes. Add the strained beans and mix gently. Check seasoning. Heat through and serve immediately.

GREEN BEAN FAGGOTS
Serves 6

This is a very attractive way of serving beans for a dinner party.

6 long green spring onion or shallot leaves to tie faggots
500 g French beans
½ tsp salt
large sprig of savory
½ tsp chicken stock powder
butter for serving

Soften onion or shallot leaves in boiling water for 1 minute. Refresh in cold water. Divide topped and tailed beans into six tidy bundles. Tie each carefully. Place faggots in a saucepan and cover with boiling water. Add salt, savory and stock powder. Cook until just tender. Carefully lift out bundles on to a warm serving platter and top with small pieces of butter. Serve immediately.

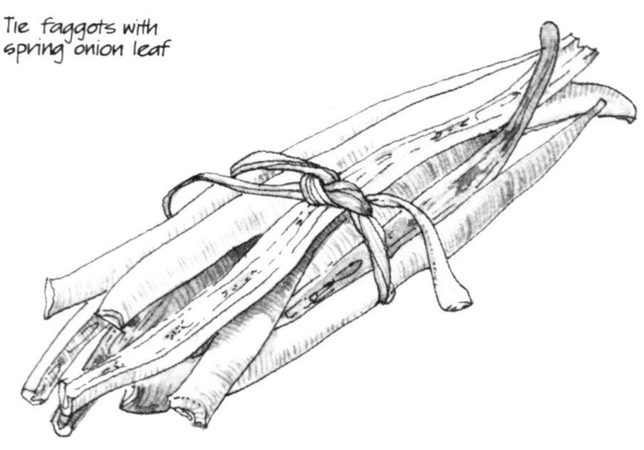
Tie faggots with spring onion leaf

GREEN BEAN SALAD
Serves 6

700 g French beans
6 tb salad oil
2 tb tarragon vinegar
freshly-ground black pepper
salt to taste
1 tb very finely chopped onion
2 tb chopped parsley
1 tsp finely-chopped, fresh tarragon (dry tarragon is not satisfactory)
½ clove garlic, very finely chopped

Top and tail beans. Bring a saucepan of salted water to the boil. Add the whole beans and simmer until just tender but still crisp to bite. Combine oil, vinegar, pepper and salt in a small bowl and beat with a fork until creamy. Stir in onion, herbs and garlic. As soon as the beans are tender, drain them in a colander and tip into a serving bowl. Pour dressing over beans while they are still hot. Toss gently and check seasonings. Serve cold.

Although we like the flavour of tarragon in this bean salad, it can be made without. Use cider or wine vinegar and chives instead of the tarragon. Nasturtium flowers make an attractive garnish.

RUSSIAN-STYLE GREEN BEANS

Serves 4

350 g French beans
100 g mushrooms
2 tb butter
4 tb sour cream
chopped parsley

Slice beans into 2 cm lengths. Cook in boiling, salted water until just tender. Drain, reserving cooking liquid. Slice mushrooms thinly and sauté in butter for a few minutes. Add two tablespoons of the cooking liquid and simmer, covered, for 5 minutes. Add beans and sour cream. Heat through gently. Serve sprinkled with chopped parsley.

Mushrooms and beans make a good combination

ITALIAN GREEN BEANS

Serves 6

Runner beans are superb cooked this way.

500 g beans
2 tb cooking oil
2 cloves garlic, finely chopped
3 medium tomatoes, peeled and chopped
salt and pepper to taste

Remove strings from beans and cut into 5 mm diagonal slices. Boil in salted water until tender-crisp. Drain. Heat oil in a medium-sized frying pan. Add garlic, beans, tomatoes and seasoning. Cook for about 10 minutes until tomatoes are soft.

RUNNER BEANS AND LETTUCE CASSEROLE

Serves 6

500 g runner beans
1 small lettuce
1 shallot or very small onion
½ tsp salt
½ tsp paprika
2 tb butter

Top and tail beans, remove any strings and cut into 5 mm diagonal slices. Shred lettuce finely. Peel and chop shallot or onion finely. Place half the beans in a well-greased oven-proof dish with a lid. Add the lettuce, shallot and seasoning. Cover with the second half of the beans. Dot with butter. Place a layer of aluminium foil over the dish and put on the lid tightly. Cook in the oven at 180°C for 1 hour.

Optional topping:

1 c soft breadcrumbs
2 tb melted butter
2 tb finely chopped walnuts
1 tb finely chopped parsley

Sauté the breadcrumbs in the butter in a small frying pan until golden and crisp. Add the nuts and parsley. Sprinkle this over the bean and lettuce casserole just before serving.

RUNNER BEANS BULGARIAN STYLE

Serves 6 as an accompaniment, or 4 as a separate course.

2 large onions
4 tb cooking oil
1 tsp paprika
500 g runner beans
2 medium carrots
4 medium tomatoes
2 green peppers
½ tsp salt
1 tb finely chopped basil, savory or parsley

Cut peeled onions in half and then slice thinly. Sauté in hot oil until golden. Use a large frying pan with a lid. Sprinkle with paprika. Remove strings from beans and cut diagonally into 3 cm slices. Scrub and slice carrots into thin rings. Add both carrots and beans to the onions. Cover tightly and simmer for 45 minutes. Stir occasionally. Skin tomatoes and chop. Remove seeds from peppers and chop flesh. Add tomatoes, peppers and salt to the beans. Simmer gently for 15 minutes. Sprinkle with finely chopped herbs.

SWEET AND SOUR GREEN BEANS

Serves 4 as a main course

This particularly attractive dish is excellent when served as a main course, accompanied by fresh wholemeal bread and cheese.

400 g French beans
4 slices bacon
1 tb flour
½ c chicken or vegetable stock
2 tb cider vinegar
2 tb sugar
1 tb very finely-chopped onion

Cook beans whole in boiling, salted water until just tender. Drain. Using scissors, cut bacon into postage stamp-sized pieces. Cook bacon in a medium-sized frying pan until lightly browned and crisp. Remove bacon and drain. Tip off all but 2 tb of the bacon fat. Add flour to the frying pan and blend in stock, vinegar, sugar and onion. Cook, stirring constantly until mixture thickens and boils. Add beans and bacon. Heat gently. Serve immediately.

Freezing

French beans can be frozen whole or cut into 2 cm pieces. Whole young beans should be blanched for 3 minutes, and cut beans for 2 minutes.

Runner beans should be frozen only when young, no more than 15 cm long. Do not slice finely as this will result in a poor texture. Cut into 2 cm pieces. Blanch for 2 minutes.

Pack cooled beans, in meal-sized quantities, in freezer bags. Do not thaw before cooking.

BEAN SPROUTS

Varieties

Many seeds can be sprouted indoors with very little effort and no specialised equipment. The resulting crisp, pale-green sprouts are both nutritious and appetizing. Our interest in seed sprouting increases each year in early spring when our gardens are falling behind the families' demands for fresh greens.

The most popular bean used for sprouting (obtainable from some grocers and most health food shops) is the mung (moong).bean. This is very small, olive green and oval shaped. Many other seeds produce tasty sprouts including alfalfa, lentils, soy beans, cress and mustard. Details on these can be found in many new recipe books on sprouting. Always buy seeds intended for sprouting, as many garden seeds are now treated with poisonous chemicals.

Cultivation

Our method of sprouting mung beans is very simple. Slightly different techniques are required for other varieites and if you are interested, check on these first.

In the kitchen

Sprouted beans should be kept immersed in a jar of cold water. Cover and store in the refrigerator. Two tablespoons of mung beans will produce about 2 cups when sprouted.

1. Soak 1-2 tablespoons of mung beans in cold water for 12 hours

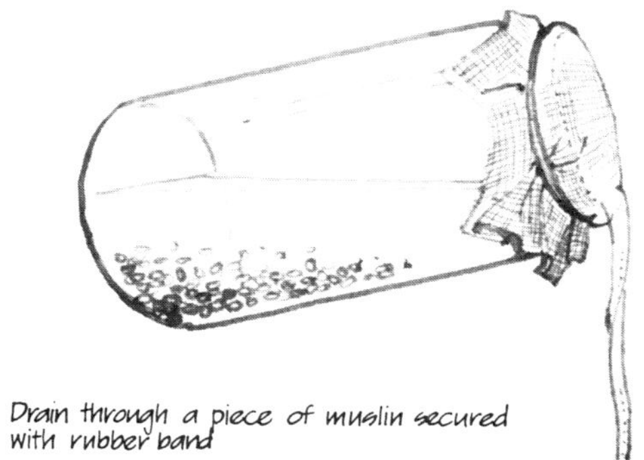

2. Drain through a piece of muslin secured with rubber band

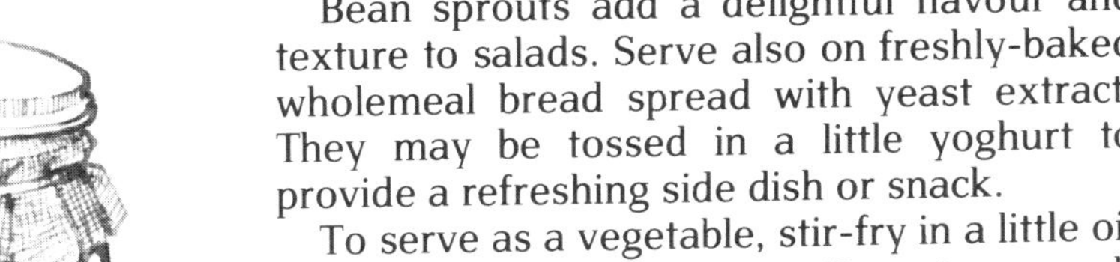

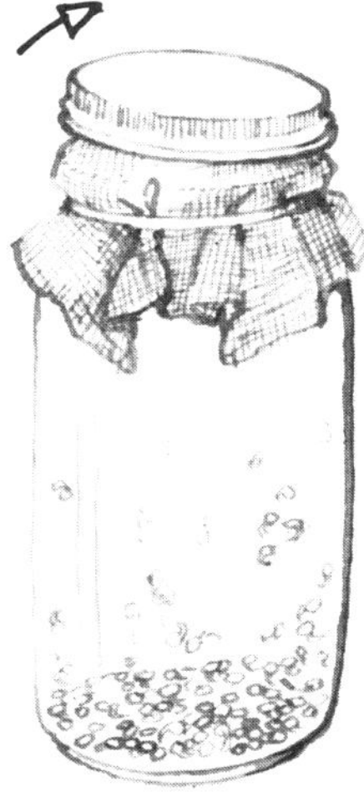

3. Screw lid on firmly over muslin and leave wet beans in a dark warm place, e.g. hotwater cupboard
4. At least 3 times a day fill jar with water and drain as in step 2

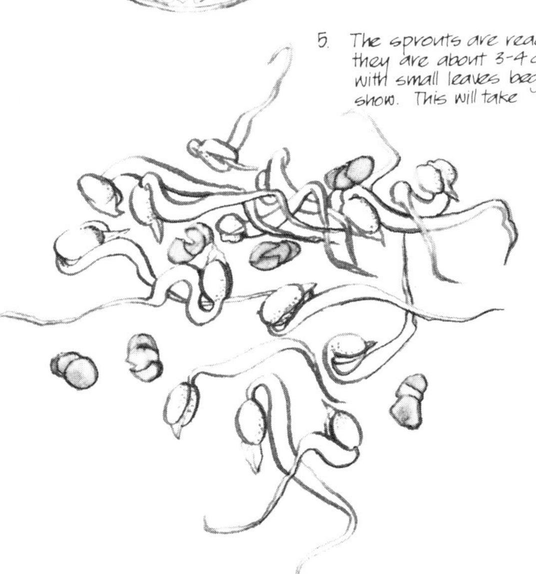

5. The sprouts are ready when they are about 3-4 cm long with small leaves beginning to show. This will take 3-4 days

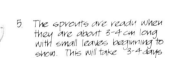

Bean sprouts add a delightful flavour and texture to salads. Serve also on freshly-baked wholemeal bread spread with yeast extract. They may be tossed in a little yoghurt to provide a refreshing side dish or snack.

To serve as a vegetable, stir-fry in a little oil over high heat for 2 minutes. Do not overcook or the crispness and delicate flavour will be lost. Stir-fry with finely-slivered, fresh root ginger and sliced spring onions for added flavour. Season with soy sauce and serve immediately. Four cups of bean sprouts will serve six.

Cook with other vegetables in Chinese-Style Vegetables (see page 206).

BEAN SPROUT, CARROT AND LEEK SAUTÉ

Serves 4

A colourful winter vegetable

1 tb cooking oil
1 c grated carrot
1 medium-sized leek, sliced finely
¼ c water
2 c bean sprouts
garlic salt to taste

Heat oil in a large frying pan. When hot add carrot, leek and water. Sauté until softened. Add bean sprouts and continue to cook for a few minutes. Season and serve immediately.

BEAN SPROUT OMELETTE

Serves 4-6

1 tb butter
2 spring onions
1 cm piece of root ginger
2 c bean sprouts
6 eggs
1 tsp soy sauce
¼ tsp salt
4 tb water

Melt butter in a large frying pan. Add finely-sliced spring onions including some of the green part. Peel ginger, chop finely and add to pan. Add bean sprouts. Sauté for 1 minute. Lightly beat eggs, soy sauce, salt and water. Tip into sprouts and cook until set. Cut omelette into sections and serve immediately.

Beetroot

*(**Beta vulgaris** var. **vulgaris**)*

Varieties

The underground, swollen stems of the beet vary in shape from globular to long and tapered like a carrot. As with so many vegetables, fewer varieties are available now than 20 years ago, but they are now generally of higher quality. However, varieties which do not bolt readily following cold weather have yet to be introduced to some countries. Early Wonder, a globe-shaped type, is usually grown as the first-sown beetroot, to be harvested in early summer. It has also been recommended for late summer planting because it is a little more tolerant of cold conditions than the maincrop types. The latter include the internationally-known Detroit Dark Red as well as Ruby Queen and Crimson Globe, all globe-shaped beetroot. Long-rooted beetroot are also grown as a maincrop to stand well until autumn harvesting. Obelisk and Cylindra (Cylindrica) are very similar varieties with roots 15 cm long. An increasingly popular variety from America is Golden Beet, which has tasty foliage and does not discolour other foods when mixed in a salad.

Cultivation

Beetroot are most successful in a sunny location and should be grown in a loose, friable soil, well supplied with humus and limed for a previous crop. Blood and bone and a light dressing of old animal manure are best dug in several weeks before sowing. For the production of sweet, tasty roots, potash applied in the form of wood ashes is recommended. Too much nitrogen impairs the flavour of the roots while encouraging luxuriant top growth.

Soak the seed for 24 hours and then plant in shallow drills, covering the seed with 1 cm of fine topsoil. For an early sowing (when the roots will be eaten golf-ball size) sow seed 2.5 cm apart in rows 20 cm apart. Thin the seedlings to 10 cm apart. Most seeds are actually clusters of two to six seeds, so don't be surprised to see small groups of seedlings. If germination is erratic in a bad spring, gaps in the rows may be filled by transplanting very young thinnings. For later sowings, place the seed about 8 cm apart in rows 30 cm apart. Leave the task of thinning until small edible beetroots have formed and then allow the rest to grow to tennis-ball (or carrot) size with 15-20 cm between plants.

Bolting occurs when mean daily temperatures are below 10-15°C for three or four weeks, so ensure that the maincrop sowing is made in warm, settled weather. Regular watering is necessary in dry weather to obtain even and tender growth.

Harvesting

Start harvesting early beetroot as soon as they

reach golf-ball size, for by the time they double in size their flavour and texture will have deteriorated. To avoid loss of colour by "bleeding", twist or cut off the tops 3 cm from the crowns.

Twist or cut off tops leaving about 3cm of stems. Do not remove rootlets

In the kitchen

The young leaves of golden beet are particularly delicious if prepared and cooked as you would silver beet.

To prepare beetroot, scrub with a vegetable brush under cold running water. Do not remove the rootlets and be careful not to pierce the skins or the beetroot will "bleed" as they cook. 750 g of beetroot will serve four to six.

Cover with water in a large saucepan and boil for 45 minutes – 1½ hours, depending on size and age. A pressure cooker comes into its own with beetroot cooking. You can reduce the time to 15-25 minutes.

The beetroot will be cooked when the largest one can be pierced easily with a toothpick. Drain, reserving cooking liquid if it is needed for a planned recipe. Slip off the skins, stems and roots by rubbing with the fingers.

HOT BEETROOT WITH HERB SAUCE

Serves 4

Golden beetroot contrast well with fresh green herbs.

4 cooked beetroot
2 tb butter
2 tb flour
1 c beetroot liquid or chicken stock
1 tb wine vinegar or cider vinegar
3 tb scissored chives
1 tb chopped parsley

Melt butter in a saucepan, add flour and cook for 1 minute. Gradually stir in beetroot liquid or stock. Stir constantly until the sauce thickens and boils. Add vinegar, herbs and seasoning. Add cubed beetroot and heat through.

HOT BEETROOT WITH ORANGE

Serves 4

4 cooked beetroot
3 tb butter
juice of 1 orange
¼ tsp salt
½ tsp paprika
1 tsp sugar
finely-shredded orange rind to garnish

Melt butter in a saucepan, add cubed or sliced beetroot, orange juice, salt, paprika and sugar. Heat through and serve with shredded orange rind.

To serve cold, slice or cube cooked beetroot and dress with vinegar or lemon juice flavoured with sugar, salt and pepper. Grated horseradish or finely chopped onion may also be added.

NANCY'S FRESH BEETROOT PICKLE

Serves 4-6

½ tsp dry mustard
1 tb sugar
½ tsp salt
½ tsp whole cloves
½ clove of garlic
⅓ c vinegar
¼ c water or beetroot liquid
400 g sliced, cooked beetroot

Combine mustard, sugar, salt, cloves and garlic. Gradually stir in the vinegar and water. When smooth pour over the beetroot. Refrigerate until chilled. Remove garlic. This beetroot pickle keeps well in the refrigerator.

Variation: layer 1 small, very thinly sliced onion with the beetroot and/or add ¼ tsp caraway seeds.

BEETROOT IN JELLY

Serves 6-8

This is a popular way of serving beetroot as a salad. It avoids any discoloration of other foods.

- 3 medium-sized beetroot, cooked
- 1 tb gelatine
- ½ c hot water
- 2 tsp sugar
- 1 c cold water
- ¼ c vinegar (wine or white vinegar if using golden beetroot)
- salt and pepper to taste

Cut beetroot into 1 cm cubes and place in a basin or jelly mould (1 litre capacity). Dissolve gelatine in hot water. Add sugar, cold water, vinegar and seasoning. Leave to thicken slightly and then pour over the beetroot. Chill. Just before serving, place mould or basin in warm water briefly. Tip out on to a serving plate, and garnish with salad vegetables.

CHILLED BORSCH

Serves 4-6

A refreshing, colourful soup for a summer dinner party. Adding the third grated, raw beetroot is an important step which gives the soup its beautiful colour. For a change use golden beetroot in this recipe.

- 1 onion, peeled
- 1 carrot, scrubbed
- 3 medium-sized beetroot, scrubbed (not cooked)
- 1 litre beef stock
- 2 cloves
- sprig of parsley
- sprig of dill or fennel
- salt and pepper to taste
- 1 tsp sugar
- 2 tb lemon juice
- 4-6 dsp sour cream and scissored chives for garnishing

Chop onion and carrot roughly. Peel and grate two of the beetroot on a coarse grater. Put onion, carrots and grated beetroot in a saucepan with the stock, cloves, parsley and dill. Bring to the boil and simmer for 30 minutes. Strain through a fine wire sieve. Add seasonings, sugar and lemon juice. Grate the third peeled beetroot and add to the soup. Leave to infuse for 2 hours. Strain again. Chill thoroughly. To serve, pour into soup bowls and garnish each with a blob of sour cream and a sprinkling of chives.

BOTTLED BEETROOT PICKLE

- 2 kg beetroot, cooked
- 1.5 litres vinegar
- 2 tsp whole cloves
- 5 cm piece of root ginger, bruised
- 2 tsp peppercorns
- 2 tsp mustard seeds
- 2 tb salt
- 2 c sugar

Boil vinegar, spices and seasonings together for 30 minutes. Have the lid on the saucepan. Strain. Peel beetroot and cut into 5 mm slices. Place in hot preserving jars. Cover with the boiling, spiced vinegar. Cover with seals and screw rings on tightly.

BEETROOT RELISH

Makes a colourful biscuit or sandwich spread. If golden beetroot are used add ½ tsp turmeric to the recipe.

- 1 kg beetroot, cooked
- 500 g onions
- 1 c vinegar
- 3 tsp salt
- 1 c sugar
- 1 tsp mixed ground spice
- pinch cayenne pepper (a big pinch if you like it hot)
- 1 tb cornflour
- 1 tb extra vinegar

Peel and mince the beetroot and onions. Place in a large saucepan with the vinegar, salt, sugar, spice and cayenne. Boil for 20 minutes. Mix cornflour and extra vinegar together. Stir into the relish. Cook for 3 minutes. Spoon into clean, hot, dry jars. Seal.

Freezing

Young cooked beetroot should be skinned and cubed before packing in convenient recipe-sized portions. Thaw for 2-3 hours before using. They are best in hot beetroot dishes.

Use bottled beetroot pickle for salads.

Broad beans

(Vicia faba)

Varieties

There are three main types of broad bean: longpod beans with four to seven seeds per pod, windsor or broadpod beans with three to five seeds and small podded types best represented by Cole's Early Dwarf with two to four seeds per pod. The longpod types are hardier and are often planted from mid to late autumn to flower in spring. They can then be picked in early summer, a time when vegetables are scarce and expensive in cool districts. Windsor beans are considered to have a better flavour but are not suitable for overwintering in frosty areas. The dwarf beans have gained popularity as gardens have become smaller and they, too, can be planted in autumn. In New Zealand, however, Cole's Early Dwarf grows at least twice as high as the 30-37 cm-high English dwarf types.

Cultivation

Broad beans need plenty of moisture when they are filling out their pods, so they are best planted in a loam containing particles of clay for water retention in early summer. However, heavy ground which is waterlogged in winter is quite unsuitable for an autumn-sown crop. It is probably better to add water-holding material like compost to the ground than to struggle with intractible clay. These beans benefit from a dressing of superphosphate worked into the soil a few weeks before sowing, at a rate of a quarter of a cup for each metre of row.

In late autumn, blood and bone does not break down very quickly and on clay loams it can become smelly. An inorganic fertilizer is therefore preferred. Lime may be added at the same rate if the soil is acid. Avoid highly nitrogenous fertilizers as too much nitrogen can lead to failure to set pods.

Broad beans are usually planted in double rows. The seeds are placed with the eye downwards at the bottom of a 20 cm wide and 5 cm deep trench, so that each seed is about 10 cm from its neighbour. The trench is then filled in with good soil, leaving a slight hollow in

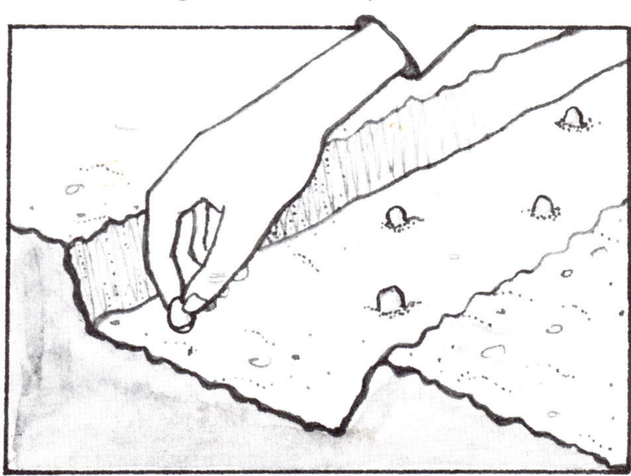

Plant beans with eye downwards

the centre for collecting water to assist germination. Leave at least a metre between each trench if you are growing longpod types, for each seed will produce four or five stalks up to 1.8 m high. Unless restrained, these bushy plants quickly turn the space between each pair of double rows into a green tunnel, fun for children but difficult for picking. In our experience, the conventional methods of securing broad beans using light stakes and twine are quite inadequate in many gardens. Fencing standards driven into the subsoil provide vertical support but spring gales may bend the soft top growth right over the top string. A light stake lashed to the upright supports to make a "top railing" on either side of the row seems to be the best solution.

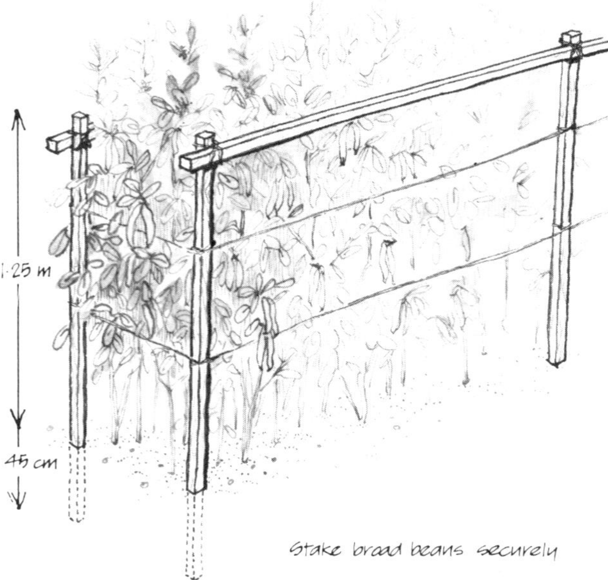

Stake broad beans securely

As the beans mature in spring or early summer, they may be attacked by black aphids which cluster in the growing tips, or by rust which spreads rapidly on the leaves and stems, eventually killing the plant. In autumn-sown crops these troubles usually strike at the end of the harvest period. To combat rust in spring-sown beans it may be necessary to spray with lime sulphur. Black aphids are usually controlled by pinching out the tips of the stalks after plenty of flowers have set. Dark brown spots are occasionally seen on leaves and stems after periods of high humidity. This fungus disease is a form of Botrytis, and can be treated with a copper oxychloride spray.

The roots of broad beans and other legumes are covered with nodules rich in nitrogen, and should either be dug back into the garden or placed in the compost heap along with the leaves and stalks. If you have plenty of seeds, grow broad beans as a green crop, digging them in when about 20-30 cm high after eating some of their tender tips.

Harvesting

Broad beans can be picked when the pods are only half grown and the seeds inside smaller than peas. Slice, pod and all, and cook like French beans. They may also be frozen at this stage. At the same time, the growing tips can be removed and cooked as spinach. Some people actually prefer them to spinach because they don't impart the "furry-teeth" sensation. As the seeds fill out they alone are eaten, provided that the outer coating of the seed is

Pinch out top 10 cm
Use as spinach

still green. When this coating turns white it develops a strong flavour, invariably disliked by children, and responsible for the bad name that broad beans have as a vegetable.

In the kitchen

Young broad bean shoots (10 cm of the growing tip) should be thoroughly washed and placed in a large saucepan with 2 tb butter, ¼ c water and 1 tsp salt. Simmer until just tender. Drain well. Serve with butter and freshly ground black pepper.

Immature bean pods should be washed, the ends removed and left whole if very small, or sliced diagonally. Boil in salted water until tender. Serve with butter and freshly ground black pepper. Finely chopped chervil, parsley and a little lemon juice are delicious additions.

Pods containing young, filled-out beans should be shelled and the pods discarded to the compost heap. Cook freshly shelled broad beans in boiling, salted water until tender. This will take from 7-20 minutes depending on age. Drain well and serve with any of the following accompaniments:

butter and freshly ground black pepper
butter, pepper and 1 tb finely chopped savory or parsley
fry finely-chopped bacon until crumbly and sprinkle over the cooked beans
parsley sauce (see page 208)
grated cheese

TURKISH-STYLE BROAD BEANS

Serves 4

Garlic and yoghurt combine well to give this dish its interesting flavour

2 c broad beans, cooked
½ c plain yoghurt
salt and pepper to taste
1 clove garlic, finely chopped
1 tsp butter
1 egg yolk

Heat the yoghurt in a small saucepan. Season with salt and pepper and the finely chopped garlic. Add the broad beans and butter. Heat through gently. Beat egg yolk lightly with a fork. Pour into the bean mixture and stir constantly until the sauce begins to thicken. Do not boil.

BROAD BEANS AND MUSHROOMS AU GRATIN

Serves 4

300 g broad beans, cooked
1 tb butter
200 g mushrooms, sliced

Sauce:

2 tb butter
2 tb flour
150 ml chicken stock
150 ml top milk
1 tb grated Parmesan cheese
salt and pepper to taste

Topping:

4 tb dry breadcrumbs
2 tb grated Parmesan cheese

Sauté mushrooms in 1 tb butter for 5 minutes. Prepare sauce. Melt the butter in a small saucepan, add the flour and cook for 1-2 minutes. Gradually stir in the chicken stock and top milk. Continue stirring until the sauce thickens and boils. Remove from heat. Add the cheese and seasoning. Grease a shallow ovenproof dish and in this, layer the beans and mushrooms. Pour the sauce over the vegetables. Top with the breadcrumbs, grated cheese and dots of butter. Bake at 200°C for about 15 minutes until heated through and the topping is golden.

BROAD BEANS AND HAM

Serves 4 as a light luncheon dish

400 g broad beans, cooked
⅓ c cream
freshly ground black pepper
1 tb finely chopped savory (or parsley)
8 slices ham

Combine beans, cream, pepper and ¾ tb savory in a small saucepan. Heat through. Place a spoonful of bean mixture on one half of each ham slice. Fold over and arrange on a serving dish. Sprinkle the remaining savory over the top and serve immediately.

BROAD BEAN SALAD

Serves 4-6

The easiest way to prepare this dish is to cook more beans than you need for an earlier meal. It is a good way of using up slightly older beans.

Slip off the outer skins after cooking and before the dressing is added. Be careful not to overcook.

500 g broad beans, cooked

Dressing:

¼ tsp dry mustard
1 tsp paprika
1 clove garlic, finely chopped
¼ tsp salt
freshly-ground black pepper
1 tb chopped parsley
1 tb wine vinegar or cider vinegar
2 tb salad oil

Combine dressing ingredients and beat until well blended. Pour over the beans. Serve with or without lettuce.

BROAD BEAN SOUP

Serves 4-5

Another way of using up slightly older beans.

1 small onion
2 medium-sized carrots
2 sticks celery
3 tb butter
300 g broad beans
800 ml chicken stock
salt and pepper to taste
a sprig of savory
3 rashers of bacon

Peel onion and chop finely. Scrub carrots and cut into thin slices. Chop celery finely. Melt the butter in a large saucepan and sauté the onion, carrots and celery for a few minutes. Add the beans, chicken stock, seasoning and savory. Bring to the boil and simmer gently until the vegetables are tender. Remove savory sprig. Put the soup through a fine sieve. Reheat. Dice bacon finely and fry until crisp. Pour soup into individual bowls and top with the crisp bacon.

Freezing

Shelled broad beans are the best vegetable we know for freezing. They have a long freezer life, retain their flavour and texture and take less time to cook than do fresh ones.

Freeze only young beans with tender skins. Blanch for 2-3 minutes depending on size. Discard any beans which are still white after blanching. Pack cooled beans in meal-sized quantities in freezer bags or snap freeze on a large tray or roasting dish for one hour, before packing in bulk in large freezer bags. With this free-flow method, sufficient beans for a meal can be removed and the bulk supply resealed. Do not thaw before cooking.

Broccoli, sprouting and heading

(*Brassica oleracea* var. *italica* and *Brassica oleracea* var. *botrytis asparagoides*)

Varieties

Sprouting broccoli produce a central head like cauliflowers and heading broccoli but, unlike them they then proceed to send up numerous small flower heads on side shoots. All these heads are picked before the flowers open. Three types exist: a hardy purple type which grows for 10-12 months before sprouting begins, a white type which is less prolific but will overwinter in sheltered gardens for spring harvesting and the popular green type, also known as calabrese, which is usually planted out in late summer for harvesting in early winter. Several named hybrids are listed, such as Dandy, Triumverate Mixture and Greensleeves. De Cicco, Green Sprouting Medium and Late take a little longer to mature. By careful selection of varieties it is possible to spread the two-month harvesting period from late autumn right through to spring.

Small side heads will soon develop
Cut off central head of sprouting broccoli

Heading broccoli look very similar to cauliflowers when picked but in the garden they exhibit some important differences. Often they have longer, narrower leaves which curl over the heart or curd, and they are both hardier and slower to mature. This makes them well suited for meeting winter and spring requirements in cool areas. Plant breeders have simplified the gardener's task of arranging for a succession by producing numbered types of the same variety which are sown and planted in one batch but mature in six, seven, eight, nine and ten months. The Pearl series comes in early, medium and late types, while the Roscoff series covers the same period in four types.

Cultivation

Sprouting broccoli like a sunny, sheltered position and a deeply worked soil which is rich in humus. Heading broccoli will tolerate a more exposed site provided the stems are earthed up. Lime is usually applied to all brassica plots two or three months ahead of sowing. In new gardens which have been well supplied with compost, animal manure and rotted turf, no extra nutrients are needed apart from the lime, but the intensively worked garden may need a dressing of fertilizer to supply the needs of these large, hungry plants.

Broccoli seed is normally sown in seed-boxes or prepared seed beds. We prefer deep boxes or beds as there is less danger of them drying out. Sow the seed in shallow drills with about 2-3 cm between seeds. Germination is rapid in warm, moist conditions and the plants can be thinned out in two to three weeks to 6-8 cm apart, pricking out the thinnings into another box if required. When four or five true leaves are present it is time for transplanting into the garden. Heading broccoli are set out in rows 60-90 cm apart with 60 cm between plants, while sprouting broccoli are grown in rows 50-60 cm apart with 45 cm between plants. Place the plants in slight hollows with the soil level up to the base of the seed leaves. Firm well (but don't stomp clay soils) and water regularly for the first week. Any setbacks experienced by the young growing plant, such as drought or root exposure, lead to premature flowering and the formation of "button" heads. Tin collars are especially useful for the first two weeks after transplanting.

White butterfly caterpillars and grey aphids are the most troublesome pests of brassicas. Discourage the caterpillars with Derris Dust and aphids with a liquid pyrethrum spray.

Harvesting

It is a good idea to grow sprouting broccoli beside a path because then they can be inspected every two or three days for sprouts which might be about to open their flowers. Once this happens they are no longer a delicacy to eat and further sprouting is inhibited. A vigorous plant will produce sprouts 10-15 cm long. Cook them as soon as possible after cutting, to retain their fresh flavour.

Cut the heading broccoli curd with a few younger leaves curled around it.

In the kitchen

For heading broccoli see cauliflower section. For sprouting broccoli remove any leaves and soak, heads down, in salted water for a few minutes to dislodge insects. Rinse thoroughly under fast, running water.

Cut the flowerets from the thick stalks leaving some stem on each. If the flowerets are large they can be sliced lengthwise through the stems. If the thick stalks seem tough, peel them thinly. Slice the thick stalks cross-wise into 5 mm slices. The flowerets, stems and thick stalks will now all take about the same time to cook. You will need approximately 150 g of broccoli for each serving.

Cook quickly in a small amount of boiling, salted water until the stalks are just tender. 5-10 mintues should be sufficient. Drain and serve immediately. If you have a recipe specifying cooked broccoli refresh in a large quantity of cold water before draining thoroughly and putting aside.

Serve broccoli hot, as a vegetable, with butter and freshly-ground black pepper or pesto sauce (see page 99). Other sauces which can be used are mornay sauce (see page 208), hollandaise sauce (see page 208) or blue vein sauce.

BLUE VEIN SAUCE

30 g crumbled blue-vein cheese
30 g butter
¼ c sour cream

Combine ingredients and stir until smooth. Heat gently, stirring constantly. Pour over freshly-cooked and drained broccoli and serve immediately.

BROCCOLI À LA POLONAISE

Serves 6

½ c dry breadcrumbs
80 g butter
1 hard boiled egg, chopped
1 tb finely-chopped parsley
1 kg broccoli, cooked

Sauté the breadcrumbs in butter in a small frying pan until golden. Add chopped egg and parsley. Mix well. Sprinkle over hot broccoli in a serving dish. Serve immediately.

Cold broccoli with vinaigrette makes a refreshing first course or accompanying salad. Pour vinaigrette (see page 209) over warm, freshly-cooked broccoli. Allow to cool. Garnish with scissored chives or chopped tarragon.

BROCCOLI AU GRATIN

Serves 4

500 g broccoli, cooked

Sauce:

2 tb butter
1 shallot or small onion, finely chopped
2 tb flour
1 tsp mild, prepared mustard
300 ml chicken stock
squeeze of lemon juice
1 egg yolk
3 tb cream
1 tb grated Parmesan cheese
salt and pepper to taste

Topping:

2 tb grated Parmesan cheese

Sauté the shallot in melted butter until soft. Add flour and mustard. Cook for one minute. Gradually add chicken stock, stirring continuously until the sauce thickens and boils. Remove from heat and add the lemon juice. Mix egg yolk and cream together and stir into the sauce. Add cheese and seasoning. Reheat without boiling. Place the broccoli in a greased, shallow, ovenproof dish. Spoon the sauce over the broccoli. Sprinkle the surface with 2 tb grated Parmesan cheese. Bake at 200°C for 15-20 minutes until heated through and the cheese is bubbly and lightly browned.

SAVOURY BROCCOLI CUSTARD

Serves 6

This colourful combination of broccoli, bacon and a rich custard makes an excellent lunch dish or first course.

700 g broccoli, cooked
3 slices bacon
½ tsp salt
freshly-ground black pepper
freshly-grated nutmeg
¼ tsp dry mustard
4 eggs
¾ c milk
¾ c cream
4 tb grated Parmesan cheese

Place the broccoli in a greased ovenproof dish (20-25 cm square). Cut bacon into small pieces, fry until crisp and sprinkle over the broccoli. Combine the salt, pepper, nutmeg and mustard in a bowl. Add the eggs and beat lightly. Stir in the milk, cream and half the cheese. Pour over the broccoli. Sprinkle the remaining cheese over the surface. Place the dish in a pan of hot water. Bake at 180°C for 25-30 minutes until the custard is just set. Serve immediately.

CREAM OF BROCCOLI SOUP

Serves 4-6

2 tb butter
1 leek
1 stalk of celery
1 small potato
500 g prepared broccoli
750 ml chicken stock
100 ml cream
salt and pepper to taste
1 tb lemon juice

Melt the butter in a large saucepan. Sauté the finely-sliced leek and celery until it just begins to soften but not brown. Add the finely-sliced potato and sauté for a few more minutes. Add broccoli and stock. Simmer until the vegetables are tender. Put through a blender or fine sieve. Return the soup to the saucepan, add the cream, seasoning and lemon juice. Reheat gently. Serve garnished with croûtons.

Freezing

Blanch prepared broccoli for 3 minutes, cool and pack into plastic containers. We find 2-litre icecream cartons are a good size. Thaw sufficiently to separate before cooking.

Brussels sprouts

(Brassica oleracea var. *bullata gemmifera)*

Varieties

This very hardy member of the brassica family probably evolved by selection from wild cabbage. Like broccoli they have been bred for a succession of harvest periods and it is possible to grow early, second-early, maincrop and late varieties. Emerald Ball is sown in mid spring for mid autumn harvesting. Jade Cross and Jade E hybrids are also considered to be early or second-early types. They grow about 70 cm high and are covered in numerous blue-green sprouts. An American strain known as Catskill is only 50 cm high, more suited to windy gardens, while the old-fashioned variety Fillbasket grows up to 1 metre. In general, tall varieties are slower maturing.

Cultivation

Brussels sprouts should be grown in well-limed, well-drained and well-firmed soil, as this vegetable cannot stand wet feet nor loose soil about its roots. The sort of friable, humus-enriched loam in which lettuces thrive will result in the formation of open sprouts consisting of a few loose leaves. The same effect is produced by too great a proportion of nitrogen compounds in fertilizer applied to the brussels sprouts. So the usual recommendation is therefore to grow them in ground enriched with compost or manure for a previous crop such as early beans or peas, without digging over the soil between removal of one crop and planting the next. A general fertilizer mixture can be raked in at planting time (see page 8). If your soil is a heavy clay loam however, an additional two to four cups of dry poultry manure could be forked into each metre of row and the area left to consolidate for two weeks before planting.

The plants are normally started in a seed bed with other brassicas and are thinned to 7 cm apart as soon as their true leaves have appeared. After seven to eight weeks when the plants are about 15 cm high they are transplanted into the garden. Spacing for dwarf types is 45-60 cm between plants and 60 cm between rows.

For taller types 75-90 cm between plants and 90 cm between rows is recommended.

The plants grow steadily through the summer and the tall varieties may need individual staking as they reach maturity. As the bottom leaves begin to yellow they are removed. With cooler weather sprout production begins and many growers apply a side dressing of one level tablespoon of sulphate of ammonia for every two plants at this time.

Brussels sprouts are troubled by caterpillars and grey aphids. The latter find their way into the tightly-folded sprout leaves and are a prime reason for children (and some adults) refusing to eat this otherwise delicious vegetable. Commercial growers use potent sprays to eliminate aphids, but for the home gardener who is unsure of their long-term effects only REGULAR spraying with pyrethrum from mid summer right through until the end of autumn will prevent aphid colonies from developing.

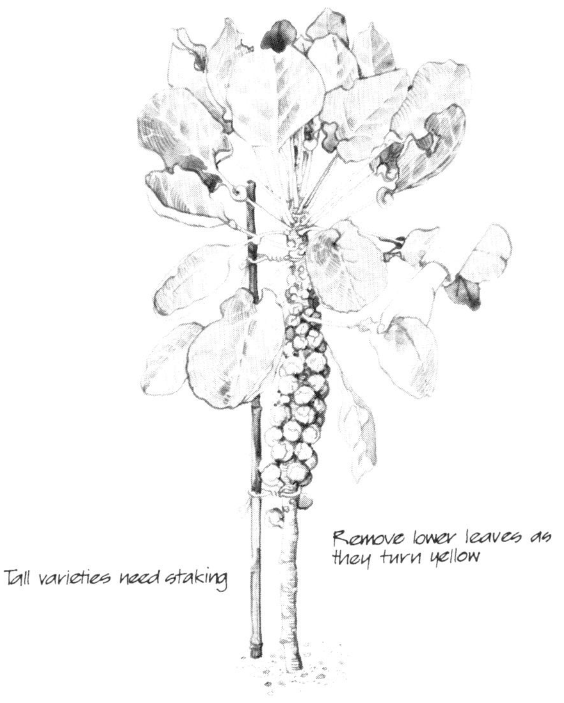
Remove lower leaves as they turn yellow
Tall varieties need staking

Harvesting

Pick the sprouts when they reach walnut size from the base of the plant up. If the lower leaves are still in position remove each one with its corresponding sprout. In early winter you may be picking every ten days while in mid winter every three weeks. From a healthy plant you can expect to pick sprouts for two to three months. When the last sprout is eaten cook the tops as they are of good flavour.

In the kitchen

Remove any loose or discoloured leaves. If tight sprouts have been affected by aphids you can usually remove enough outer leaves to reveal unaffected inner parts. Wash thoroughly and trim the stem ends. Cut a cross into the stem end to hasten cooking. Allow 100 g of Brussels sprouts to each serving.

Cook in sufficient boiling, salted water to ensure that the sprouts float. Cooking will take from seven to 12 minutes depending on size. They will be cooked when you can just pierce them with a small, sharp knife. Drain thoroughly.

Serve hot with butter and pepper or add freshly-chopped herbs.

BRUSSELS SPROUTS AND ALMONDS

Serves 4-6

An excellent dinner party vegetable. The almonds can be sautéed ahead of time.

500 g prepared Brussels sprouts
2 tb butter
2 tb blanched, slivered almonds
¼ tsp salt
¼ tsp paprika
juice of 1 lemon

Cook sprouts in a little lightly salted water until tender. While the sprouts are cooking melt the butter in a small frying pan. Sauté the almonds until golden. Drain the sprouts and season with salt, paprika and lemon juice. Tip into a serving dish and sprinkle surface with almonds and melted butter.

BRUSSELS SPROUTS WITH SPICY SOUR-CREAM SAUCE

Serves 4-6

500 g prepared Brussels sprouts
1 small onion, finely-chopped
2 tb butter
1 tb flour
1 tb brown sugar
½ tsp salt
¼ tsp dry mustard
½ c milk
⅓ c sour cream
1 tb chopped parsley

Cook the sprouts in boiling, salted water until tender. Drain. Sauté the onion in butter until soft. Stir in the flour, brown sugar, salt and mustard. Add the milk gradually. Stir until thickened and boiling. Remove from the heat. Add the sour cream and parsley. Add the sprouts and heat through gently. Do not boil.

BRUSSELS SPROUTS AND MUSHROOMS

Serves 4-6

A delicious combination of flavours.

500g prepared Brussels sprouts
3 tb butter
2 shallots or 1 small onion
150 g mushrooms
2 tb lemon juice
salt to taste
freshly-ground black pepper

Cook the sprouts in a little boiling, salted water until just tender. While the sprouts are cooking melt the butter in a medium-sized frying pan. Sauté the peeled and finely-chopped shallots or onion until soft. Add the washed and sliced mushrooms. Cook gently until the mushrooms are tender. Add the lemon juice. Drain the sprouts and add to the mushrooms. Season with salt and pepper. Heat through carefully and serve immediately.

BRUSSELS SPROUTS SALAD

Serves 6

This well-flavoured salad tastes as good as it looks.

500 g prepared Brussels sprouts
3 tb salad oil
2 tb wine vinegar
¼ tsp dry mustard
¼ tsp sugar
¼ tsp salt
freshly-ground black pepper
1 medium-sized lettuce, washed
4 small tomatoes (optional)
1 tb chopped parsley
1 shallot, finely chopped

Cook the sprouts in boiling, salted water until just tender. Drain. Combine oil, vinegar, mustard, sugar, salt and pepper in a small bowl. Beat with a fork. Pour over the sprouts and leave to marinate for two hours. Tear lettuce into bite-sized pieces. Place in a salad bowl. Arrange the sprouts evenly over the surface. Garnish with quartered tomatoes if available. Sprinkle surface of salad with parsley and shallot. Pour marinade juice over the top. Serve at room temperature. You can make this salad without lettuce by increasing the quantity of Brussels sprouts. Orange or mandarin slices can replace the tomatoes.

BAKED BRUSSELS SPROUTS WITH CHEESE

Serves 6

This is a good recipe for preparing ahead of time. Leave the baking until dinner is nearly ready.

600 g prepared Brussels sprouts
salt and pepper to taste
freshly-grated nutmeg
2 tb cream or top milk
60 g grated Cheddar cheese
2 tb butter

Cook the sprouts in boiling, salted water until just tender. Drain. Place in a greased ovenproof dish. Add seasonings and cream. Sprinkle cheese over the top and dot with butter. Bake at 180°C for 15-20 minutes until heated through and the cheese is bubbly and golden.

Freezing

Blanch small prepared Brussels sprouts in boiling water with a teaspoon of vinegar added. Cool, pat dry and pack in freezer bags. Do not thaw before cooking.

Cabbage

(Brassica oleracea var. ***capitata*** and ***Brassica oleracea*** var. ***bullata*** [savoy types]***)***

Varieties
The large number of cabbage varieties is a good indication of the importance of this vegetable to market gardeners and home gardeners in temperate countries. The long lists in seedsmen's catalogues can be simplified into four types: conical varieties which heart in spring after standing all winter, ball and drum-head varieties sown in spring for summer and autumn harvest, crinkly-leaved savoy cabbages sown in late spring for winter harvest and smooth-leaved red, pickling types which mature in autumn.

Flower of Spring is probably the best-known conical type. It is also available in a new hybrid form which is resistant to several diseases and able to be grown in summer. Wheelers Imperial is a small spring cabbage while Myatt's Early Offenham caters for larger families. Of the ball and drum-head varieties, Succession, Green Acre and Golden Acre have long been popular. Several hybrid types are also being promoted. Sentinel F.1 Hybrid is said to withstand drought and bad weather. Harvester Queen Hybrid and Stonehead F.1 Hybrid produce extremely solid cabbages which hold well. Greengold Hybrid gives medium-sized heads of great uniformity. In addition to the old Savoy Drumhead (Savoy Best of All) and the very late-maturing Savoy Omega, a hybrid type, Savoy King F.1 Hybrid is also available. It is claimed to be more resistant to heat and certain diseases. Red Dutch is the best-known red cabbage.

Cultivation
Cabbages thrive in deeply-dug, well-drained soil supplied with plenty of humus to hold moisture during summer. If no lime has been applied in the last 2 years the bed should be limed a few weeks before planting out. Strict

Drumhead

Savoy

Conical

Red cabbage

organic gardeners who wish to avoid the use of artificial fertilizers should cover the cabbage plot with a 10 cm layer of compost and old animal manure and dig it in deeply. If you don't have this quantity available supplement with a general fertilizer, for cabbages are gross feeders with very strong root systems.

Sow the seed in drills 30 cm apart in a finely-cultivated seed bed, thinning the plants to 7 cm apart when the first true leaves appear. This spacing helps to keep the plants straight-stemmed and sturdy and enables you to lift each one with a good ball of fibrous roots and soil about six weeks later. If only a few plants are required, sow a few seeds in deep plastic trays. When planting out make a deep hole with the trowel so that the cabbage taproot remains straight, and insert the plant so that the seed leaves are just above the soil. Water well. If the weather is hot and dry you could shorten the older leaves by one-third to reduce wilting. The use of tin collars makes this unnecessary. Spacing between rows and plants depends on the variety grown. Small spring cabbages may be grown 30 cm apart with 30 cm between rows, while large drumheads need 60 cm between plants and up to 90 cm between rows. To some extent you can limit cabbage size by planting medium-sized varieties closer than normal. This technique also helps to retain soil moisture and seems to inhibit the white butterfly.

Summer and autumn cabbages grown in rich ground heart up with no extra attention beyond shallow weeding and pest control. But to start spring cabbages into growth in early spring, a boost of liquid manure or foliar fertilizer, such as those made from seaweed, is often required.

Pest control is extremely important for producing crisp, well-flavoured cabbages with family appeal. Control the green caterpillar with Derris Dust, and grey aphids with regular spraying with pyrethrum. Keep the patch clean and tidy during winter as aphids overwinter on old stumps and outer leaves which have been left attached to the stumps.

Harvesting

To avoid a surplus of mature heads later on, start cutting as soon as the hearts begin to firm. Careful planning of planting times and quantities should overcome this problem, but this is only possible with a few years' experience. In the meantime choose varieties which are slow to bolt and resistant to splitting.

In the kitchen

Remove any coarse, discoloured outer leaves and trim off the thick stalk. Wash thoroughly. Cut cabbage into quarters. Slice out the core and hard midribs. Using a sharp knife slice each quarter finely. Allow 500 g of cabbage to serve four to six.

There are two simple ways of cooking cabbage: the traditional way of boiling it in a little salted water and the newer method called butter-steaming.

If you choose the first method use only a minimum of boiling, salted water and be careful not to overcook. Finely-shredded, fresh cabbage will take only three to seven minutes to reach the desirable tender-crisp stage. Drain thoroughly and season with freshly-ground black pepper.

To butter-steam, melt 2 tb of butter and 1 tb of oil in a large frying pan or saucepan with a tightly-fitting lid. When hot add the finely-shredded cabbage and 4 tb of water. Cover and steam until tender-crisp. This will take about 5 minutes depending on how full your frying pan is. Drain if necessary and season with salt and freshly-ground black pepper.

Solid, white-hearted and savoy cabbages are best cooked in the traditional way, while green, loose-hearted cabbages are superb when butter-steamed.

Serve freshly-cooked, well-seasoned cabbage with plenty of butter and, if you like, a sprinkling of finely-chopped herbs such as dill, parsley, chives, savory or mint.

Serve cooked cabbage with the following:

Mornay sauce (see page 208)
Neapolitan tomato sauce (see page 196) and sprinkled with grated cheese.
Warmed sour cream and ½ tsp of caraway seeds for those who like the flavour.

The name *cole slaw* comes from the Dutch words *kool* meaning cabbage and *sla* meaning salad. We use two different dressings to serve with our cole slaws, a creamy, boiled dressing and a well-flavoured French dressing.

CREAMY COLE SLAW DRESSING

This dressing keeps well in a refrigerator. We double the recipe as cole slaw is frequently on our menus. Do not double the salt but add a little extra to taste.

1 tb sugar
1 dsp flour
1 tsp salt
1 tsp prepared mild mustard
½ c water
½ c vinegar (a herb vinegar will give an interesting flavour)
1 egg
1 tb butter

Mix dry ingredients together in a small saucepan. Add mustard and a little of the measured water. Stir until smooth. Add remaining water and vinegar and bring to the boil, stirring continuously. Simmer for 3 minutes. Beat egg in a small bowl and add butter. Pour hot vinegar mixture slowly on to the egg and beat thoroughly. Cool. Thin with cream or top milk if desired.

OIL AND VINEGAR COLE SLAW DRESSING

freshly-ground black pepper
½ tsp dry mustard
1 tsp celery salt
2 tb sugar
½ tsp grated onion
2 tb salad oil
4 tb vinegar

Combine all ingredients. This quantity will dress 4 cups of shredded cabbage.

COLE SLAW

Serves 6

4 c very finely-shredded cabbage (Flower of Spring or drumhead type)

Select 1 or 2 of the following additional ingredients:

sliced apple (do not peel)
coarsely-grated carrot
finely-sliced celery
grated cheese
pineapple pieces
cooked whole-kernel corn
green pepper slices
plumped up raisins (raisins soaked in water or orange juice)
grated or sliced winter radishes
chopped, dried apricots, soaked in orange juice
walnuts
thin onion slices
orange or mandarin segments

Combine all ingredients, add selected dressing and toss well. Cover and leave for 1-2 hours. Pile into a salad bowl and garnish with paprika, finely-chopped mint or parsley.

Edgings and pavings are attractive and practical

Old telegraph poles
Concrete sill slabs on sand

Old bricks
Gravel

Treated timber
Old bricks on sand

Concrete cobblestones set on edge into concrete
Concrete cobblestones on sand
Railway sleepers
Non-skid concrete paving slabs
Pongas (tree ferns)
Mercury bay weed does not require mowing
Railway sleepers for a small retaining wall
and mowing strip

HOT COLE SLAW

Serves 4-5

2 eggs
¼ c water
2 tb lemon juice or cider vinegar
1 tb sugar
½ tsp dill seed
¼ tsp salt or more to taste
freshly-ground black pepper
1 tb butter
4 c finely-shredded, cooked cabbage

Break the eggs into a saucepan and beat lightly with a fork. Add the water, lemon juice, sugar and dill. Season with salt and pepper. Beat well. Add butter and place over low heat, stirring with a wooden spoon until the mixture thickens. Do not boil. Stir in the freshly cooked cabbage and reheat gently. The dressing may be made ahead of time and then reheated gently just before adding the cabbage.

SCALLOPED CABBAGE AND APPLE

Serves 6

Goes well with a roast dinner. A useful recipe to serve when wishing to avoid last minute preparations.

500 g cabbage
400 g cooking apples
1 small onion
½ tsp castor sugar
1 tsp salt
freshly-ground black pepper
1 tb butter
¾ c soft breadcrumbs
2 tb butter

Shred cabbage finely. Peel, core and slice apples. Chop peeled onion finely. Place a layer of cabbage in a large, greased casserole. Sprinkle with a little onion and then add a layer of apple. Repeat layers. Sprinkle with sugar, salt and pepper and dot with butter. Fry breadcrumbs in remaining 2 tb of butter until crisp. Sprinkle over casserole. Cover and bake at 180°C for 45-60 minutes until apples and cabbage are tender. Remove cover and brown lightly before serving.

DOLMAS (Stuffed vine leaves)

Cabbage leaves can be used instead of grapevine leaves in the recipe given on page 97. Choose a small cabbage, preferably one with a loose heart such as Flower of Spring. Remove all damaged outer leaves. Cut out the stalk. Plunge cabbage into a saucepan of boiling water and boil for 3 minutes. Lift out and carefully peel off the leaves. You will need eight to 12 depending on the size. If they become difficult to remove without tearing, plunge the cabbage back in the boiling water for a few more minutes. You may need to trim off the thick base of each leaf if they prove difficult to roll up.

RED CABBAGE SALAD

Serves 6-8

half a red cabbage
half a small onion
1 tb honey
2 tb cider vinegar
¼ tsp salt
freshly-ground black pepper

Shred cabbage and onion very finely. Red cabbage has tougher leaves than green cabbage so it is important to shred it as finely as possible. We find that the shredder on an electric mixer does a good job. Place shredded cabbage and onion in a salad bowl. Combine honey (warmed if necessary), vinegar and seasonings. Pour over the salad and toss lightly. Leave for 1-2 hours before serving.

BRAISED RED CABBAGE

Serves 6-8

This is our version of the Continental method of cooking red cabbage, which goes well with sausages and boiled bacon.

half a red cabbage
3 medium-sized cooking apples
1 small onion
½ tsp sugar
1 tsp salt
freshly-ground black pepper
4 cloves
¼ tsp cinnamon
3 tb water
3 tb butter
1 tb vinegar (herb vinegar if you have any)

Shred the cabbage finely. Peel, core and slice

apples. Chop peeled onion finely. Place a layer of cabbage in a large, greased casserole. Add a little onion and then a layer of apples. Sprinkle with some of the sugar, salt, pepper, cloves and cinnamon. Repeat layers ending up with cabbage. Pour over the water. Dot surface with butter. Cover casserole with foil and then its lid. Bake at 180°C for 1½-2 hours. Just before serving stir in the vinegar. This brightens the colour.

CURRIED CABBAGE PICKLE

This is the best way we know of using up one or two spare cabbages in the garden.

1 large, green cabbage or 2 small ones
4 medium-sized onions
50 g salt
1 litre vinegar
½ c flour
2 c sugar
1 tb curry powder
1 tb dry mustard
1 tb turmeric
½ litre extra vinegar

Shred the cabbage and onions finely. Place in a large bowl and sprinkle the salt over the surface. Leave for 24 hours. Drain. Tip into a preserving pan, add the litre of vinegar and boil slowly for 20 minutes. Mix the flour, sugar, curry powder, mustard and turmeric together. Stir in the ½ litre of vinegar and mix until smooth. Add to the boiling cabbage, stirring until thick. If not thick enough add a little more flour mixed with water. Boil for 5 minutes. Spoon into dry, hot jars and seal.

PICKLED RED CABBAGE

It is worth making pickled red cabbage for its colour alone. The flavour and texture will be at their best between one and eight weeks later. If you leave it longer it will loose its crispness. The quantities given will be enough to fill a one-litre preserving jar.

1 small red cabbage
50 g salt
spiced white vinegar (see recipe below)
freshly-ground black pepper
½ tsp ground ginger

Place the finely-shredded red cabbage in a bowl, sprinkling each layer with salt. Cover and leave for 24 hours. Drain. Rinse cabbage well and drain again. Toss in a cloth to dry. Pack into wide-necked jars. Sprinkle each layer with a little ground ginger and pepper. Cover cabbage completely with the spiced vinegar. Seal.

SPICED VINEGAR

1 litre white vinegar
1 tb whole cloves
1 tb whole allspice
3 or 4 pieces of whole nutmegs (we use up fragments too small for grating)
cinnamon bark, one 10 cm stick
6 peppercorns

Bring vinegar and spices to the boil. Pour into a bowl, cover with a plate and leave for 2 hours to infuse. Strain and bottle.

This recipe gives a spicy but mild-flavoured vinegar. If you haven't got the individual spices, use a packet (25 g) of pickling spice instead. A fairly hot vinegar will result as packaged pickling spices usually include root ginger and chillies. A solution is to remove half of the chillies from the packet.

Freezing

Frozen cabbage is a poor substitute for fresh cabbage but is better than no cabbage at all. With careful processing and the use of quickly-grown, summer drumheads the results will be acceptable. Process surplus cabbages one at a time. In other words leave them growing until the last minute. Prepare as outlined at the beginning of this section. Blanch for one minute only. Cool quickly and dry on absorbent towels. Pack in meal-sized quantities in freezer bags. Do not thaw before cooking.

Carrots

(Daucus carota)

Varieties

Few gardeners would complain about the wide selection of carrot varieties offered by seed merchants. They come in all shapes and sizes from round to long and tapering and they take from 60 to over 80 days to reach maturity. Some are deep orange-red in colour with a strong flavour, others more yellowy-orange and mild. Despite the profusion of names most gardeners have a particular preference for an early type, to supply the kitchen in early and mid summer, and a maincrop type which will be sown in quantity to be ready for autumn and winter harvesting. The early varieties also tend to be the shorter in length. Popular varieties are Oxheart and Early Scarlet Horn. Gardeners who prefer a more conventional shape than round may make a sowing of a stump-rooted, cylindrical variety such as Earlykrop, Nantes Improved or Manchester Table, all of which have excellent flavour. For the maincrop sowing, varieties described as intermediate or long may be chosen. Three names are outstanding: Egmont Gold, Autumn King and Topweight. They are long, slightly tapering and offer some resistance to virus infections and attacks by the carrot rust fly.

Cultivation and harvesting

If you plan to grow conventionally-shaped carrots the soil must be deeply dug and free from stones, large clods or lumps of bulky manure and compost which might deform the young taproot and ultimately the mature carrot. The soil should be well-drained, especially for maincrop varieties which remain in the ground through winter. Some gardeners sow their carrots in raised beds to combat rot. If plenty of compost and manure has been incorporated for an earlier crop, a dressing of blood and bone can be worked into the ground one to two weeks before sowing. Wood ash is also useful as it intensifies the colour. Pale-coloured flesh can result from over-acid soil conditions or an excess of nitrogen, so if you intend to use a mixture of inorganic fertilizer, make sure it is suited to root crops.

Sow the seed thinly in drills made with the back of the rake in the finely-worked topsoil. The rows may be 15-30 cm apart according to the type grown, closer for early carrots which are deliberately harvested immature. Keep the soil moist for the next month for germination takes three weeks and the emergent seedlings are susceptible to heat damage for another week after they appear. A mist spray from a soak hose is ideal as it does not cake the soil. As soon as the true leaves begin to show, thin the carrots to 2-3 cm apart, watering thoroughly before and after the operation. The aim is to remove the small, thin plants and any plants growing too close to each other. No

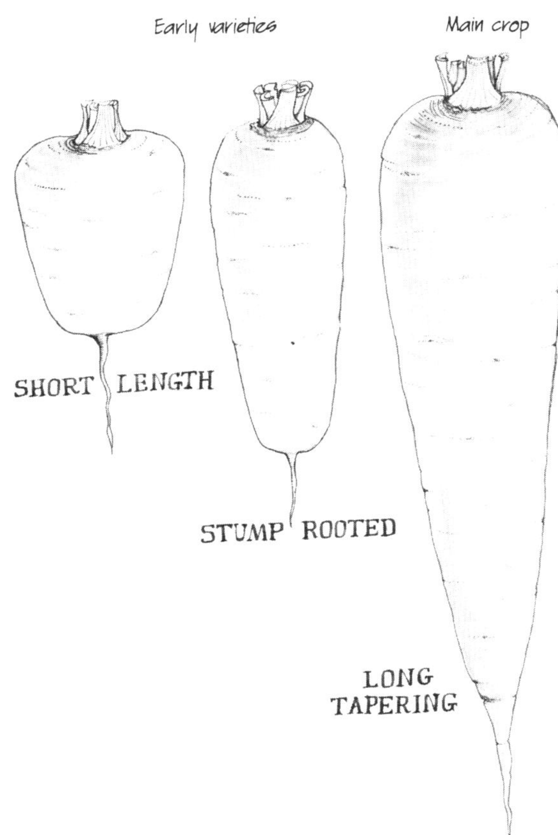

further thinning is needed with early carrots. After this, surface watering should be reduced to encourage the taproots to seek much deeper moisture. A month after the first thinning, maincrop varieties should be thinned again to 5-7 cm apart. This time save the thinnings for salads. Keep the rows weeded by light, shallow hoeing and make sure that the soil does not dry out below the loose surface layer. Otherwise the carrots may split with the next heavy rain as the interior grows faster than the skin.

Aphids occasionally infest carrot plants causing yellowing of the foliage. They can be controlled with a pyrethrum spray. However, once the larvae of the carrot fly have hatched and burrowed into the root no amount of spraying will prevent major damage. Prevention is therefore the objective, especially for gardeners in areas of light soils and hot summers where the problem is very serious. The carrot fly lays eggs in late spring and again in late summer and is attracted by the smell of carrot foliage, especially when it is bruised at thinning time. So thin on a still evening and bury the thinnings in the compost heap. Mounding the soil around the roots is also important together with a thorough watering. Many remedies have been found partially successful such as a side dressing of weathered soot or, if you can afford it, mixing freshly-ground coffee into the drill.

An American recipe suggests mixing one 600 ml bottle of crude black molasses with twelve 600 ml bottles of water and pouring it over the rows when the carrots are 5-7 cm high. Another suggestion is to spray with onion juice (1 onion crushed in 750 ml water). All these techniques aim to confuse the carrot fly's sense of smell. There is obviously plenty of room for experimentation with strong-smelling companion plants or even slow-release air fresheners.

In the kitchen

Cut enough from the top of each freshly-dug carrot to remove any trace of the stem. Stringy rootlets should also be removed. Scrub with a vegetable brush and rinse thoroughly. Scraping and peeling should be restricted to old carrots with marked skins. Allow about 100 g carrots for each serving.

Carrots can be cooked whole if small, cut lengthwise into halves or quarters, cut into sticks, diced or cut into thick or thin slices.

Cook in a small quantity of boiling, salted water. Use a heavy-based saucepan with a tight-fitting lid and be careful not to let them boil dry. Cooking times will depend on the age of the carrots and the way they are cut. Drain well.

To serve, add butter and season with pepper and a pinch of sugar. You can also add a few drops of lemon juice and freshly-chopped herbs such as chervil, dill, marjoram, mint and parsley. Hollandaise sauce (see page 208), parsley sauce (see page 208) and cheese sauce (see page 208) are also good accompaniments.

GLAZED CARROTS

Serves 4-6

500 g prepared carrots
4 tb butter
4 tb chicken stock (or water)
1 tb sugar
¼-½ tsp salt

Leave carrots whole if tiny or cut into 1 cm slices. Simmer in melted butter, stock, sugar and salt until tender. Most of the liquid will be absorbed. Drain and serve.

With herbs: sprinkle with 2 tb each of chopped parsley and chervil before serving.

Lemon glazed: add grated rind and juice of one lemon before cooking.

Oriental: add 2 tb soaked raisins before cooking.

With ginger and almonds: add 1 tsp preserved ginger and 2 tb almonds, both finely-chopped, before serving.

CARROTS AND SWEET-SOUR HERB SAUCE

Serves 4-6

500 g prepared carrots
1 c chicken stock
2 tb butter
1 onion, finely-chopped
1 tb flour
1 sprig each of parsley, savory, rosemary, thyme and marjoram (or available herbs)
1 tb honey
1 tb cider vinegar

Cut carrots into thin slices. Cook in the stock until tender. Drain, place aside, and reserve the cooking liquid. Melt the butter in the saucepan, add the onion and sauté until tender. Add the flour and stir in the reserved liquid. Continue stirring until the sauce thickens and boils. Chop herbs finely and add to the sauce with the honey and vinegar. Add the carrots and reheat before serving.

GRATED CARROT CASSEROLE

Serves 4-6

3 c grated carrot
3 tb butter
1 tsp salt
freshly-ground black pepper

Place grated carrots in a small, well-greased casserole. Cover tightly and bake at 160°C for 30 minutes. Add butter, salt and pepper and mix well. Serve immediately.

CARROT SALAD

Serves 8

150 g raisins
1 orange
500 g prepared carrots
1 tsp finely-chopped marjoram or mint
8 even-sized lettuce leaves

Dressing:

2 tb lemon juice
2 tb salad oil
½ tsp sugar
½ tsp salt
freshly-ground black pepper

Pour boiling water over the raisins. Drain. Squeeze the juice from the orange. Pour over the raisins and leave for an hour. Grate carrots into a bowl. Add the marjoram, raisins and orange juice. Mix well. Combine dressing ingredients and pour over the salad. Toss. Fill each lettuce leaf with the carrot salad and arrange on a platter.

ICED CARROT AND ORANGE SOUP

Serves 6

Simple but sophisticated.

500 g new, prepared carrots
1 small onion
2 tb butter
600 ml chicken stock
1 tsp sugar
4 oranges
salt to taste

Slice carrots thinly. Peel onion and chop finely. Melt the butter in a saucepan and sauté the carrots and onions until soft but not brown. Stir in the stock and sugar and simmer until the carrots are very tender. Put soup through a blender or fine sieve. Add the strained juice of 4 oranges. Chill for several hours.

Old cookery books contained many recipes for carrot cakes and puddings. Now with the cost of dried fruits so high, many of these old-fashioned recipes have been rediscovered. Grated carrots are a fine substitute.

STEAMED CARROT PUDDING

Serves 6-8

Although you need to remember to put this pudding on early in the day, it takes very little time to prepare.

1 c grated carrot
1 c suet
½ c brown sugar
½ c raisins
2 tb chopped peel
1 c flour
1 tsp baking soda
milk to mix

Combine grated carrot, suet, sugar, raisins and peel. Sift flour and baking soda and add to the other ingredients. Add sufficient milk to form a drop batter. Put into a greased pudding basin. Cover and steam for 3 hours. Serve with cream or icecream.

CARROT ALMOND-CRUNCH DESSERT CAKE

Serves 10

Serve with whipped cream as a rich dessert or plain as a delicious and different coffee cake.

1½ c flour
1½ tsp baking powder
1½ tsp cinnamon
¾ tsp salt
¾ c sugar
½ c salad oil
3 eggs
1½ tsp vanilla
1½ c finely grated carrot
1 c chopped, unblanched almonds
½ c honey
130 ml cream

Sift the flour, baking powder, cinnamon and salt together into a large bowl. Stir in the sugar. Add oil, eggs and vanilla. Beat until smooth. Add grated carrot and half the almonds. Beat well. Pour batter into a well-greased 20-25 cm square tin. Bake at 160°C for 45 minutes.

Meanwhile, combine honey and remaining almonds. If the honey is very stiff you may need to warm it. Remove the cake from the oven and spread with the almond-honey mixture. Return to the oven for a further 5 minutes until the cake pulls away from the sides of the tin. Cool slightly, cut into squares and serve warm, with or without whipped cream.

CARROT BREAD

Serve slices spread with cream cheese or butter.

120 g butter
1 c sugar
2 eggs
1½ c flour
2 tsp baking powder
1 tsp cinnamon
½ tsp salt
1 c finely-grated carrot
1 c raisins
½ c chopped walnuts

Prepare a greased loaf tin (5 c capacity). Line the base with buttered, greaseproof paper.

Cream the butter and sugar. Beat in the eggs. Sift flour, baking powder, cinnamon and salt. Combine grated carrot, raisins and walnuts. Stir dry ingredients and carrot mixture into the creamed butter, sugar and eggs. Stir gently to combine well. Turn into loaf tin. Bake at 180°C for 1 hour or until cooked right through when tested with a wire. Cool in the tin for 15 minutes before turning out.

Carrots are useful in jam making. Without altering the flavour to any degree, they will make other fruits go much further.

CARROT MARMALADE

You will need a blender to make this quick marmalade.

250 g carrots, prepared
1 orange
2 lemons
2 c water
4 c sugar

Chop carrot, unpeeled orange and lemons roughly. Place half at a time in a blender with ½ c of the water. Blend until finely chopped. Pour into a large saucepan. Add remaining water and sugar. Heat gently, stirring constantly until the sugar has dissolved. Boil for about 30 minutes or until setting point is reached. Pour into hot, dry jars and seal with jam covers.

CARROT AND DRIED APRICOT JAM

With the price of dried apricots so high, we were delighted to be given this recipe. The flavour is excellent.

250 g dried apricots
3 c water
500 g prepared carrots
¼ c lemon juice
1.5 kg sugar

Soak the apricots in the water for 24 hours. Tip apricots and juice into a preserving pan. Grate carrots finely and add to the apricots. Simmer gently for 15 minutes. Mash thoroughly. Add lemon juice and sugar. Bring slowly to the boil stirring constantly. Boil until setting point is reached (about 10-20 minutes). Pour into hot, dry jars and seal with jam covers.

Freezing

In most temperate areas soil and weather conditions are such that carrots can be left in the ground throughout the winter. It is seldom necessary, therefore, to preserve them.

Mature carrots freeze better than very young ones which tend to become soft. Blanch prepared, diced carrots for 2 minutes. Cool and pack in meal-sized quantities in freezer bags. Do not thaw before cooking.

Cauliflower

(Brassica oleracea var. ***botrytis cauliflora)***

Varieties

Cauliflowers are considered to be more sensitive to extremes of heat, cold, and wet weather than broccoli so in cool regions they are grown for summer and autumn harvesting. In warmer areas they replace broccoli for winter and spring harvesting. The names Phenomenal and Snowball refer to two types which have been bred for a succession of maturing times. The Phenomenals range from Phenomenal Early (ready four months after planting out) Deepheart (five months) to Phenomenal Maincrop (six months). Of the Snowball range, Snowball Early is a small plant maturing three to four months after planting and Snowball X is larger but equally early. All the Year Round (also known as All Seasons) is a popular variety in warmer areas for all seasons except summer. It takes four-and-a-half months from planting but, unlike the Phenomenal and Snowball types, does not protect the curd from bright sunshine and heavy rain with an umbrella of leaves. To overcome this, gardeners bend the inner leaves forcibly or tie the large outer leaves together at the top when the curd first appears. An unusual variety is Purple Head, ready three months after planting. Its colourful purple curds turn green on cooking.

Cultivation (See also under broccoli)

As with other members of the cabbage family, a firm, rich soil manured for a previous crop and recently limed is considered ideal for cauliflowers. Many gardeners also apply additional fertilizer. Cauliflowers are sometimes prone to suffer a deficiency in potassium so wood ash can usefully be applied at planting time.

In spring, sowing outdoors should be delayed until the air temperatures exceed 13°C, for a cold snap may lead to the formation of premature button heads. A mini-glasshouse

Bend leaves over curd for protection

allows for much earlier sowing and uninterrupted growth. The seed may be sown 6 mm deep in boxes or a seed bed which is rich in humus, worked to a fine tilth. Allow up to 30 cm between the drills in a seed bed to make transplanting easier. A well-manured soil encourages the development of a mass of fibrous roots which hold on to the soil and minimize transplanting shock. Thin the plants in the seed bed to 7 cm apart when the first true leaves appear. At transplanting time be ready to discard any spindly examples which exhibit a bluish tinge, as these usually grow into buttons.

Transplanting is best undertaken on a dull day or cool evening after the seed bed has been well watered. Space the plants 45-60 cm apart with 60 cm between rows and once more water the plants. When the plants start to develop their curds, liquid manure can be applied to increase curd size and maintain plant health. The general vigour of cauliflower plants is an important factor in deterring insect infestations, especially grey aphids and green caterpillars. It is well known that vigorous plants grown in rich ground need less spraying against pests than slower-growing specimens. Severe insect damage and drought can also lead to the development of miniature heads. Attention to watering and regular preventative dustings with Derris Dust contribute to the steady growth on which successful cauliflower raising depends.

Harvesting

Cut the head off with some of the inner leaves still curled around it. The curd should be white and very tight.

In the kitchen

(This section also applies to heading broccoli.) Trim the heavy centre stalk and wash thoroughly. If the cauliflower is a home for bugs, soak it for 15 minutes in salted water. Rinse thoroughly. One medium cauliflower, about 600 g, will serve six. The head may be cooked whole or divided into flowerets.

When cooking whole, hollow out the centre stalk to shorten the cooking time. Place stem downwards in a saucepan just big enough to hold the head. Add boiling water to a depth of 3 cm and add a teaspoon of salt. Cover tightly and simmer for about 15 minutes or until the stalk is easily pierced with a small knife. Carefully transfer the head to a colander and drain.

For cooking in floweret pieces, place the cauliflower upside down on a board and with a small sharp knife cut down through the stalk to the base of each floweret. If the flowerets are too large they may be sliced lengthwise through flower and stem. Cook in 3 cm of boiling, salted water for 5-10 minutes until stalks are just tender. Drain well.

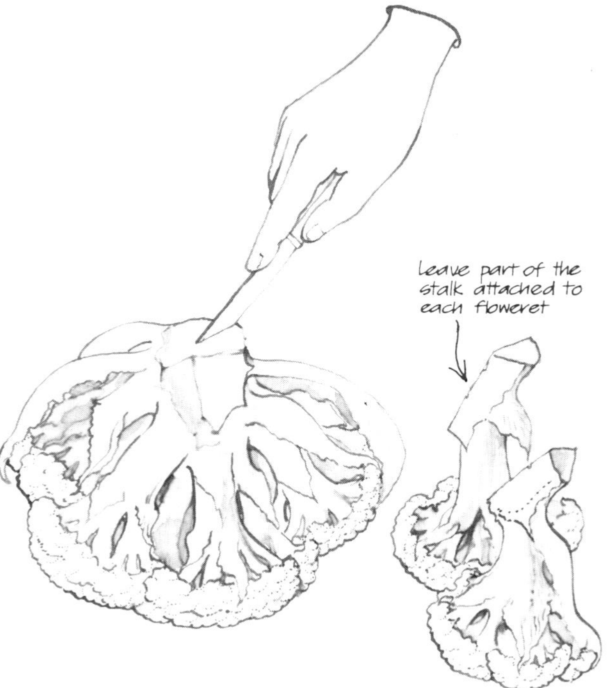
Leave part of the
stalk attached to
each floweret

A bay leaf added to the cooking water will mask the strong cooked-cauliflower odour.

Serve raw cauliflower, divided into small sprigs, as part of a vegetable platter. See page 206 for serving suggestions.

Serve cooked cauliflower with melted butter, freshly-ground black pepper and chopped parsley, chives or dill, or serve with a well-flavoured, smooth sauce such as mornay (see page 208).

A cooked, whole cauliflower looks most attractive with a polonaise topping. Use the recipe for Broccoli à la Polonaise on page 40.

CAULIFLOWER WITH HOLLANDAISE SAUCE AND CHIVES

Serves 6-8

1 c hollandaise sauce (see page 208)
2 tb sour cream
one large cauliflower, divided into flowerets
1 tb scissored chives

Before cooking the cauliflower, prepare hollandaise sauce. Add the sour cream and keep warm in a double boiler or in a small basin over hot water. Cook cauliflower. Drain. Place in a heated serving dish. Pour the sauce over the cauliflower and sprinkle with chives.

CAULIFLOWER CREOLE

Serves 6

1 small cauliflower
1 small onion
2 tb cooking oil
1 clove garlic
4 large tomatoes
1 small green pepper
salt and pepper to taste

Divide cauliflower into flowerets and cook in boiling, salted water until almost tender. Drain. Peel onion and chop finely. Sauté in oil until soft. Add finely-chopped garlic and skinned and chopped tomatoes. Cook gently until a thick sauce is formed. Add the seeded and finely-chopped pepper. Cook for 3 minutes longer. Add seasoning and cauliflower and heat through gently. Serve sprinkled with chopped, fresh basil if available.

CAULIFLOWER AU GRATIN

Serves 6 as a lunch dish or 8 as a vegetable

This is a dressed-up version of the old favourite, cauliflower cheese.

1 medium-sized cauliflower

Sauce:

3 tb butter
3 tb flour
400 ml milk
⅔ c grated tasty Cheddar cheese
½ tsp salt
freshly-ground black pepper
¼ tsp prepared mustard
¼ tsp Worcestershire sauce

Topping:

3 tb soft breadcrumbs
3 tb grated Parmesan cheese
1 tb melted butter
1 rasher bacon
3 tomatoes (optional garnish)

Cauliflower au gratin

Divide cauliflower into flowerets. Cook in boiling, salted water until just tender. Drain carefully.

To prepare sauce, melt the butter in a small saucepan and add the flour. Cook for one minute. Gradually blend in the milk and stir continuously until boiling. Remove from the heat and add ⅔ c of grated cheese, seasoning, mustard and Worcestershire sauce. Stir until smooth.

Butter a basin (about 1 litre capacity). Arrange the cauliflower flowerets in it with the stalks towards the centre. Pour over 3 tb of the sauce and, using a potato masher, press down lightly to bind the flowerets together. Carefully invert the basin on to an ovenproof plate.

Remove the basin. Spoon the sauce over the cauliflower.

Combine the breadcrumbs and Parmesan cheese and sprinkle over the cauliflower. Sprinkle well with melted butter. Cut bacon into small squares and place evenly over the surface. Slice tomatoes and arrange around the edge of the plate. Bake at 200°C for 15-20 minutes until heated through and the bacon crisp and topping golden.

Dividing the cauliflower into flowerets, cooking and then reassembling makes serving much easier than leaving it whole and dividing it at the table. For everyday occasions, simply place the cooked cauliflower in a greased ovenproof dish, pour the sauce over and sprinkle the surface with cheese and breadcrumbs.

CAULIFLOWER À LA GRECQUE

Serves 6

A delicious way to serve cauliflower cold.

1 onion
2 medium-sized carrots
3 tb cooking oil
freshly-ground black pepper
½ tsp salt
½ tsp coriander seeds
bouquet garni
1 clove garlic
250 g tomatoes
150 ml white wine
1 medium-sized cauliflower
2 tb salad oil
1 tb lemon juice
1 tb finely-chopped parsley

Peel the onion and chop finely. Scrub the carrots and dice finely. Heat the 3tb of oil in a heavy-based saucepan. Add the onion and carrots. Cook gently until golden. Remove the saucepan from the heat and add the pepper, salt, coriander seeds, bouquet garni, garlic, peeled and chopped tomatoes and white wine. Mix well. Add the prepared cauliflower divided into flowerets. Return to the heat and simmer gently with the lid on for 10-20 minutes until the cauliflower is just tender. Leave to cool.

Remove bouquet garni and garlic. Stir in the 2 tb of salad oil and lemon juice. Check seasoning. Place in a salad bowl with the parsley sprinkled over the surface. Chill lightly.

CREAM OF CAULIFLOWER SOUP

Serves 6

2 tb butter
1 large onion, chopped
2 medium-sized carrots, thinly sliced
1 small cauliflower, divided into flowerets
1 small potato, peeled and sliced thinly
800 ml chicken stock
½ c cream
freshly-grated nutmeg
salt and pepper to taste
1 tb dry sherry
1 tb chopped parsley

Melt the butter in a large saucepan. Add the onion and sauté for 5 minutes. Add the remaining vegetables and cook for a few minutes longer. Pour in the stock and simmer until the vegetables are tender. Put the soup through a fine sieve or blender. Return to the saucepan and add the cream, nutmeg, seasoning and sherry. Reheat without boiling. Serve in bowls with parsley sprinkled on top.

Freezing

Strong odour is a problem when freezing cauliflower. Use a bay leaf in the blanching water and open the freezer for 1 minute, two or three times while freezing is taking place. This allows the odour to escape without tainting other food. Blanch prepared flowerets for 3 minutes. Drain and pack in meal-sized quantities in double freezer bags (one bag inside another). Thaw long enough to separate flowerets before cooking.

Celeriac

(Apium graveolens var. *rapaceum)*

Varieties

This plant, which is also referred to as turnip-rooted celery, deserves to be better known, for it is an excellent substitute for celery in areas where sharp frosts and fungus diseases severely limit celery growth. It is a little quicker to grow, and once mature can be left in the ground until mid-spring.

Celeriac combines smooth texture and a mild celery flavour with hardness

Cultivation

It has been claimed that celeriac will grow on poorer, drier soils than celery but, as a plant of the same species, it is unlikely to produce a solid, crisp, swollen stem-base unless liberally supplied with compost and moisture. Like celery it can bolt to seed if allowed to dry out. The ground should therefore be prepared as for celery with old animal manure and compost dug into a trench beneath the row and supplemented with a general fertilizer.

The seeds can be sown directly into the garden between spring and early summer or in a seed bed or box. If sown in a box, thin the plants to 5 cm apart and transplant into the garden about five weeks after sowing, allowing 20 cm between plants and 40 cm between single rows. Direct sowing should be delayed until the ground has warmed up. When transplanting, take care to have the swollen stem-base level with the ground. As the plant grows, keep the soil away from the "bulb" and pick off any side shoots growing out of it.

Celeriac is less prone to disease than celery. Any sign of leaf spot should be treated with a copper oxychloride spray, and aphids on young plants should be controlled with pyrethrum. Use a straw mulch to protect the plants from frost damage in winter.

Harvesting

Harvesting can start when the "bulbs" reach 5 cm in diameter, usually about four months from planting.

In the kitchen

Celeriac is grown principally for its swollen root, although the stalks and leaves may be used sparingly for celery flavour in stews or salads.

Cut the stalks and rootlets from each root. Scrub thoroughly and peel just before cooking. Allow 100 g for each serving.

Cook whole, diced, sliced or cut into sticks in boiling, salted water until tender. Drain.

Serve with butter, freshly-ground black pepper and finely-chopped herbs (parsley, chervil or tarragon).

BUTTERED CELERIAC

Serves 5-6

500 g celeriac
700 ml chicken stock
1 tb lemon juice
3 tb butter
1 tb finely-chopped parsley or chives
salt and pepper to taste

Cut peeled celeriac into 2 cm cubes. Cook in stock and lemon juice until tender. Drain. Add butter, chopped herbs and seasoning. Mix gently and serve immediately.

GRATED CELERIAC SAUTÉ

Serves 6

500 g celeriac
60 g butter
1 tsp mild prepared mustard
1 tsp wine vinegar or tarragon vinegar
freshly-ground black pepper
salt to taste
2 tb chopped parsley

Peel and grate celeriac. Melt butter in a frying pan and sauté celeriac for 5-10 minutes. It should remain slightly crisp. Add mustard, vinegar, pepper, salt and parsley. Stir to combine and serve immediately.

BRAISED CELERIAC

Serves 4-6

100 g bacon rashers
2 small onions
200 g carrots
400 g celeriac
¼ tsp salt
freshly-ground black pepper
1 c chicken stock

Cut bacon into small pieces and place half in a greased casserole dish. Peel and slice onions. Place on top of bacon. Scrub carrot, slice finely and place over onions. Peel celeriac, cut in half lengthwise and then slice finely. Add to the casserole. Sprinkle with salt and pepper. Top with remaining bacon. Pour in the stock. Cover and bake at 190°C for 1 hour until vegetables are tender.

CELERIAC SALAD

Serves 6

500 g celeriac
6 tb French dressing (see page 209)
2 tb chopped parsley and chervil

Cook peeled celeriac in boiling, salted water until tender. Drain. Dice, place in a bowl and toss gently with French dressing while still hot. Allow to cool. Serve sprinkled with parsley and chervil.

Celery

(Apium graveolens var. *dulce)*

Varieties

The days of blanching tall, white celery plants by earthing them up in trenches or winding heavy paper around the stems are nearly over. Seedsmen are now promoting golden, self-blanching types which mature in 85-90 days from setting out the small plants and are harvested in early summer. There are also green, non-blanching varieties, some of which are said to mature in 125-130 days from planting out. None of the green varieties are hardy and the quality of the stalks rapidly deteriorates with the first sharp frosts of winter.

Cultivation

To compensate for the long growing season of the maincrop varieties, often seven months from seed, many gardeners sow the seed in deep boxes in a glasshouse, or in a seed bed beneath a mini-glasshouse. Protection from frosts and cold night air is essential throughout the growth period, especially when the plants are set out in the garden in summer. A cold snap at this time, when the tiny seed head is being formed within the heart of the plant, will cause many plants to bolt when warm weather returns. Celery grows well from 13-24°C, so adjust sowing times to suit this range as closely as possible.

The seed should be sown in rich, fine soil, barely covered and kept moist throughout the germination period. Thin the seedlings to 5-6 cm apart and never let them dry out in the box or bed as this, too, will lead to bolting. After two-and-a-half months they can be planted out in heavily-manured, well-drained, recently-limed ground. Many gardeners dig out a trench beneath the proposed celery row and fill it with 10 cm of animal manure (sheep, horse or cow) or 5 cm of dry poultry droppings. Superphosphate is then sprinkled over the top. The trench is filled back in and the plants are set into position with the basal crown covered by soil but without allowing soil to get into the heart.

If you have rather less manure available or only garden compost, work into each metre of row an additional cup of blood and bone and 2 tb of sulphate of potash. The plants should be spaced 20 cm apart in the case of golden types, and 30 cm between maincrop varieties. They are often grown in double rows in shallow trenches to facilitate watering, allowing 15 cm between the rows and 1 m between trenches. Mulching with sheep manure in late summer gives an added boost to growth. Alternatively, apply liquid manure or a foliar fertilizer every two to three weeks for really succulent stalks. Keep the plants well watered.

Minor aphid attacks in young plants should be controlled with a pyrethrum spray so that steady growth is not interrupted. Leaf spot may appear in autumn and can do serious damage. It is prevented by applications of a copper oxychloride spray.

Harvesting

Some gardeners still like to blanch their "self-blanching" celery for two to three weeks before cutting the whole plant. A field tile (drain pipe) can be lowered over the plant leaving the leaves protruding out the top. When cutting, use a long knife, severing the roots just below ground level and then trimming the crown. Maincrop green varieties can be harvested stalk by stalk, twisted from the plant as with rhubarb.

In the kitchen

Separate the stalks if a whole celery plant has been harvested. Discard any badly marked or tough-looking outer stalks. Trim off root ends and leaves. Young, pale leaves can be used either with the stalks, depending on the recipe, or as a flavouring for soups, stews and salads. The leaves will remain fresh for several days stored in a plastic bag in a refrigerator. Allow 100 g of celery for each serving.

The stalks may be cut into thin strips, thick or thin slices, long diagonal slices or diced.

Our favourite, simple method of cooking celery is butter-steaming. Melt 2 tb of butter in a heavy-based saucepan with a tight-fitting lid. Add thinly-sliced celery and pale leaves. Cook gently for 5-10 minutes or until tender-crisp. Season with salt and pepper and serve immediately. Finely chopped chervil or grated cheese make good additions.

Sliced celery, cooked in a small quantity of boiling, salted water, will take 5-10 minutes depending on the age and size of pieces. Drain and serve with plenty of grated cheese or a cheese sauce (see page 208).

Trim celery for the kitchen
The young leaves may be stored in refrigerator for soups, stews and salads

Raw, crisp, young celery stalks which have been finely sliced add flavour and texture to salads. Diced pieces provide a crunchy topping for soups. Celery sticks are popular as snacks with both adults and children. Large, tender stalks cut into 4-6 cm lengths and stuffed with

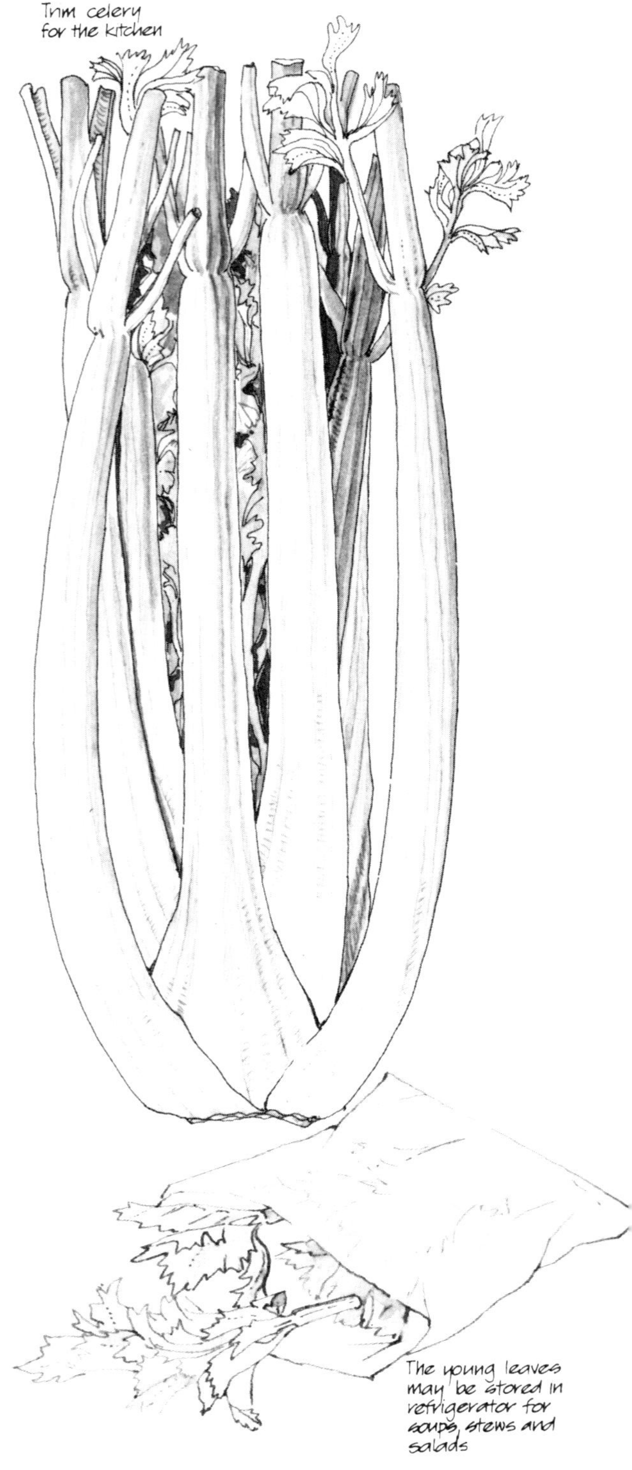

a variety of fillings make a simple appetizer. We have used meat or fish paté, cream cheese with chopped herbs and crumbled blue vein cheese mixed with softened butter. The fillings should be well seasoned.

CELERY AND TOMATOES

Serves 6

500 g celery
1 small onion
2 small carrots
2 tb butter
a half-litre preserving jar of bottled tomatoes or purée, or 400 g fresh tomatoes, peeled and chopped
½ tsp salt
freshly-ground black pepper

Cut the prepared celery into 5 mm slices. Include a few pale leaves. Peel onion and chop finely. Scrub carrots and slice finely. Melt the butter in a large frying pan with a lid. Add the onion and carrot and sauté until soft. Add the celery and cook for 3 minutes. Add the tomatoes, salt and pepper. Cover the pan and cook for about 15 minutes until the celery is tender and the sauce thick. If the sauce is not thick enough, cook without the lid for a little longer.

CÉLERI AUX AMANDES

Serves 4

The excellent flavour of this French dish is produced by the combination of celery and sautéed almonds. Serve it with roast chicken for a special dinner.

2 tb butter
30 g almonds, blanched and slivered
400 g celery
1 shallot, finely chopped
salt to taste
freshly-ground black pepper
¼ c cream or top milk

Heat the butter in a heavy frying pan with a lid. Add the almonds and sauté gently until they turn a pale golden colour. Lift out the almonds and put aside. Wash and trim the celery. Cut the stalks lengthwise into two, three or four strips, depending on thickness. Each strip should be about 1 cm thick. Slice the strips into 3 cm pieces. Add the celery and shallot to the frying pan. Season well. Cover the pan and cook over low heat for 10 minutes. Stir in the cream and continue cooking for a further 5-10 minutes until the celery is just tender. Return the almonds to the pan and stir over low heat for a few more minutes before serving.

CELERY AND APPLE CASSEROLE

Serves 6

500 g celery
2 large cooking apples
1 large onion
2 slices ham
150 ml chicken stock
salt and pepper to taste

Cut prepared celery stalks into 5 mm slices. Peel and core the apples. Slice finely. Peel onion and slice finely. Cut ham into small squares. Place half the ham in the bottom of a greased casserole dish. Cover with half the apples and onion. Add the celery and cover with the remaining onion and apples. Top with ham. Pour the stock over the vegetables. Cover and bake at 190°C for 45-60 minutes. Check seasoning before serving.

CELERY SALAD

Serves 6-8

This recipe combines celery, apples and dates with a yoghurt-honey dressing.

1 c yoghurt
2 tb honey
1 tb finely chopped mint
500 g celery
20 dates, pitted
2 rosy apples
2 tb finely chopped walnuts

Beat the yoghurt and honey together in a small bowl. Stir in the mint. Cut the prepared celery into 1 cm slices. Chop the dates into small pieces. Quarter the apples and remove cores but do not peel. Cut the apples into 1 cm cubes. Combine the celery, dates and apples together in a salad bowl. Pour in the dressing and mix gently. Chill for 30 minutes. Just before serving scatter the walnuts over the top.

CELERY SOUP

Serves 6

500 g celery
2 medium-sized carrots
1 small potato
2 tb butter
1 litre chicken stock
salt to taste
freshly-ground black pepper
½ c grated Cheddar cheese

Wash and trim celery. Reserve one or two of the small inner stalks. Cut remaining stalks and pale leaves into 5 mm slices. Scrub carrots and slice thinly. Peel potato and slice. Melt the butter in a large saucepan. Add the sliced celery, carrots and potato. Sauté gently for about 5 minutes. Add the stock and simmer until the vegetables are tender. Put through a sieve or blender. Return the soup to the saucepan, check the seasoning and reheat. Dice reserved celery finely and combine with the cheese. Serve in bowls with a spoonful of the cheese and celery added to each.

Late summer and autumn celery can be combined with tomatoes in a fresh-tasting, uncooked pickle (see page 199).

Freezing

With careful planning, we usually manage to have celery available from our gardens for nine months of the year. It is such a valuable vegetable for flavouring that it is well worth making the effort to ensure a continuous supply. When harvesting the last of our autumn-planted celery in spring, we freeze the outer stalks as a cooked and strained purée and blanch the tender centre stalks and pale leaves as follows:

Slice the small stalks and leaves. Blanch for 2 minutes. Cool and pack in small quantities for use as a flavouring in stews and soups.

Chicory

(Cichorium intybus)

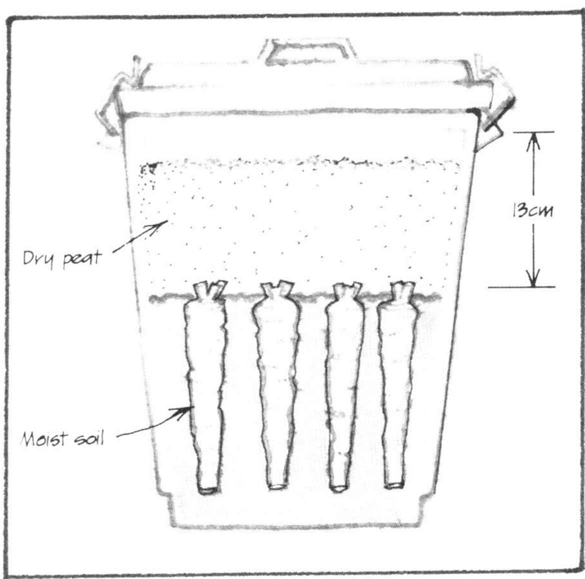

Varieties

There are two very different types of chicory. One known as Magdeburg is not used in salads but its mature root is roasted and ground for adding to coffee. Whitloof (Witloof means "white leaf") is the variety grown as a substitute for lettuce. It is forced to produce chicons (blanched heads of tightly-folded leaves) for winter consumption.

Cultivation and harvesting

Whitloof seed is sown in early summer in ground prepared as for carrots and parsnips. The drills should be shallow with 45 cm between the rows. The seedlings are thinned to 15-23 cm apart and grown on through the summer, with occasional attention to weeding and watering in dry weather.

In winter dig up a few plants at a time, discarding any larger or smaller in diameter than 2.5-4.5 cm. Cut the tops off the roots to within 2.5 cm of the crown and dry the roots in a cool shed for a week. Trim off any side shoots together with the bottom of the taproot, to

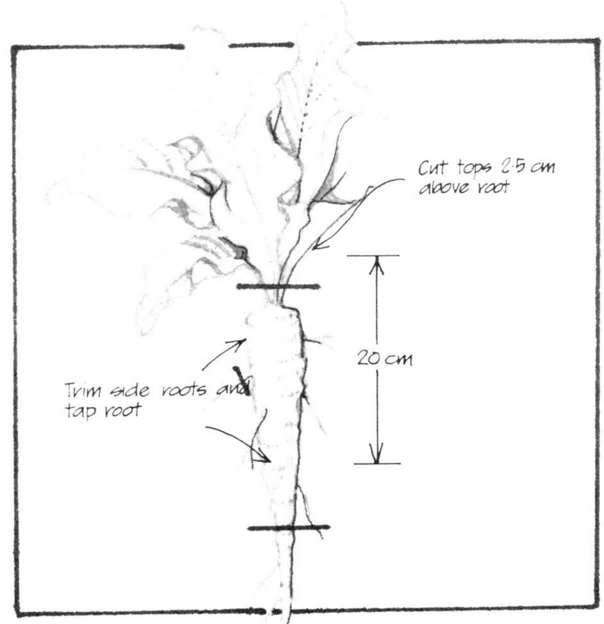

leave a parsnip-like root 20 cm long. Pack these roots in moist peat in deep boxes or plastic rubbish buckets so that the peat comes up to the base of the crown. Then pour in a layer of dry peat to cover the crowns to a depth of 17 cm. Place the box or bucket in a shed or cellar where the temperature is between 10 and 15°C. After three to four weeks the chicon tips should be just breaking the surface. Empty out the peat (it can be used again) and cut or snap the chicons from the roots. Keep them in a dark pantry or larder until required.

In the kitchen

Chicory is grown mainly for winter use as a lettuce substitute. Discard outside leaves and cut off coarse root ends with a stainless steel knife. They may be sliced crosswise into 1 cm chunks or separated into leaves. Toss lightly with French dressing made with lemon juice. Orange segments and beetroot cubes or slices make colourful additions.

Chicory may also be baked or braised to serve as a hot vegetable. Allow 2 chicons for each serving. Place them in a greased casserole with plenty of butter. Bake tightly covered at 160°C for about 1½ hours. Serve sprinkled with lemon juice, salt and freshly-ground black pepper.

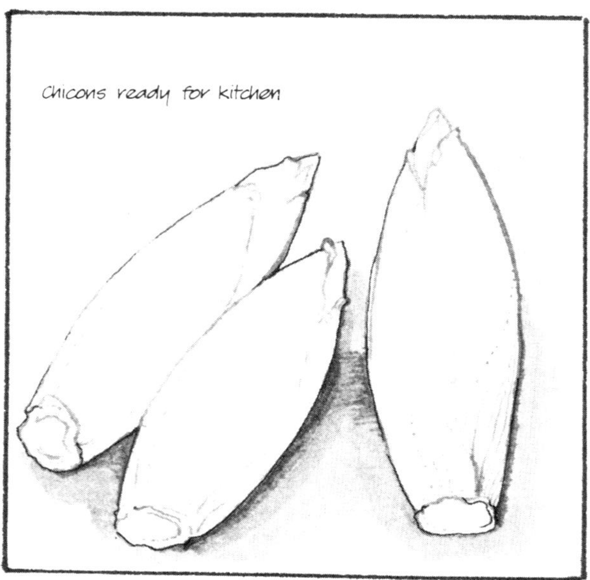
Chicons ready for kitchen

Chinese vegetables

(Brassica campestris var. ***chinensis*** (Chinese mustard), ***Brassica campestris*** var. ***pekinensis*** (Chinese cabbage))

Varieties
Many gardeners' references and seed catalogues refer to Chinese cabbage and give instructions on its cultivation. Some include a separate section on Chinese mustard while others treat it as a form of cabbage. Seldom seen are references to Chinese celery, which is a distinct variety of celery and not a brassica. Plants can be obtained from a few specialist nurseries. Of the brassica varieties which are available as seed, Pak Choi Kwang Moon is the Chinese mustard, a non-heading plant with thick, glossy, dark-green leaves contrasting with pure-white, very juicy leaf stalks. It stands nearly 30 cm tall and is ready to eat two months after sowing. Heading types of Chinese vegetables are usually described as cabbages. The smallest is Wong Bok, which stands 20-27 cm high and produces an oval heart of pale-green, crumpled leaves with white midribs. It matures two-and-a-half to three months from sowing. Chi Hi Li is taller (up to 50 cm) and is ready about 10 days earlier. Its head is of similar weight to Wong Bok, about 1.5 kg. Hybrid varieties are more commonly grown by market gardeners. China King F.1. Hybrid is one of the few listed for the home gardener. It matures in two to three months and develops a head weighing up to 2.5 kg.

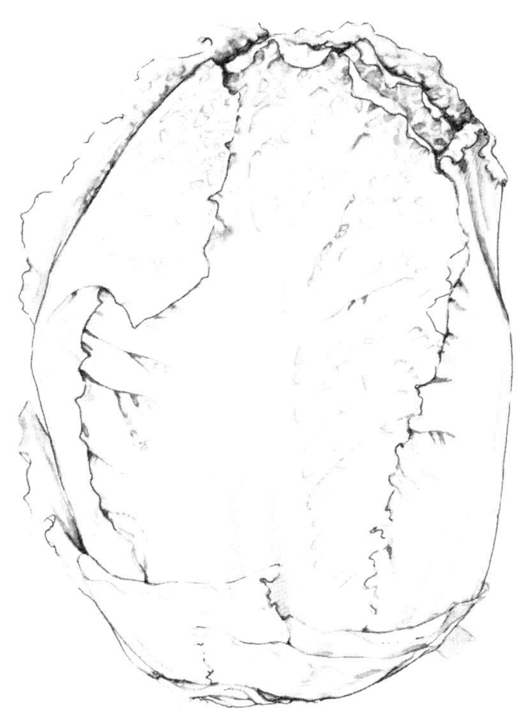

China king has a tight solid head

Cultivation
The site should be fairly open as the plants dislike overcrowding. Light shade conditions are tolerated as with summer-grown lettuces. The most important requirement is a rich soil with plenty of humus to retain moisture. A general fertilizer may be used.

Because Chinese brassicas run to seed in hot weather, they are usually sown directly in the garden from later summer to early autumn, for harvesting in late autumn and early winter. Sow the seed 2.5 cm apart in shallow drills with 40 cm between rows. When the plants have 3 or 4 leaves, thin to 30-40 cm apart. Keep the plants well watered and apply liquid manure to keep them growing vigorously. Occasionally spring sowings are made in a protected seed bed or box. The plants are set out in the garden three to four weeks later. Early sowing is important to ensure that hearting occurs before hot summer conditions set in. Transplanting is not usually recommended for any plant prone to bolt in unfavourable conditions so if an early sowing is desired, peat pots might prove as valuable for Chinese brassicas as they are for lettuces, lessening the danger of shock to the roots when they are shifted into the garden.

Harvesting

Autumn-matured Chinese mustard can be picked a few leaves at a time for eating raw in salads or for cooking like spinach. The heading Chinese brassicas are cut as cabbages when required. They stand quite well in winter provided the weather is not too wet, but if you have to harvest them they will keep for several weeks in plastic bags in a refrigerator.

In the kitchen

Chinese cabbages may be treated as cabbages or lettuces. They have a distinct Chinese cooking flavour which is less obvious when used raw.

Trim the root end and remove any tough or discoloured leaves. Wash thoroughly. Slice finely for salads or coarsely for cooking. One medium-sized Chinese cabbage weighing about 700 g will serve six.

Butter-steaming and the quick, oriental stir-fry method are the best ways to cook Chinese cabbage. To butter-steam follow the method given for cabbage on page 47 but do not add water. Season with salt and pepper. A little finely-chopped preserved ginger or sour cream and chives are good additions.

STIR-FRIED CHINESE CABBAGE

Serves 6

1 medium-sized Chinese cabbage
1 tb cooking oil
1 clove garlic, crushed
¼ tsp finely-chopped, fresh root ginger
2 tb chicken stock
1 tsp sugar
2 tsp soy sauce
1 tsp cornflour
1 tb cold water

Wash Chinese cabbage and trim. Slice into 2 cm pieces.

Heat the oil until very hot in a wok or large frying pan. Add garlic, ginger and cabbage. Stir-fry for one minute. Add stock, sugar and soy sauce. Cook for ½ a minute. Blend cornflour and water and stir into the cabbage. Bring to the boil and serve immediately.

Chinese cabbage and/or Chinese mustard make attractive and authentic additions to Chinese-Styled Vegetables (see recipe on page 206).

CHINESE CABBAGE SALAD

Serves 8

1 medium-sized Chinese cabbage
3 small sticks of tender celery
2 oranges

Dressing:

4 tb salad oil
2 tb lemon juice
1 tsp finely-chopped mint
1 shallot, finely chopped
½ tsp salt
½ tsp sugar
freshly-ground black pepper

Remove any tough or discoloured outer leaves. Slice off the thick base. Slice cabbage finely and place in a large salad bowl. Add finely-chopped celery. Peel oranges and divide into segments. Cut each segment in half. Add to the salad.

In a small bowl combine oil, lemon juice, mint, shallot, salt, sugar and pepper. Beat with a fork. Pour over the salad and toss well.

CHINESE CABBAGE SOUP

Serves 6

A pale-green, fresh-tasting soup.

- **2 tb butter**
- **1 small onion chopped**
- **1 medium-sized potato, grated**
- **1 small Chinese cabbage, sliced**
- **750 ml chicken stock**
- **juice of one small lemon**
- **salt and pepper to taste**
- **6 lemon slices to garnish**

In a large saucepan melt the butter and sauté the onion until soft. Add grated potato, sliced Chinese cabbage and chicken stock. Simmer gently until cabbage is very tender. Put through a blender or fine sieve. Return to the saucepan. Add lemon juice and seasoning. Reheat. Serve in bowls with a thin slice of lemon floating on top.

CHINESE MUSTARD

Trim root ends and wash stalks and leaves thoroughly. It may be cooked like silver beet in a minimum of boiling, salted water or cooked in the manner given above for Chinese cabbage. Very young, tender leaves add flavour to salads and the crisp, juicy stalks make good snacks for children.

Corn salad

CORN SALAD

(Lamb's lettuce, Valerianella olitorea)

Corn salad is a very useful vegetable because it matures in five to eight weeks from a late summer sowing and in up to 12 weeks from an autumn sowing. There are few varieties available.

Cultivation and harvesting

The soil should be well drained and enriched for a previous crop. Autumn sowings should be made in a sunny, sheltered location. Sow seed 12 mm deep in drills 25 cm apart and later thin to 10-15 cm apart. Keep the plants well watered. In very frosty weather a loose straw mulch or cloche protection may be needed.

As soon as each plant has four leaves or more start picking a few leaves at a time or when larger, harvest whole plants.

In the kitchen

Wash and dry leaves thoroughly. Use with lettuce or as a lettuce substitute.

WINTER SALAD

- **1 large bunch of corn salad**
- **2 cooked beetroot**
- **1 tart apple**
- **4 tb French dressing**

Place prepared leaves in a salad bowl. Cut peeled beetroot into quarters and then slice. Peel apple, cut into quarters, remove core and slice. Add beetroot and apple to salad. Toss with French dressing.

Cress

(Quick Cress) — ***Lepidium sativum***, Water Cress — ***Rorippa nasturtium-aquaticum***
American Cress — ***Barbarea praecox***

Varieties

The cress that accompanies mustard in the old-fashioned mustard-and-cress salad or sandwich is usually the only one stocked by seed merchants. It may have curled or plain leaves. Names such as Salad Curled, Curled Moss, Moss Curled and Finest Curled in seed lists indicate that the plain-leaved variety is not currently stocked.

Watercress can be grown from cuttings, root divisions or seed. Although the plant is a perennial, annual renewal is often recommended.

American or landcress is also renewed from year to year by seed. The variety Upland is described as having oval leaves like watercress and the plant grows about 10 cm high.

Cultivation

Quick cress is best sown thickly in a box filled with peat or bulb fibre. By this means the difficulties of washing soil grit from the leaves are eliminated. Press the seed into the surface and water the box thoroughly by lowering it into a water-filled container (such as an old baby's bath). Place the box in a sheltered, semi-shaded position outdoors with another box inverted

American cress

Watercress

Quick cress

over it. A few days after germination, expose the plants to light so that they begin to turn green. Harvesting takes place two to three weeks after sowing, at the seed leaf stage or just as the first true leaves appear. The box can then be resown for two more crops. Sow quick cress seed three to seven days before the mustard if you wish to harvest them together.

Watercress can be grown in a specially-prepared trench in a shady part of the garden. Dig the trench 40-50 cm deep and fill it with a 30 cm layer of compost, leaf mould or decayed straw. Cover with about 7 cm of fine soil and water until the contents of the trench are saturated. The seed is sown in the topsoil in spring and sometimes again in autumn. Once a week, during the summer, refill the trench with water but ensure that this does not become stagnant. In winter the plants can be protected from frost with a cloche or mini-glasshouse. The plants should be spaced 15 cm apart.

American cress also requires a cool, moist situation and often fails to thrive in a hot summer. Sow in rich soil and, after germination, thin the plants out to 10 cm apart. This type of cress grows about 10 cm high. If a repeat sowing is made in autumn in a protected spot it should be possible to harvest American cress for most of the year.

Harvesting

Cut quick cress just above ground level when the plants are about 5 cm high. Kitchen scissors are an ideal tool

Watercress is ready when 15-20 cm tall. Snip off the tender top growth and more will develop rapidly for the next cutting.

American cress is harvested by selectively pinching out leaves and stems. Harvesting can start four to six weeks after sowing if the weather has been mild.

In the kitchen

Wash all varieties thoroughly, drain and pat dry with a towel.

Quick cress:

Use with yeast extracts in brown bread sandwiches.

Add to salads.

Chop and use in stuffed eggs.

American cress and watercress:

Use as a garnish.

Chop and add to sandwiches and salads.

Cucumber

(Cucumis sativus)

Varieties

This ancient domesticate from India is now represented by many varieties. Twenty years ago there were three basic categories of cucumber: smooth-skinned, dark-green, long types which were usually raised in glasshouses; smooth and prickly types suitable for growing outdoors, and types grown to produce gherkins for pickling. In addition there were one or two white-skinned varieties. The glasshouse group included names like Telegraph, still available today. Members of this group matured without pollination and growers were advised to pinch out male flowers, for if pollination occurred by accident bitter fruit would result. Long Green Improved, Straight Eight and Long Green Prickly are popular old varieties of the outdoor group. Sometimes gherkin types were marketed simply as Pickling Gherkins. The most popular white variety still grown today is Crystal Apple. It produces oval creamy white fruit and is considered one of the hardiest cucumbers.

Cucumber breeders have now developed strains of gynoecious plants with fertile female flowers and sterile male ones. These crop extremely heavily and are now available in pickling and glasshouse types. Spartan Dawn, Spartan Valour and the Slicemaster hybrids are examples of gynoecious cucumbers. They are considered highly resistant to virus and mildew infections. Another new development is the "bitterfree, burpless" cucumber which is devoid of certain compounds (cucurbitacins) which cause bitterness in foliage and fruits.

Patio-Pik Hybrid is a new dwarf cucumber, very suitable for container-growing in small gardens while Japanese Climber can be grown on a trellis or bamboo cane tripod. In England it is reported to crop well even in a poor summer. Triumph F.1. Hybrid is now one of the most popular outdoor cucumbers because of its vigour and hardiness.

Cultivation

Glasshouse cultivation of cucumbers is a specialist pursuit on which whole books have been written. However, in regions where spring and early summer are cool and cloudy, a glasshouse is the only spot where cucumbers can grow in warm, sheltered conditions for the three to four months before cropping begins in mid to late summer. Moderately rich soil in the lowest corner of a small tomato house is suitable but make sure you can give extra water to the cucumbers without causing rank growth in the tomatoes. A sheet of plastic making a tent above the cucumbers may help provide the extra humidity and shade that cucumbers need when the hot weather finally arrives.

In regions where late spring is marked by dry, settled weather with plenty of sunshine, outdoor cultivation is feasible provided the plants are raised under heat, carefully hardened off and then planted under a mini-glasshouse for their first two to three months of growth. Crystal Apple is a good variety to try.

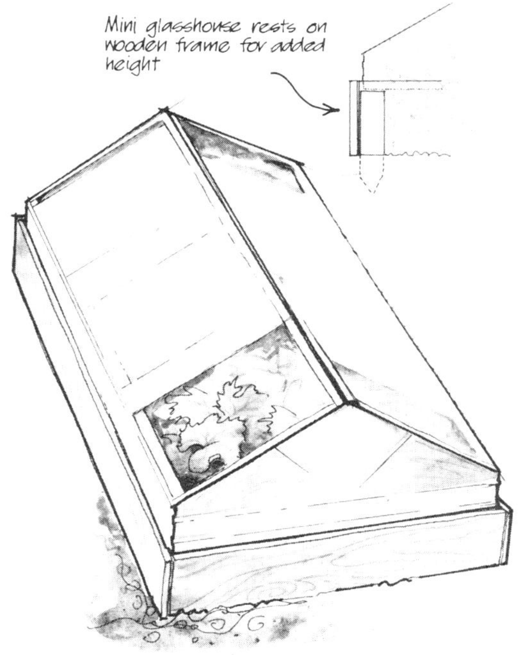
Mini glasshouse rests on wooden frame for added height

Plant cucumbers under mini glasshouse for an early start

Warmer areas offer the gardener many more opportunities for experimenting with different varieties and cultivation techniques. Even so, it should be remembered that smooth-skinned cucumbers require high growing temperatures (20-30°C) so they should not be started before late spring. Prickly-skinned, Japanese and gherkin types are more hardy. All cucumbers need a sunny, sheltered site.

The soil should be free draining and warm. A sandy loam enriched with moderate quantities of compost and a general fertilizer is ideal. A popular practice is to dig a hole 30 cm deep and 45 cm wide, half fill it with compost and old manure and cover with topsoil, forming a low mound. Germinate the seed in compressed pellet pots or larger peat pots in a warm indoor place. Two seeds are pushed into each pot so that they stand upright within the soil with their tops just below the surface. As soon as the first true leaves begin to show, cut off the weaker seedling. Pulling it out might damage the root system of the remaining plant. Cucumbers resent root disturbance at any time.

Harden off the seedlings over the next two to three weeks before planting three to four plants (in their pots) around each mound. Push the soil around the stems to encourage stem rooting. Mounds are usually spaced 1-1.3 m apart. Gherkin cucumbers grown in rows can be spaced much closer, 15-30 cm between plants and 60 cm between rows.

Frequent light watering of the ground around the plants is better than soaking the leaves with a prolonged hosing. Very wet and very dry leaves are susceptible to downy and powdery mildew. Mulching in dry weather is often recommended. If mildew is a persistent problem choose one of the resistant varieties next year.

Liquid manure is often given for boosting cucumber production. A perforated tin of animal dung set into the mound can be regularly filled with water to percolate around the roots. Avoid inorganic fertilizers with a high nitrogen content as they stimulate leaf growth at the expense of the fruit.

Training techniques usually consist of nipping off the growing points after six to seven leaves have formed. This encourages the development of side shoots after the first fruit has formed or when they reach 60 cm long. Side shoots of side shoots, known as sublaterals, are pinched out after one leaf. If you don't have time to be systematic about this, just nip off growing points when they protrude beyond each plant's allotted space.

Watch the plants for aphids and thrips, which are controllable with liquid pyrethrum, and treat fungus diseases with a sulphur spray (for dry weather powdery mildew) or copper oxychloride (for damp weather downy mildew).

Watering through a perforated tin of animal dung increases production
Nip off growing points beyond each plants allotted space
Grow plants on mounds

Harvesting
Harvest gherkins when the fruits are 5-10 cm long. Green cucumbers for slicing should always be picked before they are fully mature, for when they turn yellow they become bitter. If you discover a mature one on the vine pick it off anyway to keep production unchecked. White cucumbers are ready when you can no longer wait to eat them. The skin should be firm and creamy-white, still streaked with green.

In the kitchen
Wash and prepare according to recipe.

CUCUMBER SALAD AND VARIATIONS
To serve 4 use one medium-sized cucumber or two to three apple cucumbers.
Peeling:
Many outdoor cucumbers are best peeled with a potato peeler. To decide whether it is necessary to remove the skin, take a thin slice from one end and chew it. If the skin is at all bitter or tough, peel it. An attractive method of serving unpeeled cucumber is to score the skin with the tines of a fork before slicing.
Slicing:
We like them sliced wafer thin. The short, prickly-skinned cucumbers often have large seeds. If this is the case, they are best cut into short lengths and the seeds scooped out before slicing.
Salting:
This is only necessary if the salad has to wait. Place the slices in a colander or sieve and sprinkle with a teaspoon of salt. Leave to drain for 1 hour. Rinse slices to get rid of salt and drain well.
Dressings:
1. Combine 1 tsp salad oil, 1 tsp vinegar (cider, wine or herb), ¼ tsp salt, freshly-ground black pepper, ¼ tsp sugar and 1 tsp chopped parsley or dill. Pour over sliced cucumber.
2. Combine sliced cucumber with ½ c plain

yoghurt. Season with salt and pepper. Serve as a side dish with a curry.

3. Combine sliced cucumber with ½ c sour cream (thin with top milk if necessary), 1 tb chopped mint, pepper and salt to taste. Garnish with a little chopped mint.

FRESH CUCUMBER-AND-TOMATO PICKLE

Serves 4

1 c peeled and finely-chopped cucumber
1 c skinned and finely-chopped tomatoes
2 tb cider vinegar
1 tb sugar
½ tsp salt
freshly-ground black pepper

Leave the cucumber and tomatoes on a tilted plate to drain for about an hour. Mix vinegar, sugar, salt and pepper together in a small salad bowl. Add the cucumber and tomato. Mix gently.

SAUTÉED CUCUMBER WITH SOUR CREAM

Serves 4-6

1 large cucumber or 4 apple cucumbers
6 spring onions
1 tb butter
salt and pepper to taste
3 tb sour cream

Peel cucumber and cut into 1 cm cubes. Slice spring onions including some of the green part. Sauté cucumber and onions in butter for about 5 minutes. They should still be slightly crisp. Season. Stir in sour cream and simmer for one minute.

BAKED CUCUMBER WITH CHEESE

Serves 6

2 medium-sized cucumbers or 5 or 6 apple cucumbers
170 g grated, tasty Cheddar cheese
¼ tsp salt
freshly-ground black pepper
2 tb butter

Peel the cucumbers. Cut each in half lengthwise and scoop out the seeds. Slice halves into 4 cm chunks. Cook in boiling, salted water for 10 minutes. Drain and pat dry. Grease an ovenproof dish. Arrange a layer of cucumber at the bottom. Sprinkle with a third of the cheese and season well. Repeat layers finishing with cheese. Dot with butter. Bake at 200°C for about 30 minutes until golden brown.

LEBANESE CUCUMBER AND YOGHURT SOUP

Serves 4

This soup has a refreshing tartness which makes it an ideal starter for a rich dinner.

1 medium-sized cucumber or 3 apple cucumbers

French dressing:

2 tb oil
1 tb lemon juice
½ tsp salt
white pepper
½ tsp sugar

500 ml plain yoghurt
1 tb chopped mint and 4 sprigs for garnishing

Reserve 4 wafer-thin slices of unpeeled cucumber. Peel cucumbers and dice flesh finely. Discard any large seeds. Combine French dressing and yoghurt in a bowl. Add diced cucumber and mint. Check seasoning. Chill thoroughly. Serve in individual bowls. Garnish each with a slice of unpeeled cucumber topped with a small sprig of mint.

CUCUMBER AND SALMON BOATS

Serves 4 as a summertime entrée

1 long cucumber or 2 shorter ones
4 tb vinegar
½ tsp salt
1 c tinned salmon
1 tb mayonnaise (see page 209).
freshly-ground black pepper
1 egg, hard-boiled and chopped
1 tomato, skinned and chopped
1 tsp chopped chives

Cut unpeeled cucumber in half lengthwise. Remove flesh and discard any large seeds. Put boats aside. Dice flesh finely. Place in a bowl with vinegar and salt. Leave for 30 minutes and then drain very thoroughly. Add drained salmon, mayonnaise, pepper, egg, tomato and chives. Mix gently. Chill for 30 minutes. Dry cucumber boats with a towel. Fill with salmon mixture and serve immediately.

STIR-FRIED CUCUMBER AND BEEF

Serves 6

400 g rump or fillet steak
2 tsp cooking oil
1 tb soy sauce
½ tsp salt
½ tsp sugar
⅛ tsp cayenne pepper
2 tb sesame seeds
2 medium-sized cucumbers
1 tb cooking oil

Freeze the beef for a short time to make it firm enough to cut into paper-thin slices about 5 cm long and 1 cm wide. Put beef in a bowl with the 2 tsp oil, soy sauce, salt, sugar and cayenne pepper. Mix thoroughly. Leave for 30 minutes.

Toast sesame seeds in a dry frying pan over moderate heat. Stir constantly until golden brown. Crush with a mortar and pestle or rolling pin.

Peel cucumbers, leaving thin strips of skin running the length of the cucumber at intervals. Cut each cucumber in half lengthwise and scoop out the seeds. Then cut across into thin slices.

Heat the 1 tb of oil in a wok or large frying pan. When very hot add the meat and stir-fry for 1 minute. Add cucumbers and continue to stir-fry over high heat for another minute. Lower heat and simmer for a few minutes until cucumber is tender-crisp. Sprinkle with crushed sesame seeds and serve with rice.

PICKLED CUCUMBER FINGERS

A quickly-made, fresh-tasting preserved pickle.

3 large cucumbers
4 medium-sized onions
3 tb salt
600 ml white vinegar
170 g sugar
1 tsp celery salt
1 tsp mustard seed

Peel cucumbers and cut into fingers. Discard seeds if large. Peel and slice onions. Place cucumbers, onions and salt in a bowl. Leave for 1 hour. Drain and rinse. Combine vinegar, sugar, celery seed and mustard seed in a saucepan. Bring slowly to the boil stirring until the sugar has dissolved. Simmer for 3 minutes. Pack the cucumber fingers and onion slices into jars. Add the hot vinegar mixture to cover. Seal immediately.

PICKLED DILL GHERKINS

Home-pickled gherkins are delicious and inexpensive. Using this simple recipe you will fill 8 half-litre jars.

2 kg gherkins (small ones are best)
8 small sprays of dill or fennel
black peppercorns
8 bay leaves
8 cloves garlic
4 tsp mustard seed
5 dsp salt
8 dsp sugar
2.5 litres water
60 ml glacial acetic acid (buy from the chemist)

Pack jars with washed and drained gherkins. To each jar add a spray of dill, 6 peppercorns, 1 bay leaf, 1 clove of garlic cut into 4 slivers and ½ tsp mustard seed. In a saucepan combine salt, sugar, water and acetic acid. Bring to the boil. Pour into jars to within 2 cm of top. Process in a water-bath for 20 minutes or in the oven for 40 minutes (see page 198).

Currants

(1) BLACK CURRANTS
(Ribes nigrum)

Varieties
English gardeners have at least a dozen varieties to choose from and a few of these, including Cotswold Cross and Daniels Late September, can be obtained elsewhere.

Cotswold Cross currants are usually ready in early summer. They ripen evenly so that the entire crop can be gathered in just two or three pickings. Ripe berries hold well on the bushes if holidays delay picking, but some form of protection from birds must be supplied. The variety Goliath has very large berries which ripen over a longer period in mid summer while Daniels Late September is ready in late summer. An early summer variety known as Magnus is resistant to bud eelworm.

Cultivation
The traditional method of growing black currants is in bushes composed of canes growing up from a woody stool just above ground level. Cuttings 25-30 cm long are cut from the new wood of existing bushes just after the leaves fall. They are trimmed to just above and just below leaf joints and inserted 15 cm deep and 30 cm apart in a holding bed. From the two or three buds left above the surface strong growth is made the next summer. In autumn these young plants are moved into their final positions and the shoots are cut right down to just above ground level. After the next summer the new growth of shoots is reduced by half and the remainder bear the first crop the following summer, two-and-a-half years after the cutting was taken. This type of bush is spaced at least 1 m from its neighbours with 1.8 m between rows.

A new cultivation method is to insert three cuttings 10 cm deep in each planting position and allow them to fruit *in situ*. The shoots produced in the first summer are not pruned and produce their first fruit in the second summer, thereby shortening the process by one year. Even closer spacing is found in a method which uses black plastic over heavily-manured soil. Cuttings are inserted every 15 cm with 1 m between the rows. Fruiting occurs in the second summer and the plants are replaced every five or six years.

Whatever the method of management, all black currants need cool, moist soil which must not dry out in summer. They tolerate shade but should not be exposed to persistently-strong winds, especially when flowering. Wind discourages the insects which assist in pollination. At planting time incorporate ½ c of blood and bone and 2 tb of sulphate of potash in the bottom of each hole. Mature plants benefit from an annual winter dressing of twice these quantities, sprinkled in a circle around the base. Handfuls of old animal manure or rich compost can be spread around in early spring. Avoid root disturbance by suppressing weeds with a mulch. Even light hoeing around the bushes during flowering may prevent fruit from setting.

Both winter and summer pruning has been advocated for black currants grown on stools. In summer cut out any weak shoots cluttering up the centre of the bush. This will allow light and air into the bush to ripen the strong new shoots which will carry next summer's fruit. In winter three types of canes will be visible on the bush: strong, new canes which have grown from the woody stool, old dark-coloured canes with strong, new side shoots and old canes with new shoots at the top. Remove the last type of cane completely from the base, prune the side-shoot canes just above the junction of the side shoots and retain the new shoots growing from the stool.

Black currants are attacked by several insect pests. Eelworm infestation results in leaf buds of normal size which fail to open. Enlarged buds which also fail to open are caused by the microscopic eriophyid mite ("big bud disease") and young caterpillars of the currant clearwing moth make borer-like holes in the stems. Removal of affected portions is recommended for all these pests. Aphids may be troublesome on young foliage and these are controlled with normal insecticides.

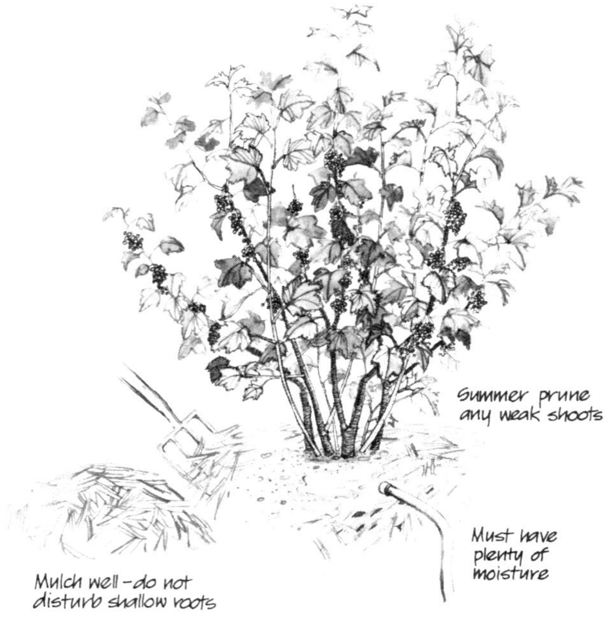

Summer prune any weak shoots

Must have plenty of moisture

Mulch well—do not disturb shallow roots

(2) RED AND WHITE CURRANTS

(Bred from three Ribes species)

Varieties

Several varieties of red currant are available, including Red Lake, Versailles and Fay's Prolific. These fruit in early to mid summer. A new Dutch variety, Johnkeer van Tets, is ready several weeks earlier. White currants have been developed by selection and breeding of red types. Although they have the least Vitamin C content of the three currants, their delicate flavour makes them ideal for use in desserts. White Transparent is a variety with large berries and White Versailles is a strong, upright type with produces early fruit. White Dutch is considered to be the best dessert variety and it can be grown on lighter soils than the other varieties.

Cultivation

Red and white currants like a deeply-dug garden soil to which compost and animal manure have been added. They need more sunshine than black currants. Shelter from strong winds in spring is also important, for new growth is easily broken off and they flower several weeks earlier than black currants. They are a little more tolerant of drought and are less vigorous in their growth. Although needing less nitrogen, red and white currants benefit from 1 c of blood and bone and 3 tb of sulphate of potash every spring. If grown as bushes they are planted 2 m apart. The spacing is wider than for black currants because the bushes are normally trained to an open-centred vase shape with nine to ten main branches. The "vase" is supported on a short leg, created by removing all but the top three or four buds on the 25-30 cm cutting before it is inserted into the ground. The lower buds are sliced off with a very sharp knife to prevent suckers growing from below the soil level.

Red and white currants fruit on short spurs which grow on the older branches, so the object of pruning is to create a framework of sturdy, mature branches and laterals on which the flower clusters appear. In winter pruning consists of removing most of the soft shoots which have grown up from the base, shortening the leading growth on each of the main branches by a third and trimming back the woody laterals to two to three buds. Old branches which may be weakened by stem-borer tunnels should be cut out and replaced by a well-situated, vigorous new branch growing from 1 m down on the bush. It is also possible to train red and white currants in cordon fashion against a fence or wall. Sometimes five or six branches from young shoots are spread out in a fan shape and tied to a suitable support to become the main branches of the mature bush.

Harvesting

(Black, red and white currants)
Currants are picked by hand or the grape-like clusters can be cut from the stems with scissors. At the beginning of harvest time it is best to pick the few early, ripe currants by hand, leaving the remainder to ripen. Later when the bulk of the crop is ripe the clusters are cut.

In the kitchen

Currants which are to be used as a purée need not be stripped from the stalks. For other recipes the fruit should be stripped off gently. Wash and drain in a sieve or colander.

Fresh, ripe red currants are delightful served raw with yoghurt or cream and sweetened with a little brown sugar.

BLACK CURRANT YOGHURT

Stew a small quantity of prepared fresh or frozen currants with a little water and sugar to taste. Cool. Fold into homemade or plain, commercial yoghurt. (150 g of currants stewed with 4 tb sugar and ½ c water will flavour 800 ml or 4 cartons of yoghurt.)

BLACK CURRANT FOOL

Serves 8
A party dessert. Serve with sponge fingers to provide a pleasing contrast in textures.
Custard:

250 ml milk
3 eggs
2 tb sugar
1 tsp gelatine
1 tb hot water

Heat the milk in a double boiler. Beat the eggs and sugar in a bowl. Pour the hot milk into the eggs and stir well. Pour the custard mixture back into the double boiler and cook until thick, stirring constantly. Dissolve the gelatine in 1 tb hot water. Add to the custard, stir well and allow to cool.
Black currant purée:

150 g fresh or frozen black currants
4 tb sugar or to taste
½ c water

Place ingredients in a small saucepan. Simmer gently until soft. Put through a sieve. Cool.
Cream:

300 ml cream, whipped until thick

When the custard is cool but not set, combine it with the cool purée. Fold in the whipped cream and pour into glasses. Chill.

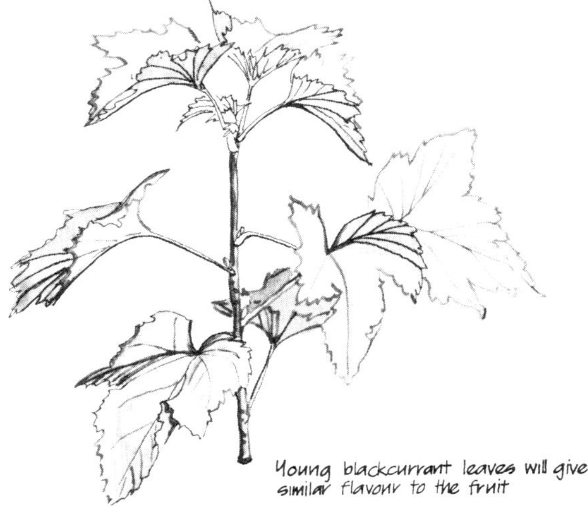
Young blackcurrant leaves will give similar flavour to the fruit

BLACK CURRANT-LEAF CREAM

Serves 8-10

The delicate perfume of young black currant leaves is used to flavour this rich dessert, which is best served in small glasses.

450 g sugar
300 ml water
1 c tightly-packed, young black currant leaves
2 egg whites
juice of 1 lemon
150 ml cream, whipped
a little preserved or crystallized ginger for garnishing

Bring the sugar, water and leaves to the boil. Simmer without stirring for 15 minutes. Beat egg whites stiffly in a large bowl. Strain hot, black currant leaf syrup. Discard leaves. Pour very slowly into the egg whites beating continuously. Stir in the lemon juice and fold in the whipped cream. Pour into small glasses and chill. Garnish with the finely-chopped ginger.

BLACK CURRANT PUDDING

Serves 6-8

Using frozen black currants, this old-fashioned pudding is a real treat on a winter's night.

225 g self-raising flour
2 tsp baking powder
¼ tsp salt
115 g butter
60 g sugar
grated rind of a lemon

Filling:

500 g black currants, fresh or frozen (stalks removed)
140 g sugar
4 tb water
1 tb lemon juice

Sift the flour, baking powder and salt. Rub in the butter. Add 60 g of sugar and the lemon rind. Stir. Add sufficient water to make a soft dough. Roll out two-thirds of the dough and line a 1.5-litre capacity basin.

Half fill with currants, add 140 g of sugar. Cover with remaining currants and add the water and juice. Fold edges of dough over the fruit. Roll out the remaining dough. Brush the folded edges of the dough in the basin with water before adding the top. Press down firmly around the edges to seal. Cover with buttered greaseproof paper tied on firmly with string, or a greased lid. Steam for 2 hours or 3 hours if using frozen currants.

RED-CURRANT CREAM FREEZE

Serves 4

150 ml cream
4 tb icing sugar
1 c red currants, stalks removed

Whip the cream and icing sugar until thick. Fold in the currants. Spoon the mixture into a freezer tray. After 1 hour stir the mixture thoroughly. Freeze for a further 30-60 minutes until the cream is just firm. Do not over freeze as the currants will be hard — they are nicest still soft. Serve in glasses garnished with crystallized red currants.

CRYSTALLIZED RED CURRANTS

Dip small clusters of perfect red currants in egg white. Shake off excess and then dip in castor sugar. Leave to dry on greaseproof paper for about half an hour.

RED CURRANT AND CREAM CHEESE FLAN

Serves 4-5

Flan:

170 g flour
pinch of salt
120 g butter
1 dsp castor sugar
1 egg yolk
2 tb cold water (approximately)

Sift the flour and salt into a mixing bowl. Rub the butter into the flour. Stir in the sugar. Mix the egg yolk and water and add to the flour. Stir with a knife to a firm dough. (You may need to add a little more water.) Chill dough for 30 minutes. Roll pastry out to 1 cm thick. Line a 20 cm flan tin or pie plate. Prick base with a fork. Chill for a further 30 minutes. Line the pastry with greaseproof paper and fill with uncooked dried beans (or rice). Bake at 200°C for 20 minutes. Remove the beans and paper.

Cook for a further 5 minutes until flan is a golden brown. Leave to cool.

Topping:

1 c red currants, stalks removed
½ c sugar
2 tb water
2 tsp cornflour

Bring the red currants, sugar and water to the boil, stirring constantly. Mix the cornflour with a little extra water. Add to the red currants and stir until thick and boiling. Leave to cool.

Cream cheese filling:

30 g butter
2 tb castor sugar
150 g cream cheese
1 tsp port wine

Cream the butter and sugar until fluffy then gradually beat in the cream cheese and port wine.

Spread the filling over the base of the cold flan. Cover with the red currant topping. Chill for an hour before serving. This dessert can be made a day ahead.

QUICK RED CURRANT JELLY

See accompanying illustration.

Red currant jelly glaze: for use with all red fruit flans or tarts. Break up the jelly with a fork and tip into a small saucepan. Heat gently until liquified. Brush the glaze over the fruit with a soft brush.

Quick red currant jelly

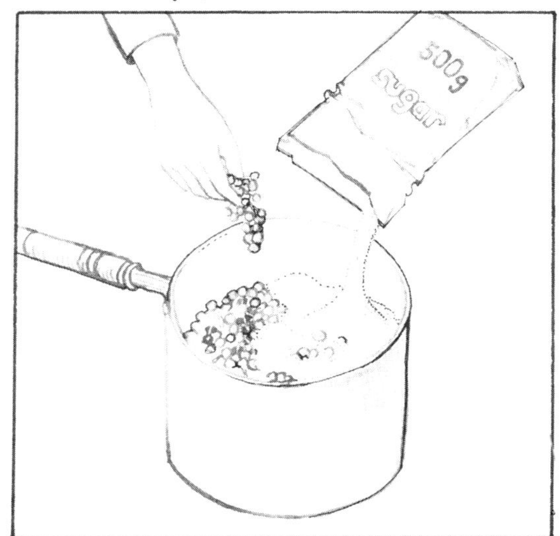

Combine 500g washed red currants with stalks and 500g sugar in large saucepan

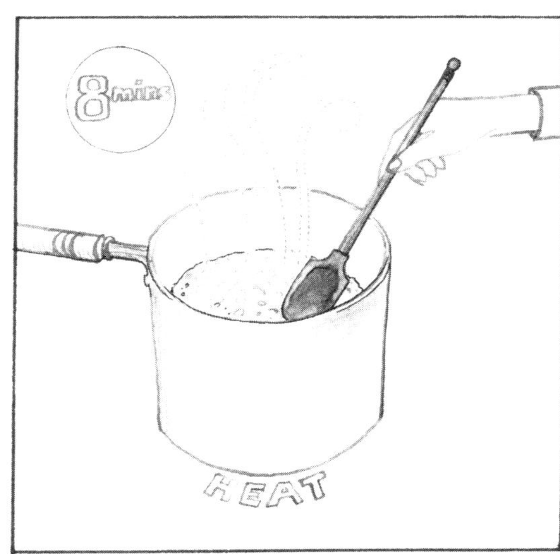

Bring slowly to the boil stirring constantly. Boil for 8 minutes stirring occasionally

Pour through wire sieve into warm jug then pour into warm small jars. Cover

Has a fresh flavour and good colour and is almost as clear as jelly strained through muslin

Red currant mint sauce: a delicious change from plain mint sauce. With a fork, break the jelly from one small jar into pieces. Turn into a glass serving dish and sprinkle with 1 tb of chopped mint and the grated rind of half an orange.

Cumberland sauce: provides a real lift for meat loaves, particularly those of pork or sausage meat.

CUMBERLAND SAUCE

This sauce can be served hot or cold as an accompaniment, or spooned over a meat loaf after cooking.

4 tb red currant jelly
4 tb brown sugar
grated rind of 1 orange
1 tb orange juice
1 tb port wine
2 tsp mild prepared mustard

Combine all the ingredients in a small saucepan. Heat and stir until the sugar is dissolved.

If you haven't a large crop of black currants but want to make jam, try the recipe given for Rhubarb and Black Currant Jam on page 164.

CURRANT MUFFINS

Makes 12-15 muffins

1¾ c flour
2½ tsp baking powder
½ tsp salt
4 tb sugar
1 egg
¾ c milk
3 tb melted butter
1 c black or red currants, fresh or thawed (stalks removed)
2 tb sugar

Stir flour, baking powder and salt into a bowl. Stir in the 4 tb sugar. Combine beaten egg, milk and melted butter. Add to the dry ingredients. Stir carefully until just mixed. Toss the currants in 2 tb sugar. Fold gently into the batter. Fill greased muffin tins two-thirds full. Bake at 200°C for 20-25 minutes.

Freezing

Currants freeze very well, retaining their full flavour. Pack washed, dried currants stripped from the stems (or not stripped, depending on intended use), into small freezer bags. There is no need to add sugar.

Egg plants

(Solanum melongena* var. *esculentum)

Varieties

Some gardeners and cooks call this plant aubergine, while others use the old term, egg plant. The large, shiny, purple-skinned fruit we grow now bears no resemblance to an egg, but there was once a white-fruited variety which bore fruit the size and shape of goose eggs.

Of the three tender members of the *Solanum* family, tomato, pepper and egg plant, the egg plant is the slowest to mature and the most sensitive to cold. It can be grown in areas with seven or more months of frost-free weather. During that period mean temperatures should exceed 15°C and there should be plenty of sunshine if outdoor cultivation is contemplated. Few varieties are offered to the home gardener. Early Long is favoured in marginal areas because it is earlier than the maincrop types such as Black Beauty and New York Purple. Its fruits are 20-25 cm long and 8 cm thick, while those of the latter varieties are shorter and thicker. Hybrid varieties are extensively used by commercial growers. Two of these, Early Prolific Hybrid and Blacknight (Blacknite F.1 Hybrid), are available for home gardeners.

Eggplants are a tropical vegetable fruit which belongs to the same family as tomatoes and peppers. Needs heat

Cultivation

It is common practice to sow egg plant seeds in peat pots and germinate them on a warm window sill or in a glasshouse. Germination is slow and erratic (as in green peppers) and takes place two to four weeks after sowing. Keep the plants under shelter, one per pot, until the garden soil is noticeably warm. Make sure they have maximum sunshine at this stage to keep them sturdy. The soil should be loose, well-drained and dressed with a tomato fertilizer. Set each pot into its prepared position, allowing 50-60 cm between plants. In windy areas, tie the stem to a 1 m stake. When the plant is about 15 cm high the growing tip may be pinched out to encourage branching.

Some four-and-a-half months after sowing,

fruiting begins. In marginal zones only four to six fruits will be allowed to develop on each plant; extra flowers and side shoots are rigorously removed. Soil moisture should be maintained at an even level as the fruits swell, while the foliage is kept dry to discourage disease. As with tomatoes, side dressings of fertilizer are recommended during this period.

Egg plants are very susceptible to verticillium wilt and other tomato diseases. For this reason garden hygiene must be maintained and soil sterilization or replacement practised if the same planting position is to be used year after year. Treat pests and diseases as for tomatoes and peppers.

Harvesting

The fruit can be picked once it has taken on a uniform, deep-purple colouring and has a surface bloom like an apple. The flesh inside should be creamy and the seeds soft and white. When the bloom disappears and the seeds become brownish, the flavour is bitter. The fruit should be handled carefully as it bruises readily.

In the kitchen

Egg plants are normally used unpeeled. Simply rinse and remove the calyx with a sharp knife. Many cooks like to salt and drain egg plants before cooking to remove excess moisture and any bitterness. If you are short of time this step may be omitted. Place egg plant slices or cubes in a colander, sprinkle with salt and leave for 30-60 minutes. Rinse thoroughly, drain and pat dry with a paper towel.

Egg plant slices can be grilled or baked. Brush 2 cm slices with cooking oil before placing under a hot grill, or on a baking tray on the top shelf of a hot oven. When they are brown, turn the slices over and brush with more oil. Slices may also be fried in a little hot oil and butter. Seal surfaces of slices before frying by dipping them in a little seasoned flour.

EGG PLANT FRITTERS

These satisfying fritters can take the place of meat without complaints from the family. Serve them hot with one or two salad vegetables to make a welcome change. One large fruit will be plenty for a family of six.

500 g egg plant (1 large, 2 medium or 3 small)
½ tsp salt
2 eggs
1 c dry breadcrumbs
½ tsp salt
freshly-ground black pepper
oil for frying

Cut unpeeled egg plant into 1 cm slices. If you have time place them in a colander, sprinkle with salt and leave for 1 hour. Drain, rinse, drain again and pat dry with a paper towel. Beat the eggs lightly with a fork to combine. Season the breadcrumbs with salt and pepper. Dip the egg plant slices first into the egg and then the breadcrumbs, making sure they are well coated. Fry in hot oil, turning slices so that both sides may become crisp and golden brown. Drain on absorbent paper and keep hot until all the fritters are cooked. Can be served with lemon wedges.

POOR MAN'S CAVIAR

This spread is delicious served on thin slices of fresh rye bread.

1 medium-sized egg plant
½ medium-sized onion
½ green pepper
2 tomatoes
½ clove garlic
3 tb cooking oil
salt and pepper to taste
1 tb white wine or dry sherry
1 tb finely-chopped parsley

Bake the egg plant at 180°C for 1 hour. Peel onion and chop finely. Remove seeds from the green pepper and chop the flesh finely. Skin tomatoes and chop the flesh finely. Chop garlic very finely. Sauté onion in oil until golden. Add green pepper, tomatoes and garlic. Peel egg plant when cool enough to handle. Chop flesh and add to the other ingredients. Simmer until fairly thick. Season with salt and pepper. Cool. Stir in white wine or sherry and the parsley. Chill.

EGG PLANT, YOGHURT AND TOMATO CASSEROLE

Serves 4

2 medium-sized egg plants
1 tsp salt
2 tb cooking oil
6 tb tomato purée
½ c plain yoghurt
freshly-ground black pepper
finely-chopped parsley for garnish

Slice egg plants into 5 mm slices. Place in colander and sprinkle with salt. Leave to drain for 1 hour. Do not rinse. Dry the slices with a paper towel. Sauté in hot oil until golden brown on both sides. Place a layer of egg plant slices in a small casserole. Cover with one-third of the tomato purée and one third of the yoghurt. Season with pepper. Repeat layers twice more. Cover casserole and bake at 180°C for 30-40 minutes. Sprinkle with parsley before serving.

STUFFED EGG PLANTS

Serves 4

1 large or 2 small egg plants (about 500g)
¼ tsp salt
1 medium-sized onion
2 tb cooking oil
1 clove garlic
2 medium-sized tomatoes
1 tb chopped parsley
½ tsp sugar
½ tsp salt
freshly-ground black pepper
½ c plain yoghurt

Cut egg plant in half lengthwise. Using a small sharp knife and teaspoon, remove flesh leaving a shell 1.5 cm thick. Sprinkle with ¼ tsp of salt. Place in a greased ovenproof dish. Chop egg plant flesh roughly. Peel onion and chop finely. Sauté onion in oil in a medium-sized frying pan until soft. Chop garlic finely and add to the onion. Peel tomatoes, discard seeds and chop the flesh roughly. Add tomatoes, egg plant flesh, parsley, sugar, salt and pepper to the sautéed onion. Mix well. Pile into the egg plant shells. Cover dish with foil and bake at 180°C for about 1 to 1½ hours. Allow to cool to room temperature. Place yoghurt in a small serving bowl to be spooned on top of each serving at the table. Cut large egg plant halves in two before dishing up.

BACON AND CHEESE-STUFFED EGG PLANTS

Serves 4

Follow the previous recipe but substitute the following stuffing.

3 rashers bacon
1 tb oil (if bacon is lean)
1 small onion, finely chopped
salt and pepper to taste
4 tb finely-grated cheese for topping

Chop bacon finely. Fry until beginning to brown. Add 1 tb of oil if necessary and onion. Continue cooking until onion is soft. Add chopped egg plant flesh and seasoning. Pile into the shells and bake. When tender, sprinkle tops with cheese and grill for a few minutes until golden brown and crisp. Serve hot.

MOUSSAKA

Serves 6

A traditional Greek dish.

500 g egg plant (or zucchini or a mixture of both)
3 tb cooking oil
2 onions
1 clove garlic
700 g lamb or beef, minced
1 tsp ground allspice
salt and pepper to taste
500 g tomatoes
2 tb chopped marjoram
¼ c red or white wine
1 c béchamel sauce (see page 208)
1 egg
2 tb grated Parmesan cheese

Sauté the sliced egg plants in oil in a large frying pan until golden. Drain on absorbent paper. If necessary add a little more oil to the pan and sauté the peeled and sliced onions and finely-chopped garlic. Add the meat and fry until brown. Add the allspice, seasoning, peeled and chopped tomatoes, marjoram and wine. Stir well. Cover and cook slowly for 20 minutes.

Prepare béchamel sauce. Separate the egg. Add the yolk to the sauce with the cheese. Beat well. Beat the egg white to a stiff foam and fold gently into the sauce.

Grease a casserole and in it place one-third of the egg plant. Cover with half of the meat. Add another third of the egg-plant slices. Cover with the remaining meat. Top with the remaining slices of egg plant. Carefully spoon the sauce over the surface. Bake at 200°C for 25-35 minutes or until topping is set and browned.

Freezing

Cut egg plants into 1 cm slices or cubes. Work quickly to prevent discolouration. Blanch for 3-4 minutes. Cool in iced water containing 2 tb lemon juice. Pat dry with a paper towel and stack slices, separating them with greaseproof paper. Pack in an airtight container or seal in a freezer bag.

Endive

(Cichorium endivia)

Varieties

The endive is a close relative of chicory and also needs blanching to remove the bitter flavour of the green leaves. The Batavian Broad Leaved variety grows like a cos lettuce with infolded, lettuce-like leaves. It is most suited for standing in the garden during winter. The Green Curled (Extra Curled) variety is usually grown for summer and autumn eating. Its leaves are extremely decorative.

Cultivation and harvesting

Soil for both types should be prepared as for lettuce and the plants should be shaded in mid summer. Avoid strongly-nitrogenous manures as they increase the chance of rot in the rosette. Both varieties need three months' steady growth to reach maturity, so make sowings of the curled type from late spring to mid summer and mid to late summer for the broad-leaved type. This will allow you to harvest the curled type before the first heavy frosts of winter.

Make very shallow sowings of endive seed in boxes of seed mix, or directly in the garden where they can be protected by glass or a PVC cloche and kept moist. If they have not germinated in four days the row should be resown. Late-germinating seedlings are supposed to grow into bitter plants, prone to bolting. Thin initially to 7 cm and then to 30-60 cm apart, the wider distance for the large, curled varieties. Never allow the plants to reach wilting point during the summer.

Start blanching the curled endive from when the rosette begins to form. If the weather is still warm and the soil surface and leaves dry, simply invert a plate over the centre of the plant and leave for five to ten days. Sprinkle soot, sand or lime around the perimeter to stop slugs crawling under for a free meal. When the rosette is pale yellow cut the plant at ground level and use for a salad as soon as possible. When winter sets in start blanching the broad-leaved variety, a few at a time. First tie the outer leaves over the centre about 10 cm from the top, after checking that the leaves are quite dry. The plant may have to be covered with a cloche for a few days to achieve this. Then invert a large flower pot with the drainage hole covered over the plant. In three to four weeks the endive will be ready for eating.

In the kitchen

Use blanched portions as a substitute for lettuce.

Feijoas

(Feijoa sellowiana)

Varieties

Feijoas are sometimes used for hedge plants because they are evergreen, have attractive red flowers and tolerate wind and salt spray. They are apparently able to withstand frosts up to minus 8°C. If grown primarily for their fruit, they are best planted as specimen trees obtained as named varieties rather than as unnamed seedlings. Named varieties such as Triumph, Magnifica, Mammoth and Coolidgei have been selected for their high quality fruit and a greater ability to set fruit by self-pollination than is possessed by most feijoas. Coolidgei is completely self-fruitful and may therefore be planted as a single specimen tree sometimes growing up to 5 m high.

Cultivation

When grown as individual trees feijoas should be planted from mid autumn to spring, 4-5 m apart in well-drained soil with 2 c of blood and bone mixed into the planting hole. A mature tree benefits from an early spring dressing of 4 c of blood and bone. The same amount is given in early summer together with ½ c of sulphate of potash, which is beneficial for fruiting. Hedge feijoas can be fed with old cow manure or compost, both rich in nitrogen, to promote extra leaf growth. A straw or grass-clipping mulch (not applied against the trunk) is better for fruiting trees since it releases less nitrogen.

Mulching is a good means of controlling weeds, for feijoas have surface roots which can be damaged by hoeing. Occasionally a sooty mould appears on the leaves, associated with small, star-shaped scales or tiny, waxy cones on the twigs. These indicate that the hard-wax scale insect is present. Spraying with summer oil in autumn is recommended.

Harvesting

Feijoas flower in early summer and their fruits ripen in late autumn to early winter. When almost mature they drop to the ground (a good reason for growing them over a lawn or a straw mulch). They need another week in storage before they reach full flavour. If stored in a cool, draught-proof place they will keep another three to four weeks before the pulp turns brown.

In the kitchen

Feijoas have a relatively short season in autumn. Many people harvest only enough to serve as fresh fruit. Cut in half and provide a teaspoon to scoop out the flesh.

If you tire of them raw they can be stewed or included in your favourite apple puddings — apple and feijoa crumble, pie or sponge.

Add three or four peeled feijoas to give interest to a stew.

FEIJOAS IN WINE

Serves 6

A delicious dinner party dessert for those who like feijoas.

6 large feijoas
¼ c red wine (burgundy type)
¾ c water
½ c sugar
1 tb cornflour
2 tb water
150 ml cream

Peel feijoas and cut in half lengthwise. Combine wine, water and sugar in a saucepan. Place over heat and stir until sugar is dissolved. Add feijoas and simmer until just tender (the less cooking feijoas have, the more flavour they retain). Using a perforated spoon, carefully lift the feijoas into a serving bowl. Mix the cornflour and 2 tb of water and add to the syrup. Stir until boiling point is reached. Simmer gently for 2 minutes. Pour over the fruit. Serve at room temperature with whipped cream.

FEIJOA AND GINGER JAM

1.8 kg feijoas
120 g crystallized ginger
2 c water
2 lemons
1.8 kg sugar

Roughly chop unpeeled feijoas. Place in a preserving pan with ginger and water. Cook until the skins are soft (about 40 minutes). Add grated rind, juice of the lemons and sugar. Bring slowly to the boil, stirring until the sugar is dissolved. Boil until setting point is reached. Pour into clean, hot jars and seal with jam covers.

FEIJOA CHUTNEY

12 medium-sized feijoas
2 onions
2 cooking apples
250 ml vinegar
1½ tb ground mixed spices
1 tb salt
450 g sugar
½ tsp cayenne pepper

Peel feijoas and onions. Chop finely. Peel, core and chop apples. Combine with remaining ingredients in a preserving pan. Bring to the boil and simmer with frequent stirring until the chutney is thick (about 30 minutes). Pour into clean jars and seal.

Bottling

Peel and then cut lengthwise in half or crosswise into thick slices. Pack in jars and cover with syrup (1 c of sugar to 2 c of water) leaving 2 cm headspace. Process in a water bath for 20 minutes (see page 198).

Gooseberries

(Ribes grossularia)

Varieties

As a native of Britain, the hardy and productive gooseberry is represented there by more than a dozen varieties with different periods of ripening, different characteristics (from drooping to upright) and of different colours. Five varieties will be discussed here. The earliest, Levin Early, is a drooping type which may collapse unless well trained to a strong framework of branches. It was bred from Farmer's Glory, a moderately-vigorous drooping type which produces heavy crops of oval, smooth-skinned berries which turn red when ripe. Billy Dean is more upright than Farmer's Glory, while Gregory's Perfection is semi-erect and produces heavy crops of round, hairy berries which are greenish-yellow when ripe. The variety Greengage is occasionally available and its yellowish ripe fruit are delicious raw.

Cultivation

Gooseberries do well in cool areas, on loams or heavy soils improved with humus. They can be grown from cuttings taken in autumn of well-ripened hardwood shoots about 25 cm long. As for red currants the lower buds are removed to prevent suckers from forming.

The cuttings are planted 10 cm deep in a nursery bed to which coarse sand has been added to encourage rooting. After the next summer's growth the branches are shortened by a half and the bushes can be planted in their permanent positions, 1-2 cm apart depending on their habit of growth. The following summer the vase shape of the future bush is created by pruning out all growths in the centre. From then on the aim of pruning is to provide regular replacements for the main branches, to keep the centre of the bush open and to remove branches which trail on the ground. Each winter, therefore, the new growth on the strong leaders of upright types is shortened by a third to outside buds. Old spurs and laterals are cut back and new lateral growths shortened to 10 cm. In drooping varieties always prune to an upward-pointing bud.

Blood and bone is a suitable fertilizer to incorporate in the soil at planting time, about 1 c for each plant. In early spring ½ c more is sprinkled around together with a mulch of garden compost. Animal manure is too rich in nitrogen, which leads to excessive leaf growth. Wood ash is more beneficial for it is rich in potash, an element which gooseberries need rather more of than many other fruit trees. An alternative to wood ash is 3 tb of sulphate of potash applied in early spring.

Gooseberries are generally among the healthiest plants in the vegetable garden. Aphids seem to avoid them and even the leafroller caterpillar does not do too much damage. If fungus disease occurs it may be an indication of overcrowding or an unsatisfactory position.

Harvesting

For most jam-making and for winter pies and tarts made from frozen gooseberries, the fruit is picked before it softens or changes colour. We pick for cooking first, leaving the smaller gooseberries on the bush to fill out and ripen as dessert fruit. They are ready three to six weeks later. One day we may be able to grow thornless gooseberries to make picking more pleasant but the other chore, topping and tailing, will always be with us. Fortunately even a three-year-old can lend a hand.

In the kitchen

Wash if necessary. Top and tail either with kitchen scissors or more quickly with your thumb nail.

To stew: prepare a syrup of 2 parts of water to 1 part of sugar. Simmer prepared gooseberries in the syrup until just tender. To obtain 2 c of stewed gooseberries use 600 g gooseberries and a syrup made from ½ c of water and ¼ c of sugar. Another method is to bake the gooseberries in a covered dish in a slow oven. They can be sweetened with 2 - 3 tb of honey.

GOOSEBERRY SPONGE

Serves 6

We had to include this old favourite which our grandmother made for us frequently in our teenage years.

2 c stewed gooseberries
2 tb butter
115 g sugar
1 egg
170 g flour
2 tsp baking powder
¼ tsp salt
½ c milk

Cream the butter and sugar. Beat in the egg. Sift the flour, baking powder and salt. Add to the creamed mixture alternately with the milk. Grease a baking dish approximately 18 cm square. Heat the gooseberries to boiling point and pour into the dish. Spread the batter evenly over the fruit. Bake at 180°C for 45 minutes.

CREAMY GOOSEBERRY TART

See recipe for Elsie's Creamy Rhubarb Tart on page 163. Use 2 cups of prepared gooseberries instead of rhubarb.

MARY'S OLD-FASHIONED GOOSEBERRY PUDDING

Serves 6

A warming pudding for cold nights. Can be made from fresh or frozen gooseberries.

225 g self-raising flour
½ tsp salt
115 g shredded suet
170 g brown sugar
55 g butter
450 g prepared gooseberries

Sift the flour and salt together. Stir in the suet and mix to a soft dough with a little water. Knead lightly. Roll out and use two-thirds to line a greased, 1.5-litre pudding basin. Cover the bottom with half the sugar and butter. Add the gooseberries. Put the remaining sugar and butter on top. Cover with the rest of the dough, sealing the edges carefully. Cover the basin with a lid or several layers of greaseproof paper tied on tightly. Put the basin in a saucepan of boiling water which should come half way up the sides. Boil briskly for 3 hours. Top up with boiling water as necessary. Serve with whipped cream, unsweetened condensed milk or icecream.

GOOSEBERRY SHORTCAKE

Can be made with fresh or frozen gooseberries.

225 g flour
1 tsp baking powder
115 g butter
1 egg
1 tb sugar
1 c prepared gooseberries
3 tb sugar

Sift flour and baking powder into a bowl. Rub in the butter. Beat egg and 1 tb sugar. Add to the flour and mix to form a soft dough. Divide the dough in half. Roll out one half to form a rectangle about 15 cm x 20 cm. Place the dough on a cold, greased baking tray. Place gooseberries on the dough leaving edges free. Sprinkle with 3 tb of sugar. Roll the remaining half out to a rectangle slightly bigger than the first. Moisten edges and place over gooseberries. Carefully seal the edges. Bake at 200°C for 20-30 minutes. The shortcake should be golden brown and the gooseberries soft when tested with a fine wire. Sprinkle with a little icing sugar and cut while hot.

Serves 4-5 as a delicious dessert or can be cut into smaller pieces to serve slightly warm with tea or coffee.

GOOSEBERRY GÂTEAU

A wholemeal sponge layered with gooseberry honey and topped with whipped fresh or sour cream.

Wholemeal sponge:

3 eggs
½ c sugar
1 tsp vanilla
¾ c wholemeal flour
1 tsp baking powder

Prepare two 20 cm sponge tins: cut a circle of greaseproof paper to fit the base of each tin. Grease the sides and lining with melted butter. Dust with flour.

Separate the eggs. Beat the whites until stiff. Add the yolks one at a time, beating well between each addition. Add the sugar, a tablespoonful at a time, beating well between each spoonful. Add essence and fold in the sifted flour and baking powder. Divide the mixture between the two prepared tins. Bake for 15-20 minutes at 190°C. Cool in the tins for 5 minutes and then tip out on to a rack. When cool split each sponge in half to give 4 layers.

Gooseberry honey:

250 g prepared gooseberries, fresh or frozen
2 tb water
130 g sugar
2 eggs
50 g butter

Place the prepared gooseberries in a small saucepan with the water. Cover and simmer until the gooseberries are tender. Put the cooked gooseberries and juice through a fine sieve or blender. In a small bowl, beat the eggs and sugar until creamy. Add the gooseberry purée slowly. Stir until combined. Return to the saucepan and add the butter. Cook over low heat, stirring constantly, until the mixture thickens. Do not boil. Cool.

These quantities will produce more gooseberry honey than you will need for the gâteau. Any left over will store well in the refrigerator. It is delicious spread on bread.

Gâteau:

4 layers of wholemeal sponge
gooseberry honey
150 ml cream, fresh or sour

Spread one layer of sponge with a generous quantity of gooseberry honey. Place a second layer on top and spread it with gooseberry honey. Repeat with the third layer. Place the fourth layer on top without gooseberry honey. Whip the fresh cream until very thick and spoon over the top layer. If you are using semi-liquid sour cream, whip as you would fresh cream. Thick, sour cream can be spread straight on to the gâteau. Chill for at least one hour before serving.

Gooseberries are rich in pectin and can be added to strawberry jam to ensure a good set. Use your surplus gooseberries to make a few strawberries go much further. See recipe for strawberry and gooseberry jam on page 179.

ELLA'S GOOSEBERRY AND LEMON JAM

Most gooseberry jams are a fairly dark red. This one is different. It remains a pleasant green.

1.4 kg green gooseberries
3 lemons
6 c water
2.3 kg sugar

Place the prepared gooseberries in a preserving pan. Chop lemons finely. (If the lemons are thick skinned, peel them thinly and shred the peel. Discard the white pith. Chop the flesh.) Add the chopped lemons (or shredded peel and chopped flesh) to the gooseberries. Add the water. Boil for 45 minutes. Add the sugar and heat slowly, stirring constantly until dissolved. Boil for 1 minute only. Pour into clean, warm jars. Seal with jam covers.

Freezing
Place weighed quantities of prepared gooseberries in freezer bags. Do not add sugar.

Bottling
Pack prepared raw gooseberries into jars. Cover with syrup (2 parts of sugar to 1 part of water) leaving 2 cm headspace. Seal and process in a water bath for 20 minutes.

Grapes

(Vitis vinifera)

Varieties

Many dessert varieties suitable for outdoor planting in sheltered positions are available from nurserymen. Choose a grafted, two-year-old, container-grown vine suitable for your area. Other gardeners in your vicinity will be happy to recommend their favourite variety. Albany Surprise is a hardy, vigorous type with almost black, sweet fruit. Chasselas Golden is an early, green-yellow variety while Chasselas Rose is similar but with light red fruit. Muscat Hamburgh produces bluish-black fruit of excellent muscat flavour.

Cultivation

Choosing the site and constructing a suitable framework are important matters to deal with as a grapevine becomes a long-lived, permanent feature of the garden. Sunshine is important to ensure the ripening of the grapes in autumn. A pergola positioned to provide summer shade over a terrace is ideal. The large grape leaves make an attractive sun filter in summer but after colouring and falling in autumn will allow full sunshine again. Sunny fences, screens or permanent-material house or garage walls also make ideal sites.

Rich soil is not necessary but good drainage should be provided. Break up any clay subsoil with a little gravel or mortar rubble. A good dressing of compost applied well before planting time will also be beneficial. Plant during late winter or early spring when soil conditions are not too wet. Spread roots out carefully in the planting hole before replacing the soil and firming the plant in position. The new vine should be pruned back to two or three buds from the graft. A mulch of peat will help to conserve moisture for the first year or two. Once a vine is well established it is tolerant of fairly dry conditions but watering will be required if the wall faces into the hot sun and has overhanging eaves.

In the first season, growth should not be checked in any way. Some temporary support may be needed to keep the leaves off the ground and to prevent wind damage. During the next winter (second year), prune the strongest shoot back to three buds and cut off all other shoots. During the following summer, one, two or three strong shoots should be selected to form the permanent framework. These should be well tied. In the winter of the third year, these main shoots should be shortened a little and all other shoots removed. Within the next year or two the vine shoots will have reached their desired size. Growth is then stopped by removing the tips. By then the vines will be quite thick and woody and should be fruiting. Any grapes which develop before the third year are best removed. Once the vine commences fruiting, summer pruning is bene-

ficial. This keeps rapid growth of side shoots in control and allows sunshine to reach the grapes. Winter pruning consists of cutting back all side growths to two buds.

Long side shoots must be pruned back to allow the sun to reach grapes

Give the vine a mulch of compost each spring, unless it is producing vast quantities of leaf. You could also give the vines a dressing of a fertilizer mixture, consisting of three parts of blood and bone and one part of sulphate of potash, applied at the rate of a quarter of a cup per square metre.

Outdoor, home-grown grapes are usually free of serious pests and diseases. In some seasons, however, they may need to be sprayed with a fungicide or insecticide. Your choice of these should be made by consulting a specialized publication on viticulture (grape growing).

If you want to grow large grapes, selective thinning needs to be carried out as soon as the largest grapes in a bunch have reached pea size.

Harvesting

Decide when each bunch is at the optimum stage of ripeness (this comes with practice) and cut carefully with kitchen scissors.

In the kitchen

For eating straight from the bunch: wash grapes well and dry with a soft tea towel. Cut large bunches into serving-sized portions.

Thick-skinned grapes which are to be added to a fruit salad or used to garnish a special recipe should be skinned and seeded. If grapes are difficult to peel, scald them as you would tomatoes. The easiest method of removing the seeds is to cut each grape in half with a small, sharp knife and flick out the seeds. To prevent discoloration, cover peeled grapes with lemon juice and wet greaseproof paper until required.

The name *véronique* is used for dishes having grapes as a garnish. A good example is Chicken Véronique: cut a roasted chicken into serving portions, coat with a gravy made from chicken stock and cream, and garnish with grapes.

Grapes can be used as part of a fruit appetizer: peel and pip white or black grapes, dress with a little French dressing made with lemon juice instead of vinegar and use to fill the cavities of small rock melon halves, or to pile on top of prepared grapefruit halves sprinkled with sugar.

DOLMAS

(stuffed vine leaves)

Serves 6-8 as a main course or 9-12 as an entrée

If you haven't got a grape vine, cabbage leaves can be used instead (see page 50).

18-24 pale-green, grape vine leaves
400 g mince
4 tb currants
juice of a small lemon
2 tsp tomato concentrate
2 tsp beef stock powder or 2 beef stock cubes, crumbled
4 tb uncooked rice
2 small onions, finely chopped
1 egg
1 c beef stock
1 dsp cornflour for thickening

Dip the vine leaves in boiling water for a few seconds until they change colour. Place flat on a board and cut off the stalk.

Combine mince, currants, lemon juice, tomato concentrate, beef stock powder or cubes, rice, onions and egg. Mix thoroughly. Place a small quantity of the mince mixture on each leaf. Fold over the stalk end first, then the sides and roll up. Place dolmas, smooth side up, as a single layer in a large casserole. Pour the stock over the dolmas. Place two or three extra grape leaves over the top and cover the casserole with a tightly-fitting lid. Bake at 180°C for 1 hour. Remove the extra leaves. Carefully pour the juices into a small saucepan. Heat and thicken with the cornflour mixed with a little water. Pour back over the dolmas and serve.

GRAPE FLAN

Serves 6

Pastry:

1 c flour
1 tsp baking powder
75 g butter
1½ tb castor sugar
1 egg
grated rind of one lemon

Sift the flour and baking powder into a bowl. Rub in the butter. Beat the egg and castor sugar together until foamy. Add the lemon rind. Pour the egg mixture into the dry ingredients and mix to form a soft dough. Chill for 1 hour before using.

Filling:

250 g grapes
½ c sugar
2 tb flour
1 egg, lightly beaten
1 tb lemon juice
1 tb butter

Wash the grapes and remove stalks. Cut each in half and flick out the seeds. Do not remove the skins. Combine the sugar and flour in a small bowl. Add the grapes, egg and lemon juice. Mix well. Roll out and line a 20 cm flan tin or pie plate. Spoon the grape mixture into the shell and dot the surface with butter. Bake at 200°C for about 30 minutes. The pastry should be golden and the filling set. Serve warm with cream.

GRAPE BUTTER

Fruit butters have the consistency of thick cream and are semi-set. They are simple to make and are delicious served with fresh scones, pikelets and some meats. Grape butter made from black grapes will be a dark-red colour while white grapes will produce a subtle-pink butter.

1 litre grapes, washed and removed from stalks
1 litre sugar
2 tb water

Combine the ingredients together in a preserving pan. Bring slowly to the boil, stirring continuously until the sugar is dissolved. Boil rapidly for 15 minutes. Put through a wire sieve. Pour into small, warm jars and seal with jam covers.

Freezing

Skin and pip grapes. Pack in syrup (200 g sugar in 500 ml water) in small plastic containers. Use thawed as a special addition to fruit salads.

Bottling

QUICK, PRESERVED GRAPE JUICE

Wash 1 c of grapes, put them into a clean, warm 1-litre preserving jar, add ¾ c of sugar, overflow the jar with boiling water and screw the scalded seal down tightly. Leave for six weeks to allow flavour and colour to develop.

Herbs

Harvesting

Herbs can be picked for daily use whenever there are sufficient leaves available. It is better, however, to wait until herb plants reach their peak of growth before harvesting for preserving. Most herbs have their fullest flavour when the flowers first open. Choose a dry, sunny morning for picking, after the dew has dried but before the sun is too hot.

In the kitchen

Avoid washing herbs unless they are particularly dirty. Flower herbs, such as nasturtium, borage and marigold, should not be washed at all and must be handled very gently. A sharp, French cook's knife and a small wooden board, or kitchen scissors are the best tools for chopping herbs finely.

Basil

Use leaves in tomato dishes, with all vegetable fruits, in tomato sandwiches and with pasta.

PESTO SAUCE

This is an Italian sauce made with fresh basil, garlic and cheese. It is traditionally served with pasta. We also add a small spoonful to some soups — particularly minestrone — to cooked vegetables and as a topping on potatoes baked in their jackets.

2 c basil leaves, packed tightly
3 cloves of garlic
4 tb grated Parmesan cheese
4 tb salad oil
¼ tsp salt
freshly-ground black pepper

Chop basil and garlic finely. Combine with cheese, oil, salt and pepper. Beat well. Store in a small jar in the refrigerator or freeze in small portions.

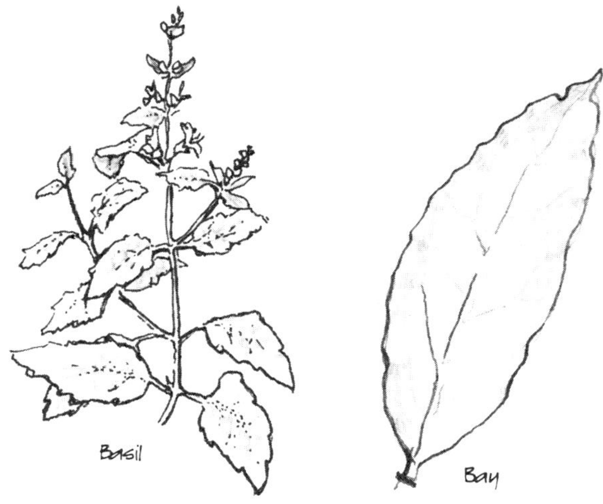

Bay

Use leaves as part of a bouquet garni, in marinades, soups and casseroles. Use in vegetable cooking water to mask strong odours.

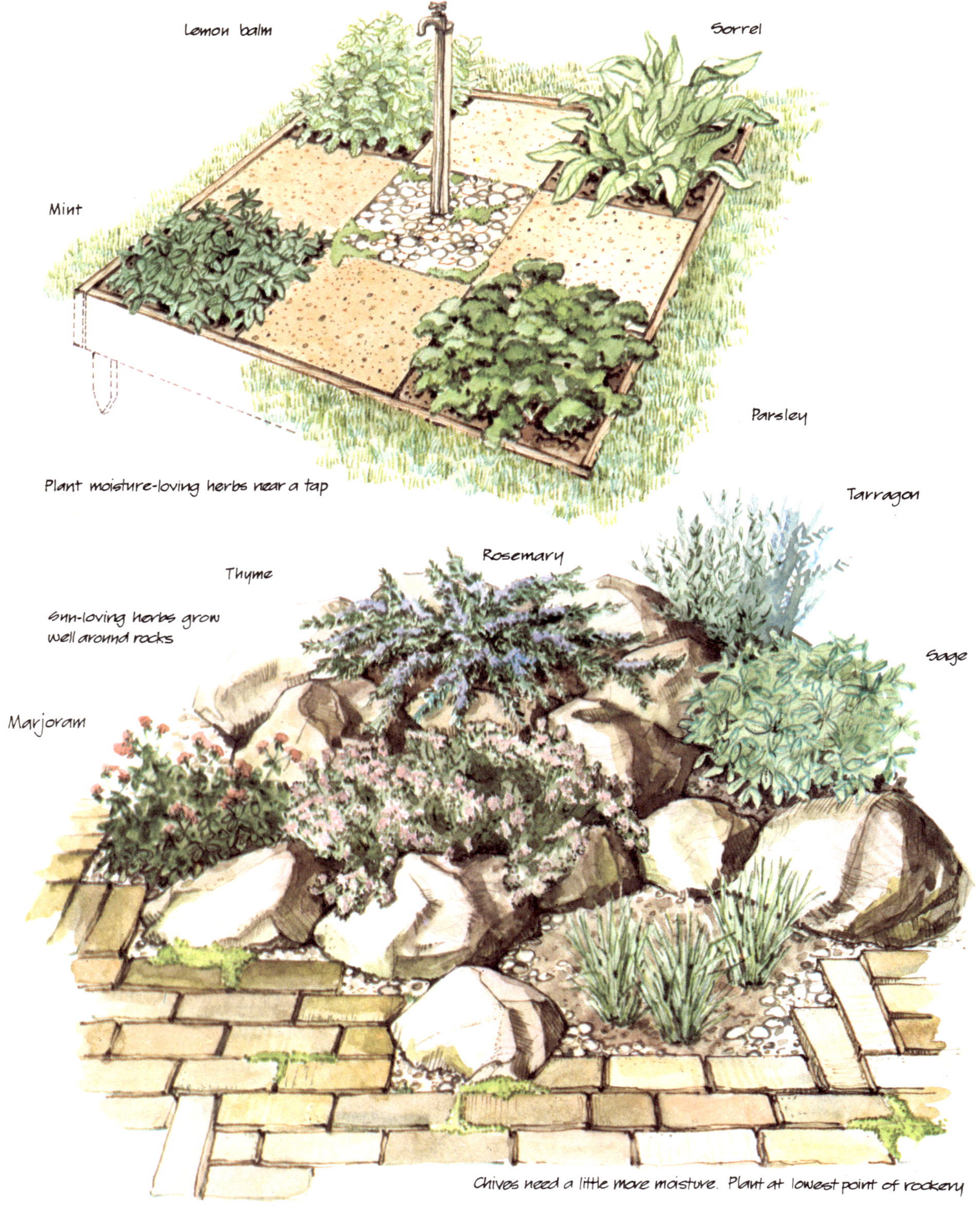
Lemon balm
Sorrel
Mint
Parsley
Plant moisture-loving herbs near a tap
Tarragon
Rosemary
Thyme
Sun-loving herbs grow
well around rocks
Sage
Marjoram
Chives need a little more moisture. Plant at lowest point of rockery

Properly cared for, most herbs do well in pots and tubs

Save space by growing some vegetables in containers

White petunias flower over a long period

HERB VARIETIES AND CULTIVATION

Common Name	Botanical Name	Sun or Shade	Soil	Moisture	Height
Basil	*Ocimum basilicum*	Sun to half shade	Well drained	Average	40-60 cm
Bay	*Laurus nobilis*	Sun to half shade	Average	Average	Shrub or tree
Borage	*Borago officinalis*	Sun to half shade	Loamy or sandy	Average	40-90 cm
Chervil	*Anthriscus cerefolium*	Part shade	Good drainage	Average Intolerant of dry conditions	30-40 cm
Chives (also see onions)	*Allium schoenoprasum*	Sun to half shade	Average to rich	Moist	20-30 cm
Dill	*Anethum graveolens*	Sun	Well drained	Average	70-90 cm
Fennel	*Foeniculum vulgare*	Sun	Light	Average	1.5 m
Garlic (also see onions)	*Allium sativum*	Sun	Light but enriched with compost	Average to moist	30 cm - 1 m
Horseradish	*Cochlearia armoracia*	Half shade	Well drained Rich Deeply dug	Moist	60 cm
Lemon Balm	*Melissa officinalis*	Sun or partial shade	Fairly rich	Moist	60 cm - 1 m
Marigold	*Calendula officinalis*	Sun	No special requirements	Average	50 cm
Marjoram Oregano	*Origanum* spp.	Sun	Not too rich	Average	20-60 cm depending on variety
Mint	*Mentha* spp.	Partial shade	Rich	Moist	20 cm
Nasturtium	*Tropaeolum* spp.	Sun	Light, moderately rich	Average	6 cm or climbing or trailing
Parsley	*Petroselinum* spp.	Sun or partial shade	Fine, rich	Moist	15-25 cm
Rosemary	*Rosmarinus officinalis*	Sun	Light, rather sandy	Fairly dry	1.5 m
Sage	*Salvia officinalis*	Sun	Light	Fairly dry	60 cm
Savory (Summer)	*Satureia hortensis*	Sun	Light, rich	Average	30 cm
Savory (Winter)	*Satureia montana*	Sun	Poor, well drained	Average	15-40 cm
Sorrel (French)	*Rumex acetosa*	Sun or shade	Light, rich	Moist	30-40 cm
Tarragon (French)	*Artemisia dracunculus*	Sun	Light Well drained	Average to dry	1 m
Thyme Lemon thyme	*Thymus vulgaris* *Thymus citriodorus*	Sun	Well drained	Dry	10-30 cm

Perennial/Biennial Annual	Propagation (Many container-grown herbs are available from nurseries)
Annual	Cool areas — sow in Jiffy Pots. Plant out in early summer. Warmer areas — sow directly in late spring. Thin to 20 cm.
Evergreen	Half-ripe cuttings in autumn. May take nine months to strike.
Annual	Sow direct in spring. Will self-sow readily.
Annual	Sow direct. Seed must be fresh. Harvest frequently.
Perennial	Sow seeds direct in spring. Root division in spring or autumn.
Annual	Sow seeds direct from mid spring to mid summer for a constant supply of fresh leaves.
Perennial	Sow direct in late spring. Thin to 45 cm. Division of roots in spring.
Perennial	Healthy cloves planted early spring or autumn.
Perennial	Crown division in spring or autumn.
Perennial	Cuttings or root divisions.
Annual	Sow direct in spring or autumn.
Perennial	Division in spring or autumn.
Perennial	New shoots in spring. Roots in autumn.
Annual	Sow direct in spring.
Biennial	Sow direct in autumn and spring for continuous supply.
Perennial	Cuttings in spring.
Perennial	Cuttings in spring.
Usually annual	Sow direct in spring. Thin to 30 cm.
Perennial	Division in spring or autumn.
Perennial	Division of roots.
Perennial	Division in spring and autumn.
Perennial	Division in spring. Side shoots can be layered.

Borage
Leaves can be cooked with other greens and the flowers used to garnish salads and desserts.

SILVER BEET AND BORAGE
Borage is inclined to come up all over the garden. A good way of using the tender, young leaves of these self-sown plants is to add them to other greens. Add 10-20 borage leaves to a potful of silver beet. Cook in the usual way. The result is a delicious, softly-textured green. The unpleasant hairs on the raw borage leaves disappear completely with cooking.

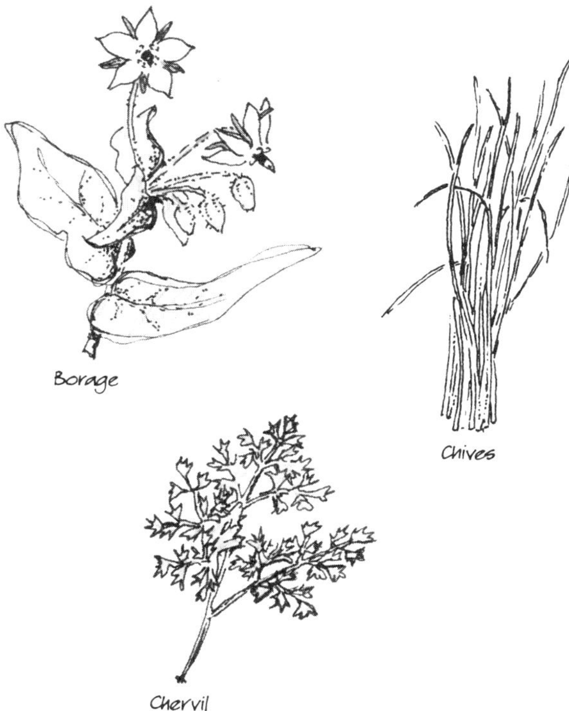

Chervil
Use leaves generously in salads, soups, sauces and as an important part of *fines herbes* (see page 107). Serve sprinkled on cooked celery.

Chives
Use in any dish requiring a mild onion flavour. Use in cottage cheese, omelettes and sprinkled on salads, tomatoes and corn.

Dill
Use leaves, flowers or seeds in fish dishes and pickles. Sprinkle on cooked cabbage, turnips, cucumber and carrots.

Fennel
Use leaves and seeds as you would dill.

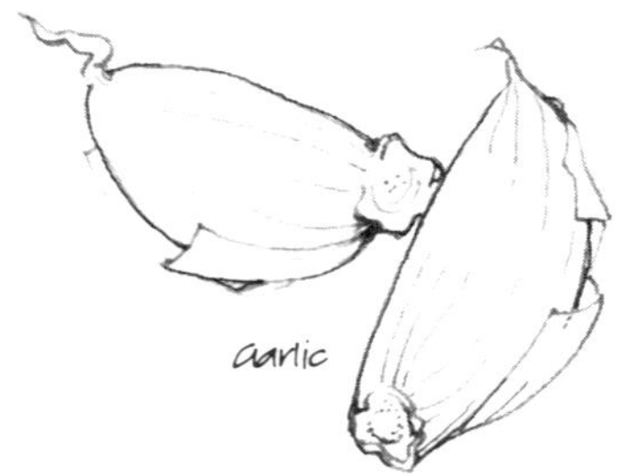

Garlic
Use cloves whole or finely chopped in meat dishes, sauces and salad dressings. Insert slivers into lamb or hogget before roasting. Rub a cut clove round a salad bowl to impart a subtle flavour. When cooking be careful not to over-brown the garlic as it develops a bitter taste.

GARLIC BREAD

2 cloves garlic
½ tsp salt
50 g soft butter
1 French loaf

Chop the garlic very finely. Cream butter with the salt and garlic until it is very well mixed. Cut the loaf part-way through into thick slices. Be careful not to cut right through the base. Spread slices with garlic butter and press together. Wrap the loaf in foil. Place on a baking tray and put in a hot oven, 200°C, for about 15 minutes until it is heated through.

Variation: substitute 2 tb of finely chopped herbs for the garlic.

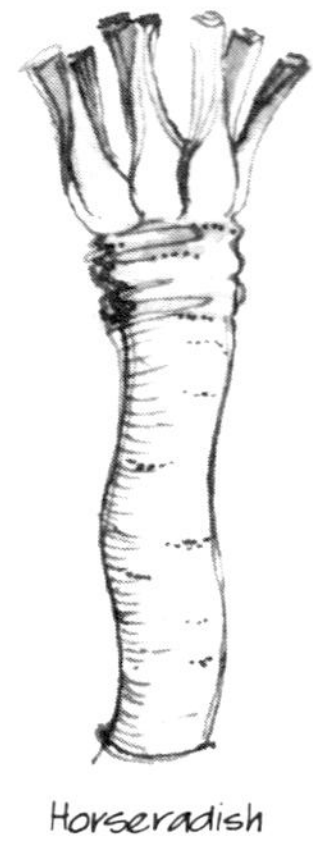

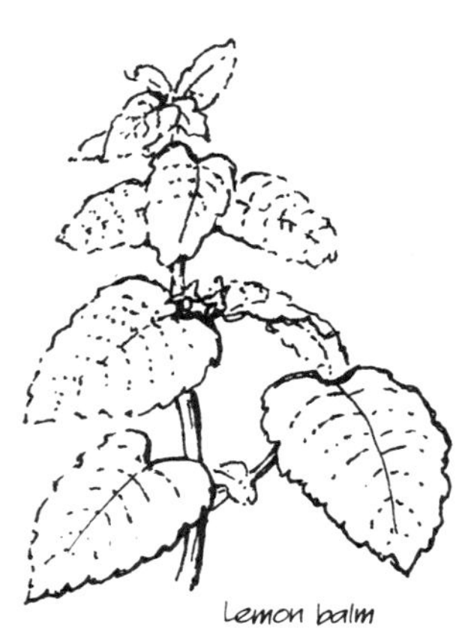

Horseradish
Use fresh, scrubbed, peeled and grated roots in dips and salad dressings. Preserve in vinegar to use as a condiment.

Lemon balm
Use the leaves as a substitute for grated lemon rind in soups and casseroles. Add to fruit drinks, salads and make into a refreshing iced tea.

Marigold
Use petals to garnish salads and flavour omelettes, breads and custards.

Marjoram and oregano
Use leaves in stuffings, sausage dishes, with most meats, cooked carrots and sprinkled on pizzas.

Marjoram and oregano

Mint
Use leaves to flavour fruit juices and soups. Sprinkle on cole slaw, cooked cabbage, carrots, peas, new potatoes and cucumber.

MINT SAUCE

1 tb finely-chopped mint
1 tb castor sugar
1 tb boiling water
2 tb vinegar

Combine mint and sugar. Add boiling water and stir until the sugar is dissolved. Add vinegar and allow to cool.

Red currant mint sauce: see recipe on page 83.

Mint

Nasturtium
Use flowers to garnish salads. Very young seeds can be pickled as a substitute for capers.

Nasturtium

Parsley
Use leaves and stalks as a garnish, either finely chopped or as small sprigs. Use to flavour practically any savoury dish. A recipe for parsley sauce is given on page 208.

Parsley

Rosemary

Rosemary
Sprinkle leaves on fried potatoes and on lamb or hogget before roasting. Add to poultry, fish dishes, cooked cauliflower, spinach, silver beet and tomatoes.

Sage
Use leaves with rich meats, sausages, cream cheese, savoury flans, onions, and stuffing.

Savory
Used as the traditional flavourer of beans. Use in stuffings, salads and with cabbage.

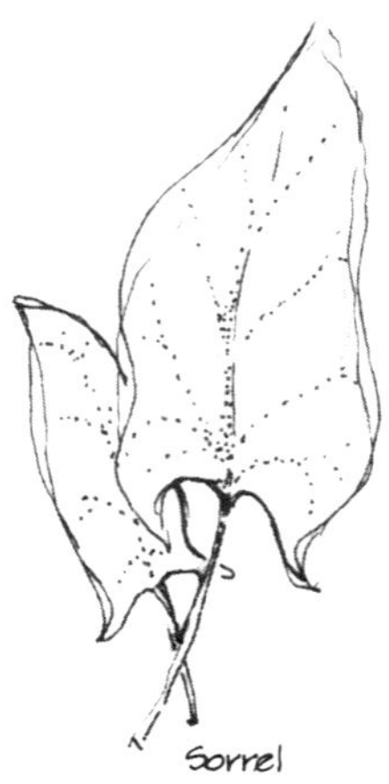

Sorrel
Use small quantities of leaves in salads, and cooked with spinach and other greens.

SORREL SOUP

Serves 6-8
If you prefer a less acid soup use lettuce leaves as a substitute for some of the sorrel.

250 g sorrel, washed
50 g butter
2 medium-sized onions, finely chopped
3 medium-sized potatoes, grated
1.5 litres chicken stock
salt and pepper to taste

Melt the butter in a large saucepan. Sauté the onions and potatoes until soft. Add sorrel, stock and seasoning. Simmer for 5 minutes. Put the soup through a blender or sieve.

Tarragon
Use leaves to flavour poultry and fish dishes. Use in marinades and sauces. Add to beans, asparagus and broccoli.

Thyme and lemon thyme
Use leaves in small quantities for adding to fish, poultry, beef, lamb, carrots, Jerusalem artichokes, tomatoes and stuffings.

"Bouquet garni" is a bunch of herbs used to flavour stews, casseroles and sauces. It is traditionally made up of two to three sprigs of parsley, a sprig of thyme and a bay leaf, but other herbs can be included. Tie the bunch with

a piece of string, having one end long enough to hang over the side of the saucepan or casserole. Another method is to tie the herbs loosely in a piece of muslin. Remove bouquet garni before taking the dish to the table.

Finely-chopped herbs are called *fines herbes*. The usual combination is parsley, chervil, tarragon and chives. Sprinkle just before serving on omelettes, scrambled eggs, baked eggs, cooked vegetables, salads and soups.

HERB BUTTER

Serve with steak, chops and baked potatoes. Toss into vegetables, use in sandwiches or on scones. Vary the herbs according to what you have available.

250 g butter, softened
2 tb chopped parsley
1 tb finely-scissored chives
1 tb chopped tarragon
1 clove garlic, finely chopped
1 tsp grated lemon rind

Blend the herbs, garlic and lemon rind into the butter. Form into a long roll on a piece of plastic film or greaseproof paper. Wrap and store in a refrigerator.

HERB MARINADE

For barbecued steak.

¼ c cooking oil
½ c wine, preferably red
½ tsp salt
freshly-ground black pepper
1 clove garlic (cut into slivers)
half an onion, sliced
1 bay leaf
sprigs of rosemary, parsley, marjoram and thyme

Combine all ingredients and pour over steak. Leave for at least two hours before cooking on a barbecue. Sprinkle freshly-gathered, scissored herbs over the steaks a few minutes before cooking is complete. We find it convenient to grow suitable herbs close to the barbecue area for this purpose.

GIRDLE HERB SCONES

We have tried cooking herb scones in the oven but the results, although acceptable, were not as light as the girdle variety. Served with slices of cheese and tomato, these scones make a simple and unusual Sunday tea.

2 c flour
4 tsp baking powder
½ tsp salt
freshly-ground black pepper
50 g butter
⅓ c chopped, fresh herbs
milk

Sift the flour, baking powder and salt into a bowl. Add pepper. Rub in the butter. Add herbs. Add sufficient milk to make a soft dough. Knead lightly, roll out to 1.5 cm thick and cut into neat squares. Heat a girdle, heavy frying pan or electric frying pan. Grease lightly. Cook scones for about 5-6 minutes on each side.

QUICK HERB LOAF

250 g self-raising flour
1½ tsp salt
½ tsp dry mustard
1 tb chopped parsley
1 tb chopped mixed herbs
100 g finely-grated, tasty Cheddar cheese
1 egg, beaten
150 ml water
1 tb butter, melted

Sift flour, salt and mustard together. Stir in the parsley, mixed herbs and grated cheese. Combine lightly-beaten egg, water and melted butter. Pour into the dry ingredients. Stir until just mixed. Spoon mixture into a well-greased loaf tin (about 1 litre capacity). Bake at 190°C for 50-60 minutes. Remove from the tin and cool briefly on a wire rack. Serve freshly baked with butter.

WHOLEMEAL HERB ROLLS

These one-hour bread rolls are the easiest and quickest we know. The results are just as good as those requiring several risings. The recipe produces nine rolls. Double or treble if you want some to freeze.

¾ c warm water (blood heat — it should feel neither hot nor cold)
1½ tsp sugar
1¼ tsp dried yeast
1 c white flour
1 c wholemeal flour
½ tsp salt
1 tb finely-chopped, fresh herbs (including parsley, lemon thyme, marjoram, rosemary, tarragon and sage)
1 tb melted butter
½ tsp dried, mixed herbs, poppy seeds or sesame seeds

Dissolve the sugar in the warm water. Sprinkle the yeast over the surface and leave in a warm place for 10 minutes until frothy. Sift white flour, wholemeal flour and salt into a bowl. Put in a warm place while you wait for the yeast mixture to froth. Warm muffin tins. Add chopped herbs to the flour. Pour the yeast mixture into the flour, adding more warm water if necessary to make a soft dough. Turn the dough on to a floured board and knead for 5 minutes. Shape into nine rolls and place in buttered muffin tins. Brush with melted butter. Sprinkle tops with dried, mixed herbs or seeds. Press lightly into the surface. Cover loosely with a large plastic bag or sheet of plastic and leave in a warm place for about 15-20 minutes, until well risen. Bake the rolls until golden-brown (10-15 minutes) in a hot oven, 220°C. Serve warm with butter.

Wholemeal rolls
Serve warm

HERB VINEGAR

1 c loosely-packed, fresh herb leaves
500 ml of wine vinegar or white vinegar

Place herbs in a bottle. Add vinegar. Cork. Leave in a warm place, such as a sunny kitchen windowsill for two to three weeks. Shake the bottle once each day. Strain and pour into a clean bottle. Cork tightly.

GARLIC VINEGAR

50 g garlic cloves
1 litre of vinegar
¼ tsp salt
3 cloves

Remove the skin from the garlic cloves and chop very finely. For a milder vinegar leave whole. Put garlic, vinegar, salt and cloves in a bottle. Cork. Leave in a warm place for two weeks. Shake the bottle each day. Strain and bottle.

Use herb vinegars in marinades, vinaigrette dressings, mayonnaise and variations, dressings for vegetable salads and pickles.

Freezing herbs

Select young, tender leaves. If necessary, wash and dry carefully with a paper towel. Wrap enough leaves for one recipe in clear plastic wrap. Staple all packages of the same herb to a small square of cardboard. Label and freeze.

To use: before thawing, cut the leaves into small pieces with scissors. Add to recipe.

Drying herbs

Dry herbs by tying them loosely in small bunches or spreading them on muslin or paper on a wire cooling rack. Hang bunches up and leave wire racks in a shady, warm and airy place. The leaves are dry when brittle to touch. Strip dry leaves from the branches and store in airtight containers in a dark, cool place (not on a decorative shelf beside a hot stove).

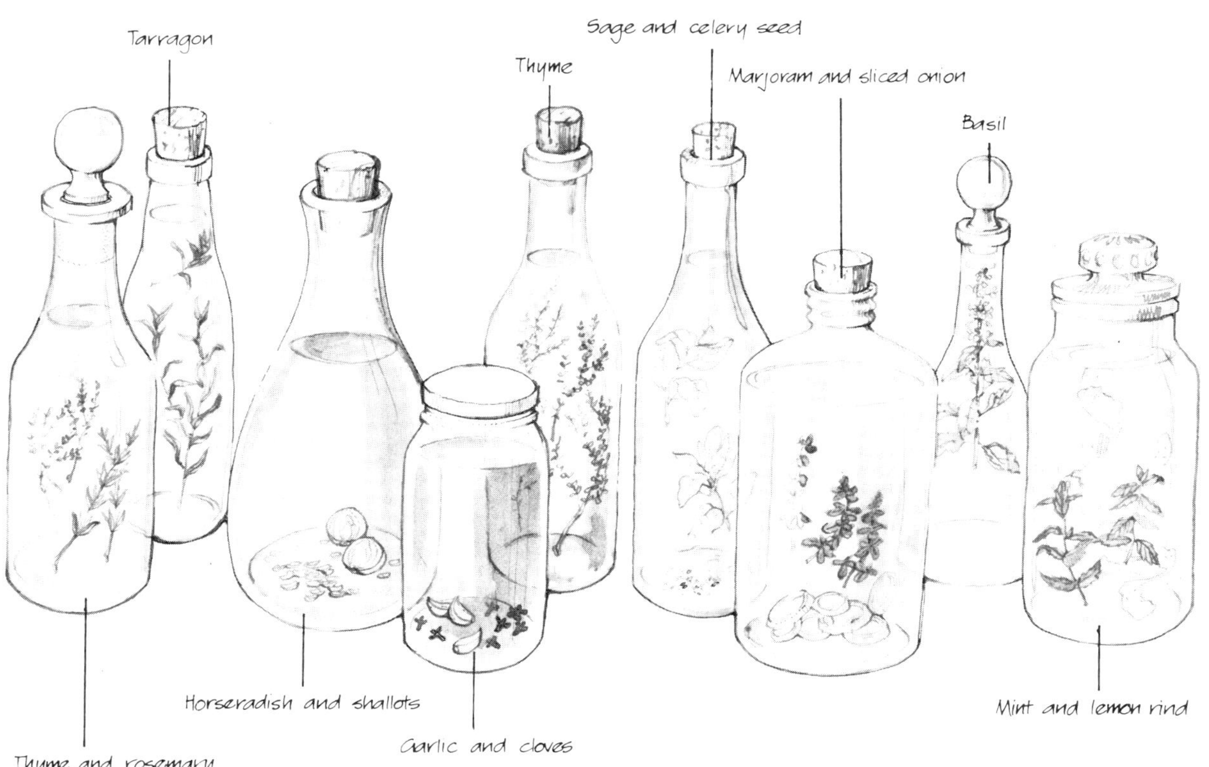

Kale

(Borecole — *Brassica oleracea* var. *acephala*)

Varieties

Kale was the first brassica to be domesticated, probably by the ancient Greeks, as early as 600 BC. Although hardy, it is not a popular vegetable today and as a result few varieties are available. Dwarf Green Curled (Scotch Kale) and Tall Green Curled are two of the most common. A highly-decorative, dwarf form is sold for flower gardens but it is not of much culinary value except for garnishing winter salads. The choice between the dwarf and tall varieties is usually made on the basis of garden size. Dwarf kale grows 30-45 cm high and the tall variety, 60-90 cm high. Both have dark, blue-green leaves which are heavily crinkled like parsley and both mature in about two-and-a-half months.

Cultivation

Kale should be grown on well-limed soil enriched with organic matter for the previous crop. It usually needs no additional fertilizer. Heavy soils are suitable provided they don't become waterlogged in winter. The seed is sown in boxes or a seed bed in late spring or early summer, or directly in the garden with 5-7 cm between clusters of two to three seeds. Thin nursery-bed plants to 4-5 cm apart. They should be set out a month later in the garden, 30-45 cm apart, with 45-60 cm between rows. Direct-sown kale can be thinned out in several stages until the plants are 30-60 cm apart, depending on their variety. The inner leaves of the thinnings can be cooked as an unusual summer "green". Tall varieties should be earthed up as winter approaches. Control grey aphids with regular sprayings of pyrethrum.

Harvesting

Start harvesting the tall variety in late autumn by cutting the central cluster of young leaves at the top of the plants. Then in mid winter, pick

The inner leaves of kale are the most tender

the side shoots that grow out from the leaf axils when they are 10-12 cm long. Older leaves are tasty but tough. They might be suitable for lining a hangi basket (for cooking in an underground oven). Harvesting is usually finished by mid spring. In some areas, the dwarf form is harvested leaf by leaf, starting from the bottom of the plant. For salads use only the young, inner leaves.

In the kitchen

After washing, remove the tough, central ribs and chop the leaves quite finely. Allow 1 kg of kale to serve six.

The two objectives when cooking kale are to achieve tenderness before the leaf colour becomes grey, and to reduce the impact of its strong flavour (too powerful for many people).

We have found that the best cooking methods are butter-steaming and cooking in a pressure cooker. These methods produce a tender, green vegetable. Kale cooked in boiling, salted water takes much longer and we suspect that the unpopularity of this nutritious vegetable is due to this unappetizing method.

The robust flavour can be masked by serving kale with a well-flavoured sauce.

Cheese sauce: (see page 208).

Tomato sauce: Neapolitan Tomato Sauce (see page 196) or Chunky Tomato Purée (see page 198).

Sour cream: add ½ c of sour cream, 1 tsp of sugar and 1 tsp of lemon juice to the cooked kale.

To cook in a pressure cooker, place prepared kale on the rack, add 150 ml water and 1 tsp of salt. Bring up to pressure and time for 3 minutes. Reduce pressure quickly and drain. Serve immediately with one of the tasty sauces suggested above.

BUTTER-STEAMED KALE

Serves 6

1 kg kale
1½ tb butter
1½ tb cooking oil
4 tb chicken stock
a sprig of dill (optional)

Prepare kale. Heat the butter and oil in a large frying pan with a lid. Add the kale, chicken stock and dill. Cover tightly and cook over low heat for 10-15 minutes, stirring occasionally. Season if necessary. Serve immediately with the chosen sauce.

When introducing the family to any new vegetable, remember that small servings have more appeal.

Kiwifruit

(Actinida chinensis)

Varieties

This strong-growing, deciduous vine can be cultivated where there are light winter frosts, but any late frosts damage the flower buds and prevent fruit setting, though they may not kill the vine. The kiwifruit used to be known as the Chinese gooseberry. There are a number of varieties on the market including Abbot, Allison, Bruno, Hayward and Monty; Hayward is recognized as the best.

To produce fruit it is necessary to plant both a male and female vine or buy a female plant which has a male scion grafted on to it. This practice has recently fallen out of favour because often the gardener would forget which was which and let the more vigorous, non-fruiting male portion take over. If you acquire a mature vine that has both male and female leaders, take a good look at the flowers (see illustration). Once the male has been identified it can be severely pruned back.

Cultivation

Choose a sheltered, sunny place, free from late

Female

Male

frosts and with rich, well-drained soil. Allow plenty of space and a very strong support (either a screen 1.8 m high with two lines of wire running horizontally, or a well-built pergola). This is necessary because the vine is very vigorous and can twine and lean as far as 6 m or more if not curbed.

When properly treated it is a very ornamental plant with large, rich, dark green leaves, white and velvety below and held on red, furry stems. If pruning is neglected it becomes an untidy, tangled, twisted mass of growth with few, very small fruits.

Plant container-grown specimens in late winter or early spring. Grafted plants are more disease resistant. Two-and-a-half cups of blood and bone should be thoroughly mixed into the bottom of each large hole and the plants should be set at the same depth as they were when growing in their containers. Firmly tread the soil around the roots. After planting, shorten the vines to about 30 cm above the bud or graft union. This will promote vigorous leaders which must be trained to radiate out over the fence or pergola.

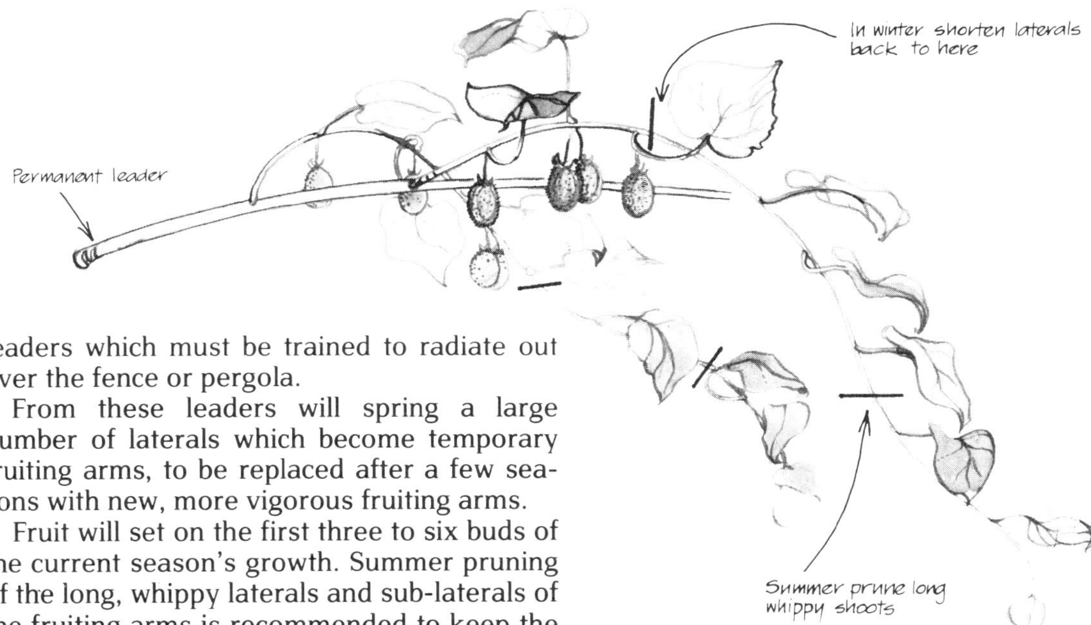
In winter shorten laterals back to here
Permanent leader
Summer prune long whippy shoots

From these leaders will spring a large number of laterals which become temporary fruiting arms, to be replaced after a few seasons with new, more vigorous fruiting arms.

Fruit will set on the first three to six buds of the current season's growth. Summer pruning of the long, whippy laterals and sub-laterals of the fruiting arms is recommended to keep the vine open and promote larger fruit. Winter pruning involves the complete removal of some of the old fruiting arms and the selection of new and vigorous arms to take their place. Bear in mind while pruning that upright growths should be removed in favour of more horizontal growths. The laterals that were pruned in summer should be shortened further.

Feed the vine with good compost in early spring and again just after fruit has set. Single, home-grown vines have few pests and diseases.

Harvesting

Three or four years after planting, a worthwhile crop will be obtained. The first fruits ripen in early autumn and harvesting continues into winter, when the vines should be pruned. Pick the large fruit first so that the smaller ones have a chance to increase in size. The fruit is picked when still hard. Like pears, they ripen and soften any time up to two months after picking. To hasten ripening, place a few hard fruit in a paper bag with a ripe apple. Within a few days they will be ready to eat.

In the kitchen

To serve as fresh fruit, cut in half and provide a teaspoon to scoop out the flesh.

To remove skin, rub hairy fruit with a cloth and then peel with a small, sharp knife or vegetable peeler.

Peeled and sliced kiwifruit makes a delicious curry accompaniment.

NEW ZEALAND FRUIT DESSERT

Serves 6

7 kiwifruit
4 tamarillos
4 tb castor sugar
6 scoops of vanilla icecream
150 ml cream

Peel and slice kiwifruit. Peel and slice tamarillos (see page 190). Layer fruit in dessert glasses, reserving 6 kiwifruit slices to use as a garnish. Sprinkle fruit with castor sugar. Place in the refrigerator for at least 2 hours. Half an hour before serving, top each dessert with a scoop of icecream and whipped cream. Return to the refrigerator. The icecream should soften but not melt. Garnish with kiwifruit and serve immediately.

WARM WINTER FRUIT SALAD

Serves 4-5

2 oranges
1 sweet eating apple
2 tamarillos
2 kiwifruit
4 tb brown sugar
2 tb brandy (optional)
whipped cream

Peel oranges and cut into circles. Cut apple into quarters, remove core and slice finely. Peel and slice tamarillos and kiwifruit.

Place orange circles in an ovenproof dish. Sprinkle with 1 tb of brown sugar. Cover with apple slices and another tablespoon of brown sugar. Repeat with tamarillo, kiwifruit and remaining sugar. Pour brandy over the fruit.

Preheat oven to 150°C. Turn off. Put the fruit salad into the oven and leave for 15 minutes to warm through. Serve warm with whipped cream.

KIWIFRUIT AND BANANA CARAMEL CREAM

Serves 8

125 g butter
1 c brown sugar
1 c water
2 tb golden syrup
1½ tb cornflour
1 tsp rum (optional)

8 small bananas
8 kiwifruit
150 ml cream
12 toasted, blanched almonds, chopped

Combine the butter and sugar in a small saucepan. Stir over low heat until the butter is melted and the sugar dissolved. Bring to the boil and simmer for 3 minutes. Combine the water, golden syrup and cornflour in a bowl. Stir until smooth. Add to the brown sugar and butter. Bring to the boil stirring constantly. Simmer for 2 minutes. Remove from the heat, add the rum and allow to cool.

Peel bananas and kiwifruit and slice into eight dessert glasses. Carefully pour the sauce over the fruit in each glass. Whip the cream and pile it on top. Sprinkle with almonds.

KIWIFRUIT CITRUS JAM

2 oranges
2 lemons
1.4 kg kiwifruit
6 c sugar

Using a vegetable peeler, skin oranges and lemons without cutting off any pith. Tie the peel in a piece of muslin. Squeeze the juice from the oranges and lemons and pour this into a preserving pan. Peel and chop kiwifruit. Add to the preserving pan with the muslin bag. Cook gently until the kiwifruit are tender. Add sugar and cook over low heat, stirring continuously until dissolved. Boil until setting point is reached. Pour into warm jars and seal with jam covers.

Freezing

Peel and slice thickly. Freeze uncovered on a metal tray. When solid, place in freezer bags.

Kohlrabi

(Brassica oleracea var. *caulorapa)*

Varieties

The kohlrabi (also called the cabbage turnip) was in cultivation in France by the fourteenth century, but only began to be grown in English vegetable gardens in the Victorian era. It has never become a popular vegetable and this may account for the lack of varieties. There are two distinct types: one with greenish-white skin which is known as White Vienna, and a purple-skinned variety which is sold under several names including Early Sweet Purple, Purple, and Purple Vienna. If properly grown, both varieties produce a mild-flavoured, bulbous formation just above the level of the ground; this is a swollen stem and the leaves grow directly out of it.

Cultivation and harvesting

Kohlrabi seed is usually sown directly in a recently-limed, sunny part of the garden, containing plenty of humus. Because the flavour is best when the plant grows quickly, decomposed animal manure or a general fertilizer mixture should be added before sowing. In cool climates maturity is reached in about eight to 12 weeks from a spring sowing. In milder areas where there is insufficient time for the stem to enlarge before hot weather sets in, a late summer to mid autumn sowing is preferable. This allows the plants to stand longer in the cool, winter conditions.

The seed is sown 1 cm deep in rows 40-60 cm apart. Thin initially to 15 cm apart and harvest alternate plants as soon as they reach golf-ball size. In dry weather water the plants regularly, for any check to growth results in a stringy, woody texture and a bitter flavour. If they are troubled by white butterflies, dust the plants with Derris Dust when other members of the brassica family are being treated.

In the kitchen

Scrub with a vegetable brush and rinse thoroughly. Cut off leaf stalks, roots and any woody parts.

Do not peel young kohlrabi. The purple skin is tender and tasty and, when cooked, turns an

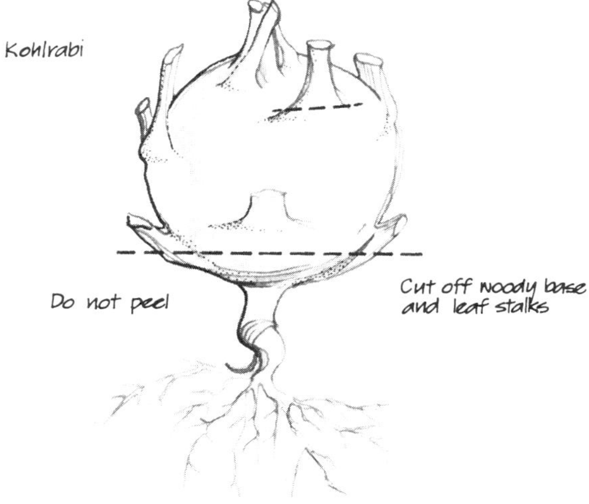
Kohlrabi
Do not peel
Cut off woody base
and leaf stalks

attractive green. Allow 100 g for each serving.

Kohlrabi can be cooked whole if very small or cut into halves or quarters. They can also be cut into sticks, diced or sliced.

Cook in a small quantity of boiling, salted water until just tender. To serve, add butter and freshly ground black pepper. You can also add a few drops of lemon juice and freshly-chopped herbs such as parsley, tarragon or chives. Hollandaise sauce (see page 208) or mornay sauce (see page 208) are also good accompaniments.

Young kohlrabi may be left raw and grated into salads to give a mild radish flavour.

CHILLED KOHLRABI

Cut young kohlrabi into thin sticks. Simmer in a little lightly-salted water until tender-crisp (about 5 minutes). Drain and, while still hot, add a little French dressing (see page 209). Toss gently. Leave to marinate for 2 to 3 hours. Add some chopped dill or fennel just before serving.

KOHLRABI AND TOMATO

Serves 4

400 g prepared kohlrabi
1 small onion, finely chopped
1 clove garlic, finely chopped
2 tb cooking oil
3 medium-sized tomatoes, skinned and chopped
¼ tsp salt
freshly-ground black pepper
½ tsp chopped basil

Cut kohlrabi into quarters and then slice thinly. Sauté onion and garlic in oil for a few minutes. Add kohlrabi, tomato and seasoning. Simmer for 10-15 minutes until kohlrabi is tender. Add basil and serve.

KOHLRABI FRITTERS

Cook whole, prepared kohlrabi in boiling, salted water until tender. Drain and cool sufficiently to handle. Cut into 1 cm slices. Dip each slice in lightly-beaten egg and then into seasoned, dry breadcrumbs. Cook in a hot frying pan with a little oil until they are golden-brown on both sides.

KOHLRABI-CARROT CASSEROLE

Serves 6

3 medium-sized kohlrabi, diced
4 medium-sized carrots, thinly sliced
1 medium-sized onion, chopped
2 tb butter
2 tb flour
½ tsp salt
freshly-ground black pepper
1½ c milk
2 tb chopped parsley
1 tb lemon juice
¾ c soft breadcrumbs
1 tb butter

Cook kohlrabi in boiling, salted water for 10 minutes. Add carrots and continue cooking until both vegetables are tender. Melt 2 tb butter in a saucepan. Sauté onion until tender. Blend in flour, salt and pepper. Add milk gradually and stir until thick and boiling. Stir in drained, cooked vegetables, parsley and lemon juice. Turn into a greased ovenproof dish. Top with breadcrumbs and dot with butter. Bake at 190°C for 20-25 minutes until heated through and the breadcrumbs are browned.

KOHLRABI SOUP

Serves 4

A thick and creamy soup.

1 large onion, chopped
4 tb butter
1½ c chicken stock
4 medium-sized kohlrabi, diced
1½ c milk
½ tsp salt
freshly-ground black pepper
1 tb scissored chives

In a large saucepan, sauté the onion in butter until tender. Add stock and kohlrabi. Cover and simmer until kohlrabi is tender. Put through a blender or fine sieve. Return to the saucepan. Add milk and seasoning. Heat through but do not boil. Serve topped with chives.

Freezing

Blanch young, diced kohlrabi for 2 minutes. Cool and pack in meal-sized quantities. Do not thaw before cooking.

Leeks

(Allium porrum)

Varieties

These hardy members of the onion family (they are actually more closely related to garlic than onions) have been in cultivation for over 5000 years. Although commercial growers have a choice of several varieties, the home gardener is limited to a very small selection. Musselburgh, one of the most popular, matures in 150 days from seed and has long, white, thick shanks growing to about 5 cm in diameter.

Cultivation

Leeks thrive in a moist clay or silty loam enriched with compost and animal manure. They seldom do well in sandy soils, which are usually free draining and low in humus. One of the best ways of preparing the ground for leeks is to dig a trench 30-40 cm deep and fill it two-thirds full with manure and compost mixed with topsoil. The plants are then set into 10 cm-deep holes in the bottom of the trench so that their roots grow within the enriched soil, not in the subsoil below. For extra-large leeks, additional fertilizer may be added plus a later side dressing of a pinch of sulphate of ammonia for each plant (in cold weather use nitrate of soda as it is more readily available to the plants).

Leeks are usually grown as a reliable vegetable for late autumn, winter and early spring use. The plants may be purchased ready for setting out in the garden in mid summer, or you may grow your own from seed. For winter-harvested leeks, sow the seed 12 mm deep in mid spring, in a protected or sheltered seed bed or a deep box. Thin the plants to 2-3 cm apart and keep them well watered. When they reach 20 cm high they should be planted out. If you are using the trench method, make a staggered, double row of holes so that the plants are 10-20 cm apart. Allow 60 cm between the trenches. They may also be planted in individual holes 15 cm deep, made from the surface with a dibble. In shallow soils, plant with the white portion of the stem just below the surface and then mound up the rows as the stems lengthen, as you would for potatoes. In the last two methods space the rows 30 cm apart.

If your leeks are planted in holes, allow the soil to fill back in by natural erosion. This allows the plants to thicken and, at the same time, increases the white or blanched portion. The walls of leek trenches fall in more slowly and may need some help from a spade. Avoid getting soil between the leaf base and the stem. If this occurs, cleaning the leeks will be much more time consuming when they are harvested. Some gardeners blanch their leeks by setting earthen drain pipes over the individual plants to exclude light.

Leek plants purchased from a nursery or seed shop are sold with the leaves and roots trimmed back. Home-sown leeks set in deep holes with the roots watered in do not seem to benefit from root trimming, but it is advisable to cut back the leaves by one-third to a half at planting-out time, as this reduces moisture loss. Keep the plants well watered, for if they dry out they are likely to bolt. Fine overhead sprinkling is recommended to avoid accelerated erosion of the trench or hole walls.

Harvesting

Leeks will stand well through the winter and are dug as required by inserting a garden fork beneath the plants to loosen the soil and then pulling up the plant. The outer, blue-green leaves should be trimmed off and discarded into the compost heap. When spring arrives, the remaining leeks can be lifted and heeled-in in a cool, shady part of the garden. This delays the formation of seed heads and thus prolongs harvesting.

In the kitchen

Trim off the root ends and most of the coarse green leaves. Remove the outer skin of the leeks and any discoloured layers. Carefully slit down both sides through the top layers using the point of a knife, and wash under cold, running water until all traces of dirt have been removed. Allow one medium-sized leek for each serving.

Leeks may be cooked, whole or sliced, in boiling, salted water until tender. Drain well.

Serve hot with butter and freshly-ground black pepper or with mornay sauce (see page 208).

Leeks make a delightful salad or appetizer. Marinate freshly-cooked, sliced leeks with a well-flavoured vinaigrette dressing. Leave to cool.

LEEK AND HAM ROLLS

Serves 4

Serve with fresh bread rolls to make a tasty luncheon dish.

4 prepared leeks (use 8 if they are thin)
250 ml chicken stock
4 large slices cooked ham

Sauce:

2 tb butter
1 tb flour
100 ml cream or top milk
1 tb grated Parmesan cheese
salt and pepper to taste

Topping:

4 tb fresh breadcrumbs
2 tb grated Parmesan cheese
1 tb butter

Place leeks in a large saucepan, add stock and simmer with the lid on until the leeks are just tender. Drain, reserving the cooking liquid. Place each leek, or two thin ones, in the middle of a slice of ham. Roll up and place in a greased, shallow, ovenproof dish.

Melt 2 tb of butter in a small saucepan, add the flour and cook for 1 minute. Gradually stir in 100 ml of the reserved cooking liquid, and the cream. Continue stirring until the sauce thickens and boils. Remove from the heat. Add 1 tb of grated Parmesan cheese and seasoning. Pour over the rolls.

Combine the breadcrumbs and 2 tb of grated Parmesan cheese and sprinkle over the surface. Dot with butter. Bake at 180°C for 20-30 minutes until the leeks are hot and the topping is golden.

LEEK AND SAUSAGE BAKE

Serves 6-8

A complete meal in a pan.

500 g prepared leeks
500 g cooking apples
120 g mushrooms
1 kg sausages
500 g tomatoes, fresh, frozen or bottled
1 tsp salt
freshly-ground black pepper

Slice leeks and place in the base of a large, shallow, greased ovenproof dish or roasting pan. Cover with thin slices of peeled and cored apples and sliced mushrooms. Arrange the pricked sausages on top and cover with the peeled and chopped tomatoes. Season. Cover the dish with foil and bake at 190°C for 45-60 minutes. Remove foil and bake for a further 5-10 minutes until the vegetables are tender and the sausages are beginning to brown.

LEEK AND POTATO CASSEROLE

Serves 6

4 medium-sized leeks, prepared
500 g potatoes, peeled
2 tb chopped parsley
1 tsp salt
freshly-ground black pepper
bouquet garni
2 leaves of sage
½ c chicken stock
2 tb butter

Slice leeks and potatoes finely. Place in layers in a greased casserole. Sprinkle each layer with parsley, salt and pepper. Finish with a layer of potatoes. Tuck bouquet garni and sage into the centre. Pour in the stock and dot with butter. Cover casserole. Bake at 180°C for 45-60 minutes until the vegetables are tender.

CORNISH LEEK PIE

Serves 6

Pastry:

200 g flour
½ tsp salt
100 g butter

Sift the flour and salt into a bowl. Rub in the butter. Add sufficient water to make a stiff dough. Chill the dough while preparing the filling.

Filling:

400 g prepared leeks
100 g sliced bacon
2 eggs
150 ml cream
¼ tsp salt
freshly-ground black pepper

Cut the leeks into 1 cm slices and cook in boiling, salted water until tender. Trim the rind from the bacon rashers with kitchen scissors. Cut the bacon into neat pieces. Beat the eggs in a small bowl and add the cream and seasoning.

Roll out two-thirds of the dough and line a medium-sized pie dish. Place the leeks in the pie, add the bacon pieces and pour the egg and cream mixture over the top. Roll out the remaining piece of pastry to form a lid. Prick the pastry lid in two or three places to allow steam to escape. Brush the top with a little milk. Bake at 210°C for 30 minutes. Serve hot.

WELSH STEW

Serves 4-6

1 kg stewing steak
700 ml beef stock
500 g prepared leeks
500 g swede turnip
2 bay leaves
a sprig of thyme
salt and pepper to taste
1 tsp sugar
flour for thickening
chopped parsley

Cut the steak into neat pieces and place in a heavy-based saucepan with the stock. Simmer gently for 1 hour. Slice the leeks. Peel and dice the swede. Add the leeks, swede, bay leaves, thyme, seasoning and sugar to the saucepan. Simmer gently for a further hour until meat and vegetables are tender. Thicken with a little flour mixed with water. Just before serving sprinkle with chopped parsley.

IRISH LEEK AND POTATO SOUP

Serves 6

4 leeks, prepared
2 tb butter
4 medium-sized potatoes
2 c chicken stock or water
bouquet garni
salt to taste
freshly-ground black pepper
2 c milk or 1 c milk and 1 c cream
2 tb chopped parsley or chives

Slice the leeks finely and sauté in butter until soft. Peel the potatoes and cut into thin slices. Add to the leeks with the stock, bouquet garni, salt and pepper. Simmer gently until the vegetables are tender. Remove bouquet garni. Put the soup through a blender or fine sieve. Return to the saucepan and add the milk or milk and cream. Reheat gently. Pour into bowls and garnish with parsley or chives.

Lettuce

(Lactuca sativa)

Varieties

Four types of lettuce are used for salads: crisphead, butterhead (sometimes grouped with crisphead and called cabbagehead), cos (also called romaine) and leaf (non-heading) lettuce. The ancient cultivars used in Mediterranean countries were pointed, narrow-leaved and non-heading. The first description of a head lettuce appeared in 1543.

Of the crisphead varieties three strains have been grown extensively: the large Webbs Wonderful (New York) was common in the early decades of this century and is still grown today; Imperial (847 for summer use and 615 and Triumph for autumn and winter) was developed after 1926 for its resistance to disease and excellent flavour and then, in 1941, the first of the Great Lakes cultivars appeared. These are rather more resistant to bolting in warm weather. Some Great Lakes types are suited for winter harvest, for example Great Lakes Gem.

Crisphead lettuce

Butterhead lettuce

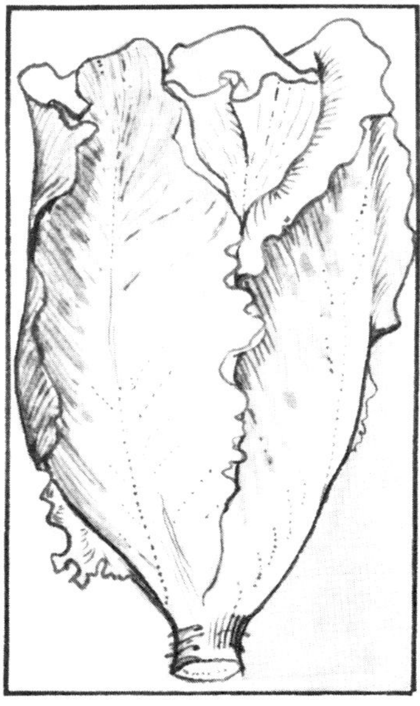

Cos lettuce

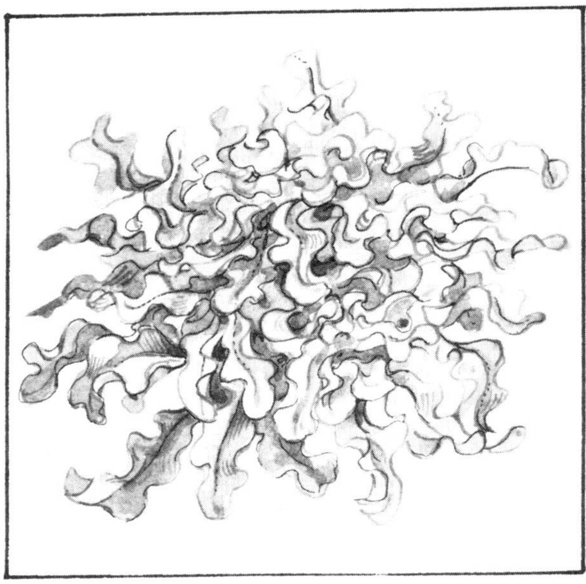

Leaf lettuce

The butterhead varieties are becoming great favourites among home gardeners today, especially Buttercrunch which is slow to bolt in hot weather and has smooth, tender leaves. Tom Thumb is an early, very small butterhead lettuce suitable for intercropping in spring. Mignonette lettuces are of this type too, and they can be obtained in both green and redleaf forms. They are small and decorative and do well in light soils and hot summers.

A standard cos lettuce grown in many areas is White Cos. It grows up to 35 cm tall and has thick, large, soft leaves. Valmine Cos is described as crisp and resistant to downy mildew.

Very few leaf-lettuce varieties are available. One in particular, Salad Bowl, deserves to be grown more often for it stands extremes of weather, can be planted out in a sheltered location in winter and is seldom troubled by pests or diseases. It is harvested as a "cut and come again" vegetable, a few outer leaves at a time. These are ideal for winter sandwiches.

Cultivation

The best soil for lettuces is a friable, well-drained loam containing sand and fine particles of well-broken down compost or peat. When this soil is watered it does not become water-logged or muddy but still feels moist just below the surface several days later.

The location of the lettuce plot is also very important. It should be sheltered and warm for winter- and spring-grown lettuce and sheltered and partly shaded during mid summer. It is better to create this shade by using old lace curtains or shade netting rather than by growing the lettuce too close to trees or hedges which may rob the plants of moisture. When buying seed make sure it is suitable for the season in which the plants will be growing — autumn-winter, early spring, or spring-summer.

Although we tend to eat more lettuce in hot weather, the plants themselves prefer the cool weather of spring and autumn. In fact, lettuce seed will not germinate above 25°C. Gardeners in warm regions may have to put the seed in a refrigerator for a few days before sowing. In cold winter weather lettuce seed will germinate but the plants grow so slowly that they have a bitter taste. Except in the warmest areas, late autumn sowings should be made under a mini glasshouse or cloche.

Bolting to seed is the bane of lettuce

growers. It may be caused by hot weather coupled with lack of soil moisture or by transplanting shock. Summer and autumn crops should therefore be sown directly in the garden where they are to mature. Place the seed in 12 mm-deep drills with 25-30 cm between rows. As soon as the first true leaves appear, thin to 10-15 cm apart and then, when birds and slugs have lost interest in getting past your protective devices, grow the remaining plants to maturity about 20-30 cm apart. The wider spacing is especially important for crisphead lettuce types. The mortality rate can be quite high for young lettuces so thinning in two stages is advisable. Tin collars are some help but they delay maturity and cannot be left on for more than seven to ten days.

In cooler districts spring-grown lettuce may have to be started on a window sill and then moved under a mini-glasshouse or cloche to achieve steady growth. The use of seedboxes increases the risk of transplanting shock so, if you wish to raise only five or six plants at a time, use peat pellet pots which can be planted out intact. Sow two seeds per pot and remove the weaker. When each plant is 5 cm high the pots should be planted out into their final position. Unless the weather is settled keep the mini-glasshouse or cloche in position until hearting begins. Whenever transplanting check that the lower leaves are just above the ground surface and not buried. Even slightly-bruised leaves in contact with the soil can provide an entrance for disease organisms.

An excess of nitrogen in the soil coupled with temperature extremes can bring about tip burn in susceptible varieties. A suitable fertilizer programme for a soil which has not been well manured for the previous crop involves an initial application of one cup of blood and bone and a half a cup of superphosphate per square metre, worked into the top 10 cm of soil. As the plants grow give one or two side dressings of dried blood (one tablespoon per plant) sprinkled beneath the plant and watered in.

Watering of cool-weather lettuce crops should be occasional and thorough, but the leaves should not be wetted. Downy mildew can become a serious problem in cool, damp weather. Hot-weather lettuces actually benefit from nightly overhead spraying as it cools the leaves and soil by several degrees and does not predispose them to rot. Their major pest is the aphid, especially if the soil is rich in nitrogen. Prevention by regular spraying with pyrethrum from mid spring is much easier than eradicating aphids from the inner leaves of a mature plant. Pull out any sow thistles growing near the lettuce patch as they often harbour aphid colonies.

Harvesting

Heading lettuce are ready when the hearts feel firm or resistant to pressure from the back of the hand. The butterhead types are rather more springy than solid to the touch. Start harvesting early as most varieties will not stand for more than one to two weeks in warm weather once they reach maturity.

In the kitchen

Trim the stalk and remove tough or discoloured outer leaves. Wash carefully, leaf by leaf. The leaves may be dried by whirling them in a tea towel, an old flour bag or a wire salad basket, or each leaf can be dried separately with a clean tea towel.

TOSSED GREEN SALAD

Serves 6

Place the leaves of a medium-sized, washed and dried lettuce in a plastic bag and refrigerate until crisp. This can be done well in advance.

Prepare French dressing (see page 209) using the best salad oil and wine vinegar that you can obtain.

Just before serving, tear the leaves into bite-sized pieces and place in a salad bowl. Beat the dressing until creamy and pour it over the salad. Gently turn the lettuce over to lightly coat each piece, and serve immediately.

Variations:

Add other salad greens when available —

young spinach, Chinese mustard or sorrel leaves, corn salad, cress, chicory or endive.

Finely-chopped garlic may be added to the dressing or, for a more subtle flavour, rub the bowl with a cut clove of garlic.

Add fresh herbs to the dressing — finely chopped chervil, basil, dill, savory, tarragon or chives.

Finely-sliced celery and green pepper can be added to give a crunchy texture.

Other additions such as sliced tomatoes, hard-boiled eggs, cheese, beetroot and radishes are best served separately if you are to appreciate fully the simplicity and sweet crispness of a fresh green salad.

Lettuce leaves are used to form the base for many salads such as Carrot Salad (see page 54) and Potato Salad (see page 156).

Serve lettuce in hot dishes to add variety and to use up a garden surplus.

CREAMED LETTUCE AND EGGS

Serves 4-5

An unusual lunch dish which contrasts the green lettuce and bright-yellow yolks to advantage. The flavour is delicate and the sauce creamy.

6 hard-boiled eggs
4 tb butter
1½ tb flour
1 c milk
300 g prepared lettuce leaves
½ tsp salt
pinch sugar
⅓ c cream
4 tb dry breadcrumbs
2 tb grated Parmesan cheese

Melt 2 tb of the butter in a saucepan, add flour and stir until bubbly. Gradually add the milk, stirring until smooth and thick. Simmer for 1 minute. Shred the lettuce finely with a sharp knife. Melt the remaining 2 tb of butter in another saucepan. Add the lettuce and cook gently for 10 minutes. Season with salt and sugar. Combine the sauce, lettuce, quartered hard-boiled eggs and cream. Turn into a buttered ovenproof dish. Combine breadcrumbs and cheese. Scatter over the top. Bake at 200°C for 10-15 minutes until heated through and the topping is golden-brown.

LETTUCE SOUP

Serves 4

A good recipe for using up outside leaves of lettuces or a lettuce that has failed to heart.

300 g lettuce leaves, washed
2 tb butter
1 small onion, chopped
1 tb flour
2 c chicken stock
salt and pepper to taste
½ tsp sugar
a little freshly-grated nutmeg
1 c milk
1 tb lemon juice
4 lemon slices

Blanch the lettuce leaves in boiling, salted water for 3 minutes. Drain and chop. Melt the butter in a large saucepan. Sauté the onion until soft. Stir in the flour and cook for 1 minute. Gradually add the stock and continue stirring until boiling. Add the lettuce, seasoning, sugar and nutmeg. Simmer for 15 minutes. Put through a blender or fine sieve. Add the milk and lemon juice and reheat gently without boiling. Serve garnished with lemon slices.

LETTUCE, MUSHROOMS AND EGGS

Serves 4

Another way of using up a lettuce surplus.

200 g mushrooms
2 lettuces, washed and dried
4 tb butter
salt and pepper to taste
4 eggs
50 g tasty Cheddar cheese, grated

Slice the mushrooms and lettuces fairly finely. Melt the butter in a large saucepan and add the mushrooms and lettuce. Cover and cook gently until both are soft. Season well. Tip into a shallow ovenproof dish. Make four hollows in the lettuce-mushroom mixture. Lightly poach the four eggs and slide one into each hollow. Cover with grated cheese and brown in the oven at 200°C.

Marrows and summer squash

(Cucurbita pepo var. *ovifera)*

Varieties

Long, green bush marrows and trailing marrows grown to maturity and then made into jam, or baked with a savoury stuffing, have been an English speciality for over a hundred years. Americans have concentrated on a rather different type of marrow which they call summer squash and eat when quite immature. In European countries courgettes and zucchini have played an important part in local cuisine.

Now, with national barriers being dissolved in the kitchen and vegetable garden, there is a major problem in the naming of the various types. For example, when Americans refer to the patty-pan squash and Englishmen refer to the custard marrow, they are both talking about the same vegetable, which may also be listed as the yellow bush scallop. Some commercial growers have standardized their terminology relating to courgettes and zucchini and this might usefully be adopted by home gardeners. Courgettes are the baby fruit of several types of marrow, harvested when about 14 x 4 cm, the size of a cigar. Zucchini are the fruit of the same plants harvested when 15-20 cm long. Marrows are the semi-mature and mature fruit which have reached full size.

If you wish to grow the traditional English marrow there is a choice of bush or trailing types. Long Green Bush produces fruit 50 x 12 cm in dimension in about 120 days. Its dark- and pale-green stripes become green and yellow when the fruit is mature. A white bush type is also available. Zucchini Black is a very popular variety for eating at all stages of maturity. In warm areas this bush marrow will produce courgettes in 45 days, zucchinis in 50 days and almost black-skinned, cylindrical mature fruit in 120 days.

A yellow zucchini/courgette marrow is now on the market. The plants are dwarf and non-spreading, ideal for a small garden. The fruit is eaten when 15-20 cm long. It develops coarse, unappetising flesh if allowed to mature further. This type is sold under the names of Sunbeam F.1. Hybrid and Goldzini Hybrid. Another F.1. hybrid marrow, Blackjack, must also be harvested before it exceeds 20 cm in length. It is a very popular variety, suitable for growing in large containers on sheltered patios or under the eaves. With this method gardeners in even cool areas can obtain a good crop of courgettes.

The fruit of bush scallops is of flattened-globe shape with a highly decorative, scalloped outer rim. St Pat F.1. Hybrid and Patty Green Tint Hybrid are names for an early, pale-green variety which is harvested after 45-50 days when the fruit is no longer than 10-12 cm in diameter. Early Golden Scallop has yellow fruit and Scallopini F.1. Hybrid bears dark-green fruit used when 7 cm in diameter.

Cultivation
It is customary to start spring-sown marrow and squash seeds in 7 cm peat pots in a glasshouse or on a sunny window sill in all except warm areas. This is because germination takes place between 15 and 32°C. To avoid problems of "damping off", the soil in the pots should be a sterilized seed-raising or potting mix. Push two seeds on end into each pot and later remove the more spindly one. Harden the plants properly before setting them out in the garden. Where spring weather is temperamental, you may need to supply extra shelter in the form of a tin collar or cloche.

Full sunshine and a rich, loamy soil are essential for marrows. Dig a hole beneath each planting position and fill it with a bucket of compost and a cup of general fertilizer before topping it with fine soil and planting the marrows. Mounds with three to four plants set around them like a pumpkin plot are a common sight in home gardens. The centres of the mounds should be 120 cm apart. If you wish to grow marrows in rows allow 60-90 cm between plants and 150 cm between rows. Any closer spacing will make regular harvesting visits into an obstacle race. Courgette growers might be advised to grow their plants beside a path

because daily inspections will be needed in mid summer to catch the fruit before it grows too big.

In the giant-marrow-growing days it was customary to pinch out growing tips and to stop laterals rigorously after a certain number of leaves. Nowadays bush types predominate and they need no pruning while trailing plants are controlled only when they exceed their available space. Marrows like frequent, light watering in hot, dry weather but, if there is a tendency for the young fruit to rot, water directly into a perforated tin set in the ground beside the plants. If courgettes or zucchini are being harvested fill the tin with animal manure as a source of extra nutrients. A black plastic, straw or pine-needle mulch also helps to keep the fruit from rotting.

Apart from "damping off' of seedling plants, marrows usually stay healthy until aphid numbers build up and weather conditions begin to favour the spread of powdery mildew. Aphids are controlled by regular spraying with pyrethrum or even a fine jet of water from the hose. Some zucchini marrows have pale-silvery blotches on their leaves which should not be confused with mildew. The strong, systemic fungicide, Benlate, may have to be applied if the old-fashioned lime-sulphur remedy is not used regularly in dry, autumn weather.

Harvesting

The desired-sized fruit should be cut from the plant with a sharp knife. Cut the stalk 1-2 cm from the fruit, taking care not to slice any adjacent leaf stalks.

In the kitchen

Most of the recipes given in this section may be made with either courgettes or zucchini. When a large vegetable marrow weighing as much as 3 kg is required, the recipe will specify this type. Bush scallop marrows may also be used in several of the recipes.

Wash gently and remove the stem and blossom ends. There is no need to peel courgettes or zucchini. Large vegetable marrows and mature scallop marrows have tougher skins which should be removed. Allow 100 g for each serving.

Courgettes, zucchini and small squashes may be sliced thickly or thinly, diced or left whole. Scoop out the seeds of larger, more developed marrows.

COURGETTES WITH TOMATOES

Serves 4-6

This is our favourite simple courgette recipe. It is best with fresh courgettes and tomatoes but is also a welcome change in winter using frozen courgettes and tomato purée.

500 g courgettes or zucchini
2 tb cooking oil
1 tb butter
4 medium-sized tomatoes (or 1 c tomato purée)
1 clove garlic, finely chopped
salt to taste
freshly-ground black pepper
1 tb mixed, freshly-chopped herbs (parsley and basil)

Cut courgettes into 5 mm slices. Melt the butter and oil in a heavy frying pan. Add the courgettes and cook gently, stirring occasionally until they are almost tender. Peel the tomatoes and chop roughly. Add to the courgettes with the garlic. Cook slowly until the tomato is soft but not mushy. Season. Add the chopped herbs and serve immediately.

COURGETTES WITH FRESH HERBS

Serves 4-6

Delicious served with lamb or chicken

500 g courgettes or zucchini
2 tb cooking oil
1 tb butter
2 tb mixed, chopped, fresh herbs (parsley, chervil and chives)
1 tsp lemon juice
salt and pepper to taste

Cut courgettes into 5 mm slices. Melt the butter and oil in a frying pan. Add the courgettes and cook gently for 5-10 minutes until they are just tender. Turn the slices over once or twice during cooking. Stir in the herbs, lemon juice and seasoning. Serve immediately.

GLEN'S COURGETTES WITH SHRIMP STUFFING

Serves 8

This pretty dish makes an elegant lunch course or dinner-party entrée.

8 small zucchini (about 15 cm long)
4 medium-sized tomatoes
1 shallot or 2 spring onions
2 tb butter
½ tsp paprika
salt and pepper to taste
200 g tin of shrimps
300 ml mornay sauce (see page 208)
2 tb grated Parmesan cheese

Top and tail the zucchini. Cook for 4 minutes in a large saucepan of boiling, salted water. Drain. Leave to cool. Remove a thin slice lengthwise from each zucchini. Using a coffee spoon, scoop out the flesh. Chop the flesh and reserve. Leave the zucchini cases upside down on a paper towel to drain.

Skin the tomatoes, remove the core and seeds and chop the flesh. Chop the shallot or spring onions finely. Melt the butter in a frying pan. Add the shallot and sauté gently until tender. Add the paprika, courgette flesh and tomatoes. Cook for 2-3 minutes. Season. Cool slightly before adding the drained shrimps.

Fill the zucchini cases with this mixture. Place them carefully in a shallow ovenproof dish. Spoon the hot mornay sauce over the zucchini and sprinkle with cheese. Brown at 200°C for about 10 minutes.

COURGETTES AND HAM

Serves 4

Serve with warm, crusty rolls, fresh fruit, an interesting cheese and lightly-chilled rosé wine for a special occasion summertime lunch.

500 g courgettes or scallop marrows
2 tb cooking oil
150 g ham, cut into strips
1 clove garlic, finely chopped
freshly-ground black pepper
1 tb chopped parsley

Dice unpeeled courgettes or scallop marrows into 1.5 cm cubes. Sauté in oil in a heavy-based frying pan for 5 minutes. Add the ham, garlic and pepper. Cover the frying pan and cook gently for 10-15 minutes until just tender. Sprinkle with parsley just before serving.

ZUCCHINI FRITTERS AND TARTARE SAUCE

Serves 4

Tartare Sauce (best made several hours before serving):

150 ml mayonnaise (see page 209)
2 tsp finely-chopped gherkins
1 tsp chopped parsley
1 tsp chopped tarragon
1 tsp chopped chervil
salt, pepper and súgar to taste

Combine all ingredients and chill.

Batter:

1 c flour
½ tsp salt
2 eggs
⅔ c milk

Sift the flour and salt into a bowl and make a well in the centre. Combine the milk and egg yolks. Pour sufficient of this liquid into the flour to make a thick batter. Beat until smooth. Beat the egg whites until stiff and fold into the batter.

500 g zucchini or small scallop marrows, cut into 1 cm slices.

Heat a little cooking oil in a large frying pan. Dip the slices in batter. Cook each side until golden brown. Drain on absorbent paper. Serve hot with tartare sauce.

COURGETTE AND TOMATO OMELETTE

Serves 4-6

500 g courgettes or small summer squash
1 medium-sized onion, finely chopped
2 cloves garlic, finely chopped
½ tsp salt
freshly-ground black pepper
2 tb cooking oil
1 tb butter
500 g tomatoes
1 tsp chopped basil
4 eggs
4 tb grated tasty Cheddar cheese
2 tb chopped parsley
freshly-grated nutmeg

Cut unpeeled courgettes into 1 cm cubes. Cook with onion, garlic, salt and pepper in the oil and butter until just tender. Skin the tomatoes and chop the flesh roughly. Add to courgettes and continue cooking until soft but not mushy. Add the basil.

Beat the eggs, add the cheese, parsley and nutmeg. Mix this gently into the vegetables.

Either bake at 190°C until the eggs are set and golden-brown or cook gently on top of the range until the eggs are set and lightly browned on the bottom.

STUFFED MARROW

This versatile recipe can be used for a large vegetable marrow or three smaller marrows.

This year our gardens produced an abundance of a new scallop marrow, Scallopini. Their size is ideal for one stuffed half per serving.

1 large vegetable marrow (1.5 kg) and twice the stuffing recipe will serve 8.

3 scallop marrows (7-10 cm diameter) or 3 zucchini marrows will serve 6.

Peel a large vegetable marrow, cut off the ends and use a spoon to remove the seeds.

Do not peel smaller marrows. Cut evenly in half and remove the soft centres and any seeds.

Stuffing: (double the recipe to stuff a large marrow):

1 small onion, finely chopped
2 tb butter
250 g mince
60 g mushrooms, chopped
1 tb chopped parsley
½ tsp chopped thyme
50 g soft breadcrumbs
freshly-ground black pepper
½ tsp salt
1 small egg
2 tb butter, melted

Melt the butter in a frying pan, add the onion and sauté for a few minutes. Add the mince and mushrooms and continue to cook until browned. Remove from the heat. Add the remaining ingredients except for the melted butter. Mix thoroughly with a fork.

Pack the stuffing carefully into the marrow or marrows. Place in a large roasting pan and brush with melted butter. Cover with a piece of foil. Bake at 190°C. A large marrow will need 1½ hours and small marrows 45 minutes. When cooked the marrow flesh will be tender. Serve with freshly-made Neapolitan sauce (see page 196).

KATHY'S VEAL AND ZUCCHINI

Serves 4-6

500 g zucchini
500 g thinly-cut veal or topside steak
seasoning — salt, pepper and freshly-grated nutmeg
100 g grated cheese
50 g butter

Cut unpeeled zucchini into 5 mm slices. Sprinkle lightly with salt and leave to drain on an absorbent towel for 1 hour. Cut the thinly-sliced veal into pieces, 4-5 cm square. Grease a deep casserole. Put in a layer of zucchini. Season and cover with slices of meat. Sprinkle with cheese and dot with butter. Continue layering, finishing with zucchini, cheese and butter. Bake uncovered at 180°C for 1½ hours.

COURGETTE SOUP

Serves 4

A delicately-flavoured, creamy soup.

1 small onion
1 small potato
500 g courgettes or frozen purée
2 tb butter
½ tsp chopped fresh tarragon (if available)
2 c chicken stock
salt and pepper to taste
¼ c cream

Peel the onion and potato. Slice these and courgettes finely. Heat the butter in a large saucepan. Add the vegetables and tarragon. Sauté gently for 3 minutes. Add the stock and simmer until the vegetables are tender. Put through a blender or fine sieve. Return to saucepan, check seasoning and reheat. Serve with a teaspoon of whipped cream in the centre of each bowl.

Note: if frozen purée is used, add it to the sautéed vegetables with the chicken stock.

COURGETTE SALAD

Serves 6

This salad can be prepared well before it is needed. We find it useful for serving at dinner parties.

- 500 g courgettes
- 3 tb salad oil
- 2 tb lemon juice
- 1 tsp sugar
- ½ tsp salt
- freshly-ground black pepper
- 1 tb scissored chives
- 1 tb chopped parsley

Cut courgettes into 5 mm slices. Boil until they are barely tender in lightly-salted water. Be careful not to overcook. Drain. Mix the oil, lemon juice, sugar, salt and pepper and pour over the courgettes while they are still hot. Cover and leave for at least 1 hour. Just before serving, add the herbs and mix thoroughly.

Courgettes can be eaten raw in salads or sandwiches. Slice wafer thin and season well. The new yellow marrow looks very attractive in green salads.

DARK ZUCCHINI BREAD

Makes 4 small loaves

This recipe comes from the United States. It is dark, moist and keeps very well. Don't be tempted to put in more than the stated ¼ tsp of baking powder and 1 tsp of baking soda — the loaves rise beautifully.

- 3 eggs
- 2 c brown sugar
- 1 c cooking oil
- 1 tsp vanilla
- 3 c peeled and grated zucchini
- 1 tb treacle
- 4 c flour
- 1 tsp baking soda
- ¼ tsp baking powder
- 2 tsp cinnamon
- 1 tsp allspice
- ½ c chopped walnuts

Beat the eggs and brown sugar together until creamy. Gradually beat in the oil. Add the vanilla, grated zucchini and treacle. Beat well. Sift the flour, baking soda, baking powder, cinnamon and allspice. Add to the liquid ingredients. Stir in the nuts and combine thoroughly. Bake in three or four small, greased loaf tins (2-3 c capacity). Fill each two-thirds full. Place in the oven at 180°C for 1 hour. Cool in tins for 5 minutes and then tip on to a rack.

ZUCCHINI PICKLE

- 1 kg zucchini
- 4 large onions
- 1 red pepper
- 1 green pepper
- ½ c salt
- 2 c sugar
- 2½ c white vinegar
- 1 c water
- 2 tsp turmeric
- 2 tsp celery seed

Chop unpeeled zucchini finely. Peel and chop the onions. Remove the seeds from the peppers and chop the flesh. Combine the vegetables in a large bowl. Sprinkle the salt over the surface and cover with water. Leave for 2 hours. Drain. Rinse thoroughly with cold water and drain again.

In a preserving pan boil the sugar, vinegar, water, turmeric and celery seed for 3 minutes. Add the vegetables and cook for 15 minutes. Spoon into hot dry jars and seal.

MARROW JAM

If you have to buy all the fruit you need for making jam this recipe will appeal because it costs so little to make.

- 1 large vegetable marrow (about 1.5 kg)
- 4 tb water
- 50 g bruised root ginger
- 1.5 kg sugar
- 3 tb lemon juice
- 120 g chopped crystallised ginger
- 1 bottle liquid pectin (225 ml) or equivalent made from pectin powder

Peel the marrow and remove the seeds. Chop the flesh finely. Place the marrow and water in a preserving pan. Simmer, covered, until the marrow is tender (about 20 minutes). Tie the root ginger in a piece of muslin. Add to the marrow with the sugar, crystallised ginger and lemon juice. Bring slowly to the boil stirring until the sugar has dissolved. Boil hard for 2 minutes. Remove from the heat. Take out the muslin bag and stir in the liquid pectin. Allow to cool before pouring into clean, dry jars. Seal with jam covers.

PICKLED COURGETTES

Whole or sliced courgettes may be pickled in the same way as gherkins (see page 78).

Freezing

Large vegetable marrows keep for months in their hard skins and do not need to be frozen.

Courgettes, zucchini and scallop marrows may be frozen as part of a cooked dish, for example Ratatouille (see page 205), frozen as a purée for soup or in slices to use as a vegetable. This last way is acceptable but the slices tend to go mushy when thawed.

To freeze as a purée, cook courgette or zucchini slices in a minimum of water, put through a blender or fine sieve, cool, pour into plastic containers and freeze. Directions for making this into soup are on page 128.

To freeze as a vegetable, cut unpeeled courgettes or zucchini into 1 cm slices. Blanch for 3 minutes, cool and snap freeze (see page 38). Pack in meal-sized quantities. Cook with tomato purée for the best results.

Melons

Varieties

Melons are tender annuals belonging to the pumpkin-squash-cucumber group. Most rock melon varieties produce oval to round fruit with pale-green skins which appear to be covered in a tightly-woven net. Inside, sweet orange or salmon-coloured flesh surrounds a small seed cavity. Desert Sun, Hales Best, Sampson F.1 Hybrid and Saticoy F.1 Hybrid are examples of this type. Honey Dew is slower to reach maturity (18 weeks instead of 15) and has pale-green flesh and a creamy-white rind.

Watermelons vary in shape from oblong to almost round. Their seeds are distributed through the deep-pink, edible centre and the skins are smooth, dark green and sometimes striped with a lighter green. A number of varieties are currently available to the home gardener. Most take 14-16 weeks to mature. One of the largest is Cannonball which may grow to 18 kg. Charleston Grey is a little smaller but still not suitable for a small family. Sugar Baby at about 4 kg is a home-garden favourite. The hybrid Sugar Doll is earlier and more prolific and this hybrid vigour is coupled with disease resistance in Red Crisp F.1 Hybrid. Some gardeners swear by Crimson Sweet or Candy Red, both well-tried varieties.

Cultivation

If your area is suitable for outdoor tomatoes, egg plants and peppers it should be possible to grow water and rock melons, provided the soil is a well-watered, rich loam. Like cucumber and pumpkin seeds, melon seeds should be started indoors in peat pots in spring. Push two seeds into each pot 2-3 cm deep and in an upright position, later removing the weaker. The plants get away to a good start if soil temperatures are maintained just above 21°C. Cloches or mini-glasshouses are invaluable where spring weather is temperamental.

Rock melons are often grown on mounds which provide good drainage and warm up quickly. Allow 1.3 m between the hills and 25 cm between individual plants (two or three per hill). Space the plants 90 cm apart if you are growing them in a straight row rather than on mounds. A black plastic or straw mulch will keep the fruit off the damp ground and retain moisture in dry weather. Feeding the plants with liquid manure is recommended for heavy crops. This should not be watered on to the leaves in case it encourages the spread of mildew, but applied in a furrow around the base of the mound or in a perforated tin sunk into the ground beside each plant.

Watermelons require nearly twice as much space and are usually grown in a flat, enriched bed covered with black plastic. Place the peat pots and plants into holes cut in the plastic 1.5 m apart. Watering is done through sunken tins or a soak hose left in place under the plastic.

Harvesting

Rock melons are ready when the fruit falls away from the stalk. In some varieties skin colour under the "netting" turns yellow. Their flavour is best if left for another two to three days in a warm room. Watermelons are ripe and ready for picking when the skin in contact with the ground begins to yellow, when the surface texture looks a little bumpy and when the fruit sounds hollow when knocked. Some gardeners use their nose to detect the characteristic aroma of the ripe melons.

In the kitchen

Unless you are lucky enough to have a surplus of melons you will probably prefer to serve them with just a squeeze of lemon juice.

Watermelons produce seeds throughout their flesh. Cut into slices without peeling and flick out the seeds.

Cantaloupes or rock melons have their seeds in a central cavity. Slice in half and scoop out the seeds with a spoon. Cut into unpeeled wedges.

Melon flesh can also be cut into cubes or balls using a special ball cutter. Dress with lemon juice, French dressing, rum or port wine. Melon combines well with other fruits such as dates, grapes or grapefruit to make an attractive appetizer or dessert. Serve in dessert glasses or use the melon shell as a container.

Mix with tomato and cucumber as a delicious salad.

GINGERED MELON

Serves 6

We serve melon dressed this way as a simple appetizer for a summer dinner or as a refreshing dessert to follow a rich party meal.

4 c diced melon flesh with seeds removed (watermelon, cantaloupe or rock melon)
2 tb honey, warmed if necessary
2 tb lemon juice
¼ tsp freshly-grated nutmeg
¼ tsp ground ginger

Garnish:

2 tb chopped preserved ginger or 6 tiny sprigs of mint

Place the prepared melon in a bowl. Combine the honey, lemon juice and spices. Pour over the melon. Chill well. Serve in individual glasses. Garnish with mint sprigs or chopped preserved ginger.

MELON, TOMATO AND CUCUMBER SALAD

Serves 6-8 as an appetizer

1 large cucumber or 4 apple cucumbers
1 tsp salt
1 medium-sized cantaloupe or rock melon
500 g tomatoes

Dressing:

2 tb wine vinegar
6 tb salad oil
½ tsp salt
¼ tsp castor sugar
freshly-ground black pepper
2 tb mixed, chopped herbs (mint, parsley and chives)

Peel the cucumber and cut the flesh into neat cubes. Remove any large seeds. Sprinkle with salt and leave for ½ an hour to drain. Rinse and drain. Cut the melon in half and scoop out the seeds. Cut the flesh into cubes of a similar size to the cucumber. Skin the tomatoes, cut into quarters, flick out the seeds and remove any hard core. Cut into pieces, a similar size to the cucumber. Combine the melon, tomato and cucumber in a deep serving bowl.

Mix all the dressing ingredients together and pour over the salad. Chill for 2 hours. Just before serving sprinkle with herbs. Ladle salad into small soup bowls or glasses. Provide spoons.

Onions

(*Allium* spp.)

Many members of the onion family are used as vegetables. The most popular are large onions and shallots (*Allium cepa* var. *cepa* and *Allium cepa* var. *ascalonicum*), leeks (*Allium ampeloprasum* var. *porrum*) and chives (*Allium schoenoprasum*).

There is a growing interest in garlic (*Allium sativum*). Some gardeners grow tree onions (also called top or Egyptian onions). These are actually two or three varieties of *A. cepa* which bear clusters of small cocktail onions on long stalks, as well as flowers. Some varieties are also capable of producing large onion bulbs at ground level. Being perennials, they are extremely useful to have in the garden as their top onions can be harvested in autumn and pickled or stored while the bases remain in the ground for times when other onions are scarce. They need dividing every two to three years. Unlike other varieties of *A. cepa* they are virtually disease free.

Another group of onions are the Welsh or bunching perennial types (A. *fistulosum*) which supply immature sprouts as substitutes for spring onions throughout the year. They, too, should be divided every two to three years. The seeds of bunching onions, chives, large onions and leeks are available from seedsmen but those members of the family grown from small bulbs (shallots, garlic and tree onions) can be obtained from garden shops, friends or neighbours. A real onion enthusiast might be able to find a source for potato onions, Egyptian leeks, Chinese chives, and sand leeks (rocambale).

The following section will deal with large onions, pickling onions, spring onions and shallots. Leeks have their own section while chives and garlic are discussed under the heading, "Herbs".

Varieties

Large onions fall into two categories, early and maincrop. The early varieties are usually sown in late autumn and they mature in late spring to early summer.

The most popular is California Early Red which has deep-red skin and white flesh. It is not a good keeper and has a tendency to grow thick necked (a sign of imminent flowering) but most cooks will be using these early onions just as fast as they reach an edible size. They are a very mild onion combining well with tomatoes, peppers and zucchini. The best strain of maincrop onion in our part of the world is undoubtedly Pukekohe Long Keeper. Its golden-brown-skinned bulbs will last for up to ten months if stored in a cool, dry and airy shed or porch. In districts where late summers and early autumns are dry and warm, it is sown in mid spring to be harvested in mid autumn. Where autumns are humid and winters mild, it should be sown in late winter so that it is out of

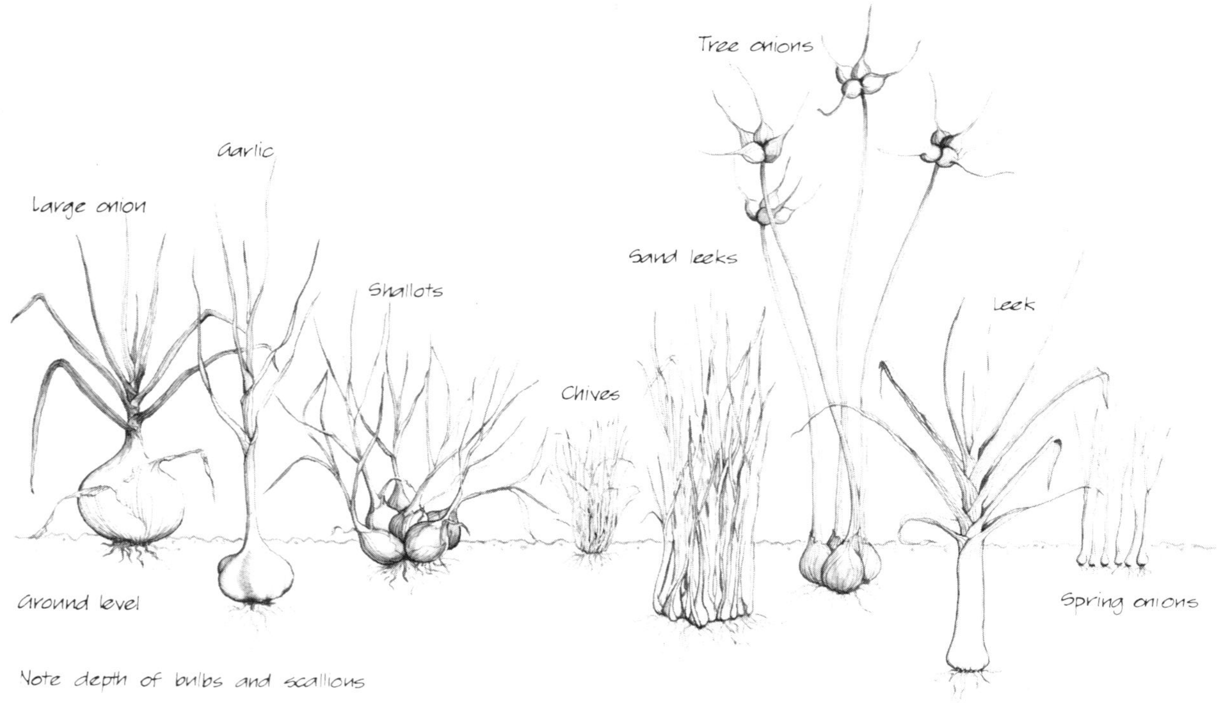

the ground in late summer before downy mildew becomes widespread. Other maincrop varieties are Abundance Hybrid and Coopers Gold.

Pickling onions with names like Early White Cocktail, White Pearl and Queen Pickling Silverskin are usually sown in spring in ground of only moderate fertility. They are sown in very shallow drills only 10 cm apart and the plants are not thinned. Harvest time is mid to late summer.

Spring onions listed in seed catalogues may be perennial bunching onions without basal bulbs (White Bunching) or varieties with bulbs which will eventually flower (White Valencia and White Lisbon). They are ready for harvesting in 60-90 days and are sown in autumn or early spring. Those from an autumn sowing should be of pencil thickness by early winter if they are to be harvested as genuine "spring" onions.

Two varieties of shallot are briefly available in garden shops from late autumn to early winter, ready for the traditional planting time in mid winter. These are yellow skinned and red skinned, both of similar size and both quite long keepers.

Cultivation and harvesting

Onion roots form a shallow mat spreading within a radius of 15 cm from the bulb so the aim of soil preparation is to have a firm topsoil without lumps. It should also be well supplied with nutrients. Prepare the ground in an airy and sunny part of the garden during autumn, working in mature compost and lime. By spring, when seed is sown or autumn-raised plants set out, the soil should have compacted considerably. If you do not have much compost available, make a 5 cm flat-bottomed trench beneath each row and sprinkle a general fertilizer along it. Fill back the topsoil and firm it down before sowing the seed in shallow drills.

Onion seed should always be fresh and the seed bed must be kept moist for even germination. For later transplanting, sow the seed in beds or boxes in drills 10 cm apart. The seedlings should be planted out before they exceed

6 mm across the stem just above ground level. Delayed transplanting is just one of the causes of thick necks in the mature onion. Others include using the wrong variety, sowing too early, an excess of nitrogen, planting out too deep, dry soil in the early growth period, excessive shade and loose soil. Large onions should be thinned or transplanted to 7.5-10 cm apart in the row with 20-30 cm between rows. Pickling and spring onions are grown with the plants virtually touching one another in rows 10 cm apart.

A useful transplanting technique to prevent over-deep planting is to make holes with a dibber. Trim any long, straggly roots, lower the seedling into the hole and then pull upwards until the base of the bulblet is just 12 mm below the surface. Plunge the dibber into the soil beside the first hole. This will push the soil firmly around the seedling, holding it at the right level. Keep the young plants watered and well weeded, preferably by hand, as their roots are so close to the surface.

About mid summer bulbs of maincrop varieties will begin to expand and no further leaf growth is made. If the weather stays warm and the rainfall light, the tips of the leaves will begin to yellow and in a few weeks the foliage will flop over on to the ground. It is possible to bend over the tops yourself to hasten the drying-off process. Lift the onions if you suspect that the dry, settled weather is coming to an end, even if the tops are still fairly green. Provided the bulbs are full and firm and the necks thin, the final ripening can be achieved in a sunny porch or airy greenhouse, anywhere that is warm and dry. The foliage should not be removed until it is completely withered, otherwise the onions will not keep more than a few weeks.

Shallots are much less fussy and any gardener who cannot provide the right conditions for large onions should concentrate on them as a source of good keeping onions for autumn and winter use. Provided the soil is not waterlogged, plant out small, firm shallot bulbs or cloves any time from mid winter to early spring for mid summer to late summer harvesting. Set each shallot 12-20 cm from its neighbours in rows 30 cm apart. The bulbs should be pushed half-way into firm, moderately rich soil. Keep them well weeded and do not allow soil to build up around the necks of the bulbs.

Onions are subject to several fungus diseases including downy mildew, white rot and neck rot. These are not easily controlled by spraying and it is better to keep them at bay by crop rotation and by choosing a breezy, sunny part of the garden for the onions. Remove and burn any young onions or shallots that have yellow-streaked and stunted leaves.

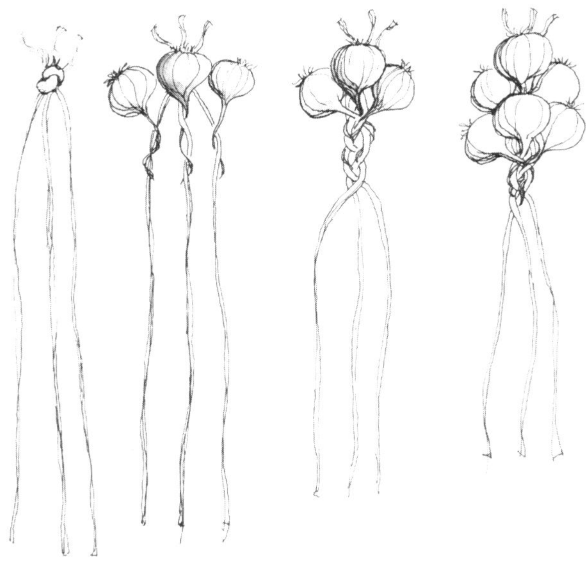

How to string onions

Cut 3 lengths of twine or strips of flax about 60 cm long and tie them tightly at one end. Place 3 dry onions on top and plait the twine and the withered stalks together twice. Then lay 3 more on top and plait again the stalks and twine. Continue plaiting-in 3 more onions at a time. To finish tie one strand tightly round the last three and then tie all three strands together to make a loop from which the bunch will hang. Cut off onions as required

In the kitchen

Onions play such an important role in flavouring dishes that we cannot imagine a kitchen without a supply. Their use as a main dish or vegetable accompaniment, however, is often forgotten. Baked in their jackets, sautéed with cheese and in pies and soups they make a warming addition to winter meals.

Trim the top and root end and peel off paper-like skins. Allow a medium onion for each serving. Tiny onions are more easily peeled if they are first scalded in boiling water and then plunged into cold water.

To slice finely or dice, cut the onion in half and lay, cut side down, on a wooden board. Using a French cook's knife, slice or chop.

The best way to stop streaming eyes is to ensure good kitchen ventilation or, better still, take your chopping board, French cook's knife and onions out into the garden.

FRIED ONIONS

Blanch onion rings for 1 minute. Cool quickly. Fry in oil. Sprinkle with a little sugar to hasten browning. Drain on absorbent paper and serve piled on and around grilled steaks.

ONIONS IN WHITE SAUCE

The traditional accompaniment to boiled meats, especially mutton.

Boil 4-6 roughly chopped onions in salted water until tender. Drain. Add to a well-seasoned white sauce and heat through. Use the recipe for Parsley Sauce on page 208 but omit the parsley.

BAKED JACKET ONIONS

The onion-loving members of our families are very enthusiastic about this recipe. Onions take longer to bake than potatoes so allow plenty of time. Cut a thin slice from the base of each unpeeled onion. Brush the skins with oil. Place in a shallow baking dish. Bake at 180°C for approximately 1½ hours or until tender. Using a small, sharp knife cut a shallow cross in the top of each onion. Peel back the outer layers to expose the onion flesh. Place a small teaspoon of sour cream in the top of each and sprinkle with paprika.

SAUTÉED ONIONS AND CHEESE

Serves 6

A simple onion dish with lots of flavour.

6 medium-sized onions
4 tb butter
¼ tsp salt
freshly-ground black pepper
½ c chicken stock
½ c grated Cheddar cheese

Slice the onions into thin rings. Melt the butter in a large frying pan. Add the onions and seasoning. Sauté gently for about 10 minutes until the onions are almost tender. Add the chicken stock and simmer for 5 minutes. Add the cheese, stir to combine and serve immediately.

CORNISH APPLE AND ONION PIE

Serves 6

Serve warm with cold meat and a salad, or cold for a picnic snack.

Rich shortcrust pastry:

225 g flour
¼ tsp salt
140 g butter
1 egg yolk
water if necessary

Filling:

3 medium-sized onions
3 cooking apples
salt and pepper to taste
1 tsp chopped sage
¼ tsp mixed spice
3 tb sour cream

Sift the flour and salt into a bowl. Rub in the butter until the mixture resembles coarse breadcrumbs. Stir in the egg yolk and sufficient water to make a stiff dough. Knead until smooth. Chill for 30 minutes. Roll out two-thirds of the pastry and line a 20-25 cm flan ring or pie plate.

Peel and slice the onions. Blanch in boiling water for 1 minute. Drain and cool. Peel, quarter and slice the apples. Place a layer of apples in the flan, cover with onions and season with salt, pepper, sage and mixed spice. Cover with the remaining apples. Spread the sour cream over the surface. Roll out the remaining pastry to cover the pie. Moisten the edges and press them together. Bake at 200°C for 30-40 minutes.

ONIONS À LA GRECQUE

Serves 4-6

A delicious cold onion dish.

500 g small, even-sized onions
1 c water
½ c white wine
2 tb cooking oil
1 tb tomato concentrate
50 g raisins or sultanas
1 tb sugar (omit if wine is sweet)
bouquet garni
4 peppercorns
salt to taste

Peel the onions and place them in a saucepan. Add all the ingredients and simmer gently for about 45 minutes until the onions are tender but still whole. Cool and chill for several hours before serving.

FRENCH ONION SOUP

Serves 6

600 g onions
3 tb butter
2 tb cooking oil
½ tsp sugar
1.5 litres beef stock
salt and pepper to taste
1 tb brandy (optional)
½ tsp mild prepared mustard (optional)
12 tb grated Cheddar cheese
6 rounds of French bread, toasted (optional)

Peel the onions, cut them in half and slice thinly. Heat the butter, oil and sugar in a large saucepan. Add the onions and cook over moderate heat for about 15 minutes, stirring frequently. The onions should be a rich golden colour. Stir in the stock. Simmer for 30 minutes. Season and add brandy and mustard.

Serve with 2 tb of grated cheese added to each bowl. Alternatively, sprinkle cheese on the toasted bread rounds and place them under a hot griller for a few minutes until the cheese is bubbly and golden. Float one round in each bowl of soup. Serve immediately.

PICKLED ONIONS

3 kg small pickling onions
½ c salt
2 litres spiced vinegar (double the recipe on page 51 but use malt vinegar)
½ c sugar

Peel the onions and place them in a basin. Sprinkle with salt and leave overnight. Rinse well and dry. Combine the spiced vinegar and sugar in a saucepan. Bring to the boil. Add the onions and bring back to boiling point. Pack in jars and overflow with boiling, spiced vinegar. Cover. Try to leave for 2 months before use.

Parsnip

(Pastinaca sativa)

Varieties

Parsnips are not popular vegetables and this is often blamed on their sweetness. But if this was really the case, no-one would like sweet potatoes. Certainly they take four to five months to grow and are slow and erratic in germination, but they make up for this by sitting out the worst winter weather in the garden without rotting or cracking and even improving in flavour after heavy frosts. They come in short, medium-long (25 cm) and long (30-35 cm) sizes.

If you have shallow soils or haven't had time to sow your seed until early summer, choose the Oxheart variety. This has a hollow crown and a stout tapered root. It is ready before the very popular medium-long variety, Hollow Crown, which grows to about 25 cm. Student is also of medium length. Freshman is a longer parsnip which matures a little earlier than Hollow Crown. Smoothie and Supersnip are recommended for their smooth white skins. They are both long parsnips.

Cultivation

Long parsnips obviously need deeply-dug soil or else specially-prepared planting holes 30 cm apart. These should be made with a crowbar and filled with potting soil. Raised beds or soil-filled field tiles (drain pipes) are other methods of achieving a deep topsoil. The soil should have been limed within the past twelve months and manured for a previous crop. Fresh manure (as well as clay lumps and clods) often causes the roots to fork. A general fertilizer (see page 8) may be worked into the soil just before sowing.

The seed should be very fresh to ensure good germination. In clay-based soils it should be sprinkled thickly on to a thin layer of sand in the seed drill and covered with sand to a depth of 12 mm. This helps to prevent rotting in the two to four weeks before germination. In cool areas sowing should be completed by late spring to ensure good-sized parsnips for the next winter. Gardeners in warmer regions may sow in autumn for a spring harvest. Thin in one or two stages to 10-20 cm apart, with 40 cm between the rows.

Parsnips need very little attention as they grow slowly to maturity needing only occasional hoeing between the rows to control weeds. Carrot fly may be a pest in certain areas and the same precautions should be taken as for carrots. It is claimed that canker or crown rust can occur if the soil is too rich in nitrogen or if the seed is sown too early in spring.

Harvesting

When winter frosts set in the top growth begins to die back. Some gardeners wait for this to occur before beginning harvest. From a mid-

Pull parsnip sideways
to avoid breaking
Trench

spring sowing, however, parsnips will be ready in autumn. Pulling parsnips by their leaves from hard or heavy ground often results in a harvest of tops with the roots breaking off just below the surface. It is advisable to harvest from the ends of the rows, working from a slowly advancing trench and pulling the parsnips towards you from the face of the trench. In spring, signs of re-growth in the tops is a signal to lift all remaining parsnips from the ground. Trim the tops close to the crowns and store them in dry sand in a shed or cellar. They should be eaten as soon as possible before they develop a woody core.

In the kitchen

Trim off the tops and root ends. Peel thinly. Allow 100 g for each serving. To prepare as chunks, slice parsnips into thick sections and then cut each section through the core to make even-sized pieces. Parsnips may also be thinly sliced or diced. Quarter old parsnips lengthwise and remove hard central cores before cutting to the desired size.

Sliced, chunked or diced parsnip should be cooked in plenty of boiling, salted water until tender and then drained. Serve simply with butter, pepper and finely-chopped parsley. For variety, try fresh or sour cream and a little Worcestershire sauce or brown sugar. Parsley sauce and cheese sauce (see page 208) are also good accompaniments.

Cooked parsnips may be mashed and seasoned with pepper, chopped parsley, a pinch of cinnamon and cream or butter to make a delicate purée.

A particularly tasty and easy method of cooking parsnips is to roast them with a joint of meat. If they are old, blanch large chunks for 5 minutes and then tuck around the meat and roast for 45-60 minutes, turning them over once or twice.

PARSNIP CHIPS

Serves 6

May be served instead of potatoes.

800 g prepared parsnips
3 tb butter
½ tsp salt
freshly-ground black pepper

Cut the parsnips into "chips", about 6 cm long and 1 cm thick. Cook in a large saucepan of boiling water until just tender. Do not overcook. Drain. Melt the butter in a large frying pan and sauté the chips until golden-brown. Season well.

Cut parsnip sections
through their cores

PEG'S PARSNIP CUTLETS

Serves 6-8

A good way to use up left-over mashed parsnip.

2 c mashed parsnips
1 c grated Cheddar cheese
1 tb melted butter
½ tsp salt
freshly-ground black pepper
¼ tsp ground mace
1 egg, lightly beaten
½ c dry breadcrumbs
2 tb butter
1 tb cooking oil

Combine the parsnip, cheese, butter, seasoning and bind with the egg. Form the mixture into 6-8 cutlets and coat with the breadcrumbs. If possible chill for 30 minutes. Fry in hot butter and oil turning the cutlets so that both sides become crisp and golden-brown.

BAKED PARSNIPS WITH HONEY

Serves 6

500 g prepared parsnips
salt to taste
freshly-ground black pepper
1 tb butter
1 tb honey

Quarter the parsnips lengthwise and then slice into 6-8 cm chunks. Blanch for 7 minutes. Drain. Place in a greased ovenproof dish. Season. Melt the butter and honey in a small saucepan. Pour over the parsnips. Bake at 180°C for 30-45 minutes until golden-brown and tender. Turn the parsnip chunks once or twice during the cooking time.

CHEESY PARSNIPS

Serves 6

600 g prepared parsnips
2 tb butter
¼ tsp salt
freshly-ground black pepper
freshly-grated nutmeg
120 g grated Cheddar cheese

Cut the parsnips into thin slices. Cook in boiling, salted water until just tender. Drain well. Place in a greased ovenproof dish. Dot with butter. Add the salt, pepper and nutmeg. Sprinkle with grated cheese. Bake at 200°C for 15-20 minutes until golden-brown.

PARSNIP AND TOMATO BAKE

Serves 4

2½ c diced parsnip (2 medium-sized parsnips)
2 tb butter
1 small onion, finely chopped
2 tb flour
½ tsp salt
freshly-ground black pepper
1 tsp sugar
1¼ c tomato juice
1 c soft breadcrumbs
1 tb butter

Boil the parsnip in a small quantity of salted water until tender. Drain. Melt the butter in a saucepan, add the onion and sauté until soft. Add the flour, salt, pepper and sugar. Cook for 1 minute then gradually pour in the tomato juice. Stir constantly until thick and smooth. Add the parsnip to the sauce. Spoon into a greased ovenproof dish. Sprinkle the top with breadcrumbs and dot with butter. Bake at 200°C for 15 minutes until the topping is golden.

SCALLOPED PARSNIPS AND POTATOES

Scalloped parsnips and potatoes is a tasty variation of scalloped potatoes (see page 155)

). Use roughly half parsnips and half potatoes and substitute 2 rashers of bacon for the onion.

PARSNIP LOAF

Serves 6

This dish makes a substantial main course. Serve it with a colourful winter salad.

- **1 kg prepared parsnips**
- **3 tb butter**
- **4 rashers of bacon**
- **1 medium-sized onion**
- **130 g grated Cheddar cheese**
- **8 tb cream**
- **salt and pepper**

Topping:

- **50 g grated Cheddar cheese**
- **5 tb dry breadcrumbs**

Quarter the parsnips lengthwise and slice into 5 cm chunks. Cook in boiling, salted water until tender. Drain.

Melt the butter in a saucepan. Add 3 rashers of finely chopped bacon and the peeled and chopped onion. Sauté until the onion is soft. Add the parsnips and mash with a fork. Add the 130 g of grated cheese and the cream with salt and pepper to taste. Beat well.

Tip the creamed parsnips into a greased baking dish. Smooth with a spatula. Combine the 50 g of grated cheese with the breadcrumbs. Sprinkle evenly over the surface. Cut the remaining rasher of bacon into small squares and place on top. Bake at 200°C for 25-35 minutes until the topping is golden-brown.

PARSNIP CHOWDER

Serves 6

- **3 rashers of bacon**
- **2 tb butter, if bacon is lean**
- **2 small onions, chopped**
- **2 c finely diced raw parsnip (2 small parsnips)**
- **½ c finely diced raw potato (1 small potato)**
- **2 c chicken stock**
- **2 c milk**
- **salt and pepper to taste**
- **2 tb chopped parsley**

Chop the bacon finely and fry with or without butter in a large saucepan. When lightly browned add the onion. Continue cooking without further browning until the onion is soft. Add the parsnips, potato and chicken stock. Simmer until the vegetables are tender. Remove from the heat. Add the milk and seasoning. Reheat gently. Serve sprinkled with parsley.

PARSNIP FLAN

Serves 8

The natural sweet flavour of parsnip is enhanced in this recipe. It is a dessert for parsnip lovers.

Pastry:

- **225 g flour**
- **½ tsp baking powder**
- **pinch of salt**
- **115 g butter**

Filling:

- **2 c mashed parsnip**
- **1 tb honey**
- **¼ tsp ground ginger**
- **¼ tsp mixed spice**
- **1 egg yolk**
- **2 lemons**

Topping:

- **1 egg white**
- **1 tb castor sugar**

Sift the flour, baking powder and salt into a bowl. Rub in the butter until the mixture resembles coarse breadcrumbs. Mix to a stiff dough with cold water. Roll out and line a 25 cm pie plate. Reserve left-over pastry to make a lattice topping.

Combine the parsnip, honey, ginger, mixed spice and egg yolk with the grated rind and juice of the lemons. Mix well. Spoon into the flan shell. Smooth the surface. Add thin strips of left-over pastry for a lattice topping. Bake at 190°C until the pastry is golden-brown.

Beat the egg white until stiff. Add the castor sugar and continue beating until it becomes stiff again. Place teaspoons of meringue mixture around the edge of the hot flan. Return to the oven (160°C) for 10-15 minutes to allow the meringues to dry a little and to be tinged brown.

Passionfruit

(Passiflora edulis)

Varieties

This beautiful and productive evergreen vine grows easily in warm, frost-free climates. If it is tucked under the eaves facing the morning sun it will flourish in areas subject to light frosts.

Cracker Jack is one of the most popular varieties with extra-large, sweet fruit. Nelly Kelly has smaller fruit but these have a stronger passionfruit flavour, smaller seeds and may be easier to grow. Hawaiian Yellow is not as popular and the yellow fruit often have a diseased appearance.

Cultivation

Finding the right site for this vine is most important. Passionfruit need rich soil, summer moisture, shelter from frosts and shelter from strong winds. If grown under the eaves they should not be exposed to excessive heat reflected back from the wall behind. Morning sun in this case would be more than adequate. Given ideal growing conditions the vine becomes a tangled mass of densely foliaged stems, unless allowed plenty of room. A screen or trellis 1.8 m high and 3 m long is suitable, or an overhead support system like a pergola. The vine climbs by tendrils and should be provided with wide-meshed netting on a screen or stout wires stretched across a pergola.

Buy grafted, container-grown plants as a precaution against collar rot. This disease can destroy a thriving ungrafted plant quite suddenly. The best time to plant is from late spring to early summer. Two cups of blood and bone should be mixed thoroughly into the planting hole and the vine should be set at the same depth as it was when growing in the container. Firm the topsoil around the roots and water well. Well-rotted compost or a balanced general fertilizer should be applied early in spring and again in early summer. Make sure the vine is well watered during summer dry spells, especially if it is growing under the eaves. Lack of water will cause the fruit to shrivel on the vine.

Young plants can be trained up the trellis in a fan shape with four leaders branching into approximately eight secondary leaders. Pinch out the growing tips when they reach the tops or ends of the support. This will encourage lateral fruiting growths.

Annual pruning of excess growth will ensure a healthier plant. The passionfruit vine bears its fruit on the current season's growth, so cut back old laterals 15-25 cm (or two buds) from the leader vine in the early spring. At the same time remove any weak or unwanted growth. After three to four growing seasons start replacing the main leaders one at a time.

The passionfruit vine is shallow rooted and should be cultivated carefully by shallow hoe-

Passionfruit
Each spring, cut laterals back to 2 buds from the leader
Leader

ing or weeding by hand. Keep the base well clear of foliage to maintain plant hygiene and lower the chance of disease. Watch out for snails and slugs — they love a young, tender vine.

Many serious diseases have made commercial production difficult but these diseases do not usually affect a lone passionfruit vine.

Harvesting

Harvesting the fragrant purple fruit takes place at the end of summer and continues through autumn. The fruit usually falls off when it is ripe and can sometimes be helped with a gentle shake. If required, a fully-coloured fruit can be picked with a small piece of stalk attached.

In the kitchen

Cut the fruit in half with a sharp knife. Remove the pulp with a teaspoon. Discard the skins.

Serve whole as fresh fruit, leaving the pulp to be scooped out with a teaspoon. You may like to sprinkle each half with a little sugar.

Use sweetened raw pulp as an icecream topping.

Add the pulp to fruit salads.

Use slightly sweetened as a cheesecake topping.

Add the pulp to breakfast muesli.

Mix the pulp with apples for a crumble pudding.

A favourite special occasion cake with our families is passionfruit sponge. We make a rich two-layer sponge, fill it with 300 ml of whipped cream and spread passionfruit icing on top.

PASSIONFRUIT ICING

1 tsp melted butter
1 c icing sugar
2 passionfruit

Add the melted butter to the sifted icing sugar. Add the passionfruit pulp gradually until the mixture is of spreading consistency.

PASSIONFRUIT CHIFFON PIE

Serves 8
Biscuit crumb shell:

2 c crushed vanilla biscuits (225 g packet)
115 g butter, melted
½ tsp grated nutmeg, optional
½ tsp cinnamon, optional

Combine the ingredients thoroughly and press into a 20-25 cm diameter tin with a removable base. An aluminium foil pie plate can also be used. Chill for 1 hour.

Filling:

1 c sugar
1 c water
2 eggs, separated
1 tb gelatine
2 tb water
½ c passionfruit pulp

Combine the sugar and cup of water in a small saucepan or a double boiler. Add the egg yolks and cook gently until the mixture thickens. Stir constantly and do not boil. Remove from the heat. Soften the gelatine in the 2 tb of water and add to the hot sugar mixture. Stir to dissolve thoroughly. Cool until the mixture begins to set. Add the passionfruit pulp and fold in the stiffly-beaten egg whites. Pour into the biscuit-crumb shell. Chill until firm. Garnish with whipped cream and a little extra passionfruit pulp sweetened with sugar.

PASSIONFRUIT HONEY

Delicious on bread or sponges or in tartlet cases.

pulp from 6 passionfruit
2 eggs
2 tb butter
1 c sugar

Combine all the ingredients in a pyrex measuring jug or the top part of a double boiler. Place in a saucepan of boiling water. Cook for 20 minutes, stirring continuously. The butter will become thick and creamy. Pour into small jars and seal when cold.

Freezing

Combine 50 g of sugar with1 c of passionfruit pulp. Mix thoroughly. Pour into plastic containers or ice-cube trays. Freeze. Store the cubes in freezer bags.

Bottling

Mix together thoroughly 1 c of sugar and 1 c of passionfruit pulp. Leave for 1 hour and stir again to dissolve the sugar. Pour into a clean jar. Cover with a plastic lid and store in a refrigerator.

Serve preserved passionfruit pulp with icecream, fruit salads, cheesecakes or pavlovas. It can be used instead of fresh pulp in most recipes but the quantity of sugar specified should be reduced.

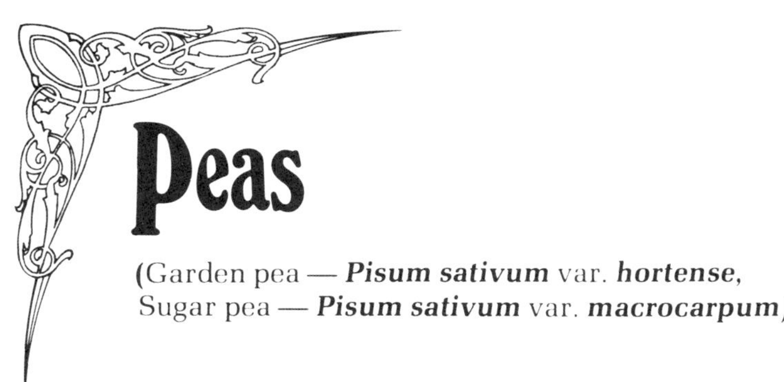

Peas

(Garden pea — ***Pisum sativum*** var. ***hortense***,
Sugar pea — ***Pisum sativum*** var. ***macrocarpum***)

Varieties

Most of our modern pea varieties are descendants of strains developed by British breeders over the last two centuries. The tall climber Telephone, for example, was the parent of Giant Alderman, one of the few climbers now available. Many variety names are actually synonymous such as Kelvedon Wonder, W.F. Massey, Earlicrop and Gem. The names Lincoln and Greenfeast also refer to a single variety.

Nowadays peas are sold according to the length of time they take to reach maturity. Hence early peas are described as maturing in 68-75 days in warm temperate areas (77-84 days in cool areas), second early peas are ready about one week later and maincrop peas one week later still. In fact the distinction between second early and maincrop is often not maintained in the home garden situation nor in seed catalogues, which describe Greenfeast as both second early and maincrop.

The most popular early pea is undoubtedly Kelvedon Wonder. It grows to 66 cm (less in cool areas) and once it has germinated it tolerates unsettled spring weather and the ravages of sparrows and slugs. Kelvedon Monarch (selected from Victory Freezer) is a good second early, growing up to 80 cm. Greenfeast is a little shorter (75 cm) and is one of the most popular peas of all. The standard maincrop pea is Onward, of similar height. Its pods are straight and blunt ended, unlike Greenfeast's curved, pointed ones.

Sugar peas, sometimes called mangetout or Chinese snow peas, are also available. Mammoth Melting Sugar grows to 150 cm and Dwarf Grey Sugar is about the same height as Greenfeast (75 cm).

Cultivation

Early crops of peas for harvesting at the beginning of summer should be grown in light, friable soil that warms up quickly but does not become waterlogged in heavy spring rains. This soil is not suitable for mid-to-late summer maincrop peas, however, because it is unable to hold the necessary moisture.

According to the soil type, the best compromise for a home gardener might be to lighten a clay loam with sand and compost and warm it with cloches for early sowings, and to enrich a sandy loam with large quantities of compost or peat to hold water in summer.

The ground should be deeply dug as pea roots penetrate right down through the topsoil in search of food and moisture. At sowing time a trench should be dug out 10 cm deep with a general fertilizer (see page 8) sprinkled along it. This trench should then be filled with friable topsoil. Lime may be needed if the ground has not been limed in the last year.

In most areas the first sowing is made in mid spring. If the ground is cold and wet (below 10°C) germination will be slow and uneven. This can be avoided by covering the bed with cloches or black plastic two to three weeks in advance. Otherwise delay sowing until late spring. Autumn sowings are made in areas where summers are too hot for a successful pea crop. They can also be made in cool, coastal areas where winters are not severe and spring sowings are delayed by cloudy weather and frequent light rain.

The traditional method is to make a flat-bottomed drill, 15-20 cm wide (a hoe's width) and 5-7 cm deep, into which the seeds are sown about 5 cm apart. For ease of picking space these drills at least 50 cm apart. Cover the seed with friable soil, water thoroughly and then cover the rows with wire netting or black cotton to prevent bird damage. Sparrows usually spot an emerging pea seedling before the gardener does, so protection must be arranged in advance.

When the plants are 10 cm high and growing strongly set up a framework to support them. Even dwarf peas benefit from a brushwood fence on either side of them or a series of stakes and strings. A single, central wire-netting support is not suitable for modern varieties which do not cling very tightly. A double row of fine-mesh netting with the peas inside is also inadvisable as it makes picking very awkward. We prefer 2 m hoops of strong fencing wire straddling the row at about 30 cm intervals. Peas need thorough watering at two critical times during growth: when the first flowers appear and when the pods are swelling. Keeping the ground moist around the roots in hot weather is important to prevent powdery mildew.

Harvesting

Holding a basket in one hand and pulling on the pods with the other usually breaks or bruises the pea vine. The two-handed approach is therefore essential — one pulling the pod and one firmly supporting the pod stalk. An old-

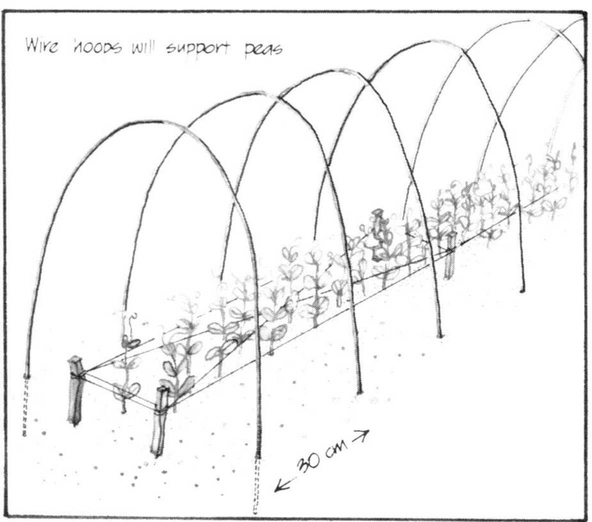
Wire hoops will support peas
30 cm

fashioned peg apron with a big deep pocket below the waist is ideal for pea picking, which should be done at regular intervals to keep production high. Once the pods begin to crinkle, the sugar in the peas converts to starch and the tender pea-flavour is lost. It is therefore most important to eat fresh peas as soon as possible after picking. If they must be kept overnight, store them in the refrigerator. When flowering is over keep any crinkled pods you may find. These can be dried on the vine for sowing next spring or for use in soups.

Sugar peas should be picked while the pods are still quite flat, with no sign of the pea seeds visible from the outside.

In the kitchen

Shelling peas is a pleasant task if carried out in the garden. Reserve a few pods to flavour soups and throw the remainder on the compost heap. Five hundred grams of unshelled peas yield about a cup of peas or sufficient for two servings.

Add the peas to a small quantity of boiling, salted water. A teaspoon of sugar and a sprig of mint may be added. Cover and simmer gently until they are just tender but still bright green. The simplest way to be sure they are cooked is to eat one or two — the cook's privilege.

Freshly-cooked peas are sweet and delicious when served with butter and pepper. A little finely-chopped mint further enhances the flavour. *Lemon and mint butter* is worth preparing if peas are to be on the menu often. Use 2 tb of finely chopped mint and the grated rind and juice of a lemon to flavour 100 g of softened butter.

Cold, leftover peas may be added to salads or mashed and seasoned to make a tasty sandwich filling.

PEAS IN ORANGE SAUCE

Serves 6

1 tsp cornflour
1 tb sugar
½ tsp salt
grated rind and juice of 2 oranges
1 tb butter
3 c shelled peas

Mix the cornflour, sugar and salt together in a small saucepan. Add the orange rind and juice and mix well. Heat, stirring constantly until thickened. Add the butter and stir until it is melted. Cook the peas, drain and tip them into a serving dish. Pour the hot sauce over the peas and serve immediately. The sauce may be prepared ahead of time and reheated before serving.

FRENCH-STYLE GREEN PEAS

Serves 6

Use the youngest peas possible, either straight from the garden or your own frozen supply. This dish is best served as a separate course so that its superb flavour can be appreciated.

2 rashers of bacon
6 spring onions (or 1 small mild onion)
2 tb butter
1 small lettuce
500 g shelled peas
½ c chicken stock
freshly-ground black pepper
¼ tsp sugar
salt to taste (if necessary)
sprig of parsley
sprig of mint
1 tb butter
1 dsp flour

Dice the bacon. Trim the spring onions and cut them in half. If you are using an onion, chop it finely. Melt the butter in a saucepan and sauté the bacon and onions until they are just beginning to colour. Shred the heart of lettuce and add to the saucepan. Add the peas, stock, seasoning and herbs. Cover the saucepan and simmer gently until the peas are just tender. Stir the contents of saucepan once during cooking time. Remove the parsley and mint stalks. Mix the butter and flour together and then add in small pieces to thicken the peas. Bring back to the boil. Turn into a serving dish.

PEAS AND HAM WITH CREAM

Serves 4-6

A dinner party vegetable dish.

120 g ham
1 medium-sized onion
1 tb butter
500 g peas, cooked
⅔ c cream
salt and pepper to taste
120 g grated cheese (Cheddar and Parmesan mixed)

Sauté the diced ham and finely-chopped onion in butter until the onion is soft. Add the cooked peas, cream and seasoning. Heat through gently. Pour into a greased, shallow ovenproof dish. Sprinkle with the cheese. Cook under a grill until the top is golden-brown. If you prefer you can make this dish ahead of time. Reheat it in a moderate oven for 15-20 minutes before browning the top, if necessary, under a grill.

PEAS AND PASTA

Serves 6

A colourful and satisfying lunch dish.

1 small onion, finely chopped
1 clove garlic, finely chopped
4 tb cooking oil
6 tomatoes, skinned and chopped
800 g peas in the pod
salt and pepper to taste
250 g spaghetti
1 tsp finely-chopped basil
1 c grated Cheddar cheese

Sauté the onion and garlic in the oil for 5

minutes. Add the tomatoes and cook until they start to soften. Add the shelled peas and seasoning. Cover and simmer, stirring occasionally, for 20-30 minutes until the peas are tender. Meanwhile, cook the spaghetti in a large saucepan of boiling, salted water until it is just tender. Drain. Dish up the spaghetti into a warmed serving bowl, cover with the pea and tomato sauce and sprinkle with basil and grated cheese.

QUICK PEA SOUP

Serves 6

A family soup to serve on a cold day

3 c shelled peas, fresh or frozen
4 c chicken stock
a large sprig of mint
1 tsp sugar
salt and pepper to taste
1 c milk
2 tb butter
1 tsp cornflour
6 small frankfurters

Put the peas in a large saucepan and add the stock, mint, sugar and seasoning. Bring to the boil and simmer until the peas are tender. Put through a fine sieve or blender. Return to the saucepan and add the milk and butter. Mix the cornflour with a little water. Add to the soup and stir until it is just boiling. Remove from the heat. Skin the frankfurters and slice thinly. Ladle the soup into bowls and garnish with the frankfurters.

Sugar Peas

Rinse freshly harvested pods. Top and tail and remove the strings. Allow 100 g for each serving.

Cook in a little boiling, salted water until tender. Drain and serve with plenty of butter, freshly-ground black pepper and a pinch of sugar.

Sugar peas may also be butter-steamed. Melt 2 tb of butter in a heavy-based frying pan with a lid. Add the sugar peas and 4 tb of water. Cover tightly and cook until just tender. Season well with salt, pepper and sugar and serve immediately.

Sugar peas are most attractive in Chinese dishes. Add to Chinese-Style Vegetables (see page 206).

Freezing

Deterioration is rapid after harvesting so speed with processing is important. Blanch shelled peas for 1 minute, cool rapidly and pack into freezer bags in meal-sized quantities. Do not thaw before cooking.

Sugar peas may also be frozen. Blanch prepared pods for 2 minutes.

Peppers

(Capsicum annuum var. *annuum)*

Varieties

The mild sweet pepper which has become increasingly popular in the last ten years was first domesticated in Mexico, possibly a thousand years before the beginning of the Christian era. The most popular standard varieties are California Wonder which grows about 60-76 cm high and Yolo Wonder, slightly shorter at 45-60 cm. New hybrids have been developed for earlier cropping and reliable fruit setting under cool conditions. Wondergiant F.1. Hybrid is particularly adaptable and grows into a sturdy plant 45-50 cm high with glossy green fruits which eventually turn red. Golden Bell F.1. Hybrid (50-60 cm) produces early crops of extremely attractive, dark-golden fruit.

Hot pungent chilli peppers form a separate branch of the Capsicum family. Long Red Cayenne is one of the few varieties available to the home gardener. It grows 45-60 cm high and its long thin fruits start off glossy dark green, ripening to red.

Cultivation

If tomatoes and cucumbers can be successfully grown outdoors in your area, peppers are worth trying in a warm sheltered position. The main problem to overcome is the very long growing season from seed to harvest. The temperature should stay about 15-18°C if growth is to be steady during the eight to ten weeks when the seedlings are in peat pots. Once they are out in the garden or in patio tubs the weather should be settled and warm for the nine to 12 weeks that they need to fill out the first fruit. Even in warm areas seed is therefore usually raised indoors or in a glasshouse for planting out in late spring to early summer. Because the plants resent root disturbance, Jiffy pots almost buried in coarse sand or gravel-filled trays make ideal nursery beds. The pots are sunk in the ground to discourage the growth of green algae during this long period. Sow three seeds per pot and retain the strongest.

The garden site should be a friable, warm, rich loam, well drained but with enough fine peat or compost worked into it to release moisture slowly. A tomato fertilizer mixture should be scuffled into the ground just before planting. The plants should be spaced 30-60 cm apart with 60 cm between rows. Six or eight plants are usually sufficient for a family of four.

Peppers thrive in warm, humid conditions and they will not set fruit readily in very dry weather. The soil beneath them should therefore be kept moist and the plants sprayed with a fine mist when the flowers are open. Swelling fruit benefits from a liquid foliar fertilizer. This will also inhibit aphid and red spider infestations.

Big bushy plants grown in subtropical con-

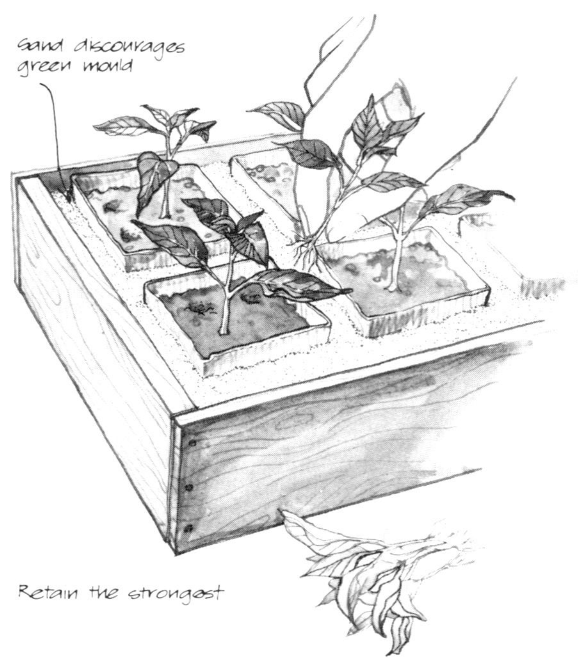
Sand discourages
green mould
Retain the strongest

ditions should be allowed to set as many peppers as possible. These are picked while green skinned in order to keep the plant in production until winter. Growers in marginal areas often restrict their plants to four to six fruits to enable these to attain a good size before cold weather stops growth in autumn.

Harvesting
Sweet peppers are usually picked green, early in the season, while later they may be left to change to their bright-red or yellow autumn colourings. Hot peppers are usually left until they turn bright red, to develop their pungent flavour.

In the kitchen
Wash the peppers. Cut around the calyx and ease out the stem, core and most of the seeds. If the pepper is to remain whole rinse out any remaining seeds. Using a small spoon, trim away any bitter white pith. For sliced or diced peppers, cut in half, remove any seeds, trim away the pith and cut into the desired size. Allow a half to one whole pepper for each serving.

Finely-diced or sliced raw peppers add texture to green salads. To serve as an appetizer, slice into thin rings, add French dressing and a few black olives. Thin rings can also be used to garnish many vegetable dishes. Bright-green, red and now yellow peppers, provide vivid colour contrasts.

PEPERONI
Serves 4-6
This colourful vegetable dish may be served with grills. When peppers are plentiful it is a good dish to freeze. Double or treble the recipe and divide the mixture among foil containers. To serve, place unthawed in the oven at 180°C for 20-30 minutes until heated through.

2 green peppers
2 red peppers
2 tb butter
1 medium-sized onion, sliced
1 clove garlic, finely chopped
½ tsp salt

Slice the peppers very thinly. Blanch for 3 minutes. Drain. Melt the butter in a medium-sized frying pan. Add the onion and garlic and sauté until soft. Add the peppers and salt and continue cooking until they are tender.

PIPÉRADE
Serves 4-6
This egg dish from the Basque region of France can be served on toast as a simple lunch dish, or dressed up for a more formal meal with a slice of grilled or fried ham.

2 red or green peppers
2 tb butter
2 small onions, thinly sliced
2 cloves garlic, finely chopped
4 large tomatoes
2 medium-sized potatoes, boiled and diced
6 eggs
salt and pepper to taste
chopped parsley to garnish

Cut prepared peppers into strips and blanch for 5 minutes. Drain well. Melt the butter in a large, heavy frying pan and cook the onions and garlic until they are soft and golden-brown. Add the pepper strips and cook gently for 10 minutes. Peel the tomatoes and chop roughly. Add to the frying pan and cook for 5 minutes. Add the cooked, diced potatoes. Beat the eggs and seasoning. Stir into the vegetable mixture. Cook as you would scrambled eggs until the mixture is just set and creamy. Sprinkle with parsley for serving.

STUFFED PEPPERS

Peppers make colourful containers for serving savoury mixtures. We have included two different versions which we enjoy. They can be served as a luncheon dish or instead of the usual meat course at dinner. They are too filling to serve as an entrée.

Blanch prepared peppers for 3 minutes. Lift them out carefully and cool under running water. Drain upside down. Pat dry. Fill with the selected stuffing. Stand closely together in a greased ovenproof dish with a lid. Cover and bake at 180°C for 20-30 minutes until the filling is heated through and the pepper is tender.

Corn and rice stuffing (for 4 peppers):

1 onion, finely chopped
2 tb butter
2 chopped tomatoes
1 c cooked rice
1 c whole-kernel corn, cooked
½ tsp salt
freshly-ground black pepper

Sauté the onion in butter. Add the tomatoes and cook until they are tender. Add the rice, corn and seasoning. Cook as above.

Ham, mushroom and rice stuffing (for 5 peppers):

1 onion, finely chopped
2 tb butter
120 g raw, long-grained rice
50 g mushrooms, sliced
100 g cooked ham, chopped
salt and pepper to taste
400 ml chicken stock
400 ml tomato purée

In a small ovenproof dish with a lid, sauté the onion with 1 tb of the butter. Cook until soft. Add the rice and stir over a low heat for 2 minutes. Add the mushrooms and ham. Pour in the stock, check the seasoning and bring to the boil. Cover and bake at 180°C for about 20 minutes or until the rice is tender and the stock is absorbed. Stir in the remaining 1 tb of butter. Fill the peppers and pack them upright in a casserole. Heat the tomato purée and pour this over and around the peppers. Cook as above.

BEEF WITH RED AND GREEN PEPPERS

Serves 6

1 kg braising steak
oil for frying
1 large onion, thinly sliced
1½ c stock
100 g mushrooms, sliced
2 sticks of celery, cut into pieces 3 cm long and 0.5 cm thick
1 green pepper
1 red pepper (or another green pepper)
1 tsp cornflour
1 tb soy sauce
salt and pepper to taste

Cut the meat into neat 2 cm cubes. Fry until brown in hot oil in a large frying pan. Take out the meat. Add the onion and fry until golden. Return the meat to the pan with the stock. Cover and simmer gently for 50-60 minutes until the meat is tender. Add the mushrooms and celery. Simmer for 5 minutes. Dice the prepared peppers and add to the pan. Mix the cornflour with a little water. Stir into the meat mixture. Add the soy sauce and check the seasoning. Cook for 2 minutes. Serve on boiled rice.

Freezing

Peppers freeze very well. They can be frozen whole for stuffing or cut into slices or diced for adding to casseroles and egg dishes. Cooked dishes such as Peperoni (see page 150) or Ratatouille (see page 205) also freeze well. Blanching is optional. We only blanch whole peppers for stuffing.

Potatoes

(Solanum tuberosum)

Varieties

There are many varieties of potato grown in home and market gardens. Most home gardeners make their choice from "early" varieties which are harvested and used soon after flowering while the skins are still very thin. Early potatoes are much more expensive to buy than maincrop ones so gardeners with small plots concentrate on raising one or two rows as an early summer treat and money-saver. It is advisable to check that the variety you have chosen is suitable for your soil type and locality, for some varieties produce large watery tubers in wet regions while others crop poorly in light soils. Garden shops, farmers' supply stores and neighbours will be able to build up a list of what can be grown locally. Popular early varieties include Jersey Bennes in cool areas, Epicure and Cliffs Kidney (good on medium soils or peat). These should not be grown to maturity as they are very susceptible to blight, break up on boiling and lose their fine flavour.

Some potato varieties, such as Arran Banner, are good for eating at all stages. This type is suited to light soils while Katahdin (sometimes called Chippewa) is suited to alluvial soils and Ilam Hardy to medium to heavy soils. Katahdin is waxy while immature, later becoming floury and good for baking. In cool areas, Red King Edward can be grown both for early and maincrop harvesting but, as an early potato, it does not have the "new potato" flavour nor the waxy flesh of Jersey Bennes.

Dakota Red and Glen Ilam are often grown for maincrop potatoes in areas of light soils, but both require regular spraying against blight. Tahi is blight resistant, however, and thrives on light soils which receive abundant spring rainfall but dry out in summer and autumn. Arran Chief and Arran Consul are suited to medium to heavy soil but are now not so commonly grown as Ilam Hardy. One of our favourite New Zealand varieties is the Rua which is blight resistant, keeps for months and has an excellent flavour. It boils and bakes equally well and its tendency to mature into very large tubers can be controlled by closer planting.

Occasionally one can obtain varieties of considerable historical interest. In our part of the world for instance, the "Maori" potato is still grown in certain areas. It is purple skinned with deep eyes and delicious waxy flesh. It sometimes shows signs of virus infection (yellow streaks on leaves and small tubers) and infected plants of this or of any non-commercial variety should be eliminated as soon as the symptoms appear. As a general rule, government certified seed should be used at least every second year for your main potato requirements.

Cultivation

It is widely recognised that potatoes grown in a deeply-dug, friable loam enriched with abundant organic matter, taste better and show more resistance to disease than those fed with inorganic fertilizers. The best preparation for a potato patch is to dig it roughly in autumn and cover it with leaves, sawdust, stable manure or seaweed which will break down over the winter months. Alternatively, dig in a late summer-sown green crop such as mustard, oats or lupins.

At planting time, cultivate the soil thoroughly and make 15 cm-deep trenches with a draw hoe. Sprinkle the bottom of the trench with equal quantities of superphosphate and blood and bone (½ c of each per plant) and then half-fill with peat or fine compost. The seed potatoes are then pushed into position, eyes (or sprouts) uppermost, and the trench filled with friable topsoil. The top of each tuber should be about 5 cm below the surface. In "no dig" gardens place the tubers on a bed of moist, decomposed hay or leaves and cover with dry straw at least 10 cm deep (see page).

For an early start some gardeners plant pre-sprouted potatoes. In late winter place the tubers (with the old stem scar end underneath) in flat boxes in a light sunny position where the temperature is fairly steady between 5 and 10°C. In six to eight weeks several sprouts will be protruding from each tuber. These should be short and thick. Leave two to three sprouts on each tuber, rubbing off any weaker ones. Check the sprouts occasionally for aphid infestation, spraying if necessary with pyrethrum or dipping them into soapy water. Sprouted tubers should be planted very carefully with soft soil pushed around the sprouts before the trench is refilled. Otherwise they can be damaged by any hard lumps in the soil.

Spacing depends on whether you are growing early or maincrop potatoes and also on the particular variety. If you have plenty of seed potatoes and want the maximum return for a given area plant 30 cm apart in rows 60 cm apart. To obtain a maximum yield from each plant increase the space to 45 cm between plants and 75 cm between rows. Varieties which display a tendency towards very large tubers (so big they are hard to peel) should be planted with the closer spacing.

It is still common practice to earth up potatoes. This keeps the tubers well away from light which turns them green and poisonous. Earthing up can be done in one or two stages when the plants are 25 cm tall. Using a hoe or cultivator, draw soil from between the rows until the tops are about two-thirds buried. This

Pre-sprout potatoes in light spot for early start

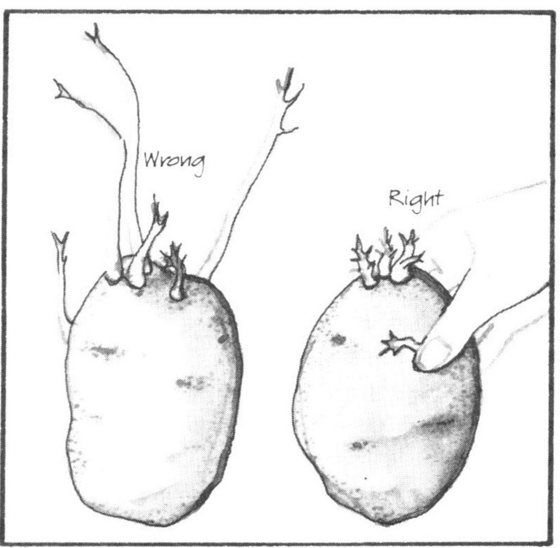

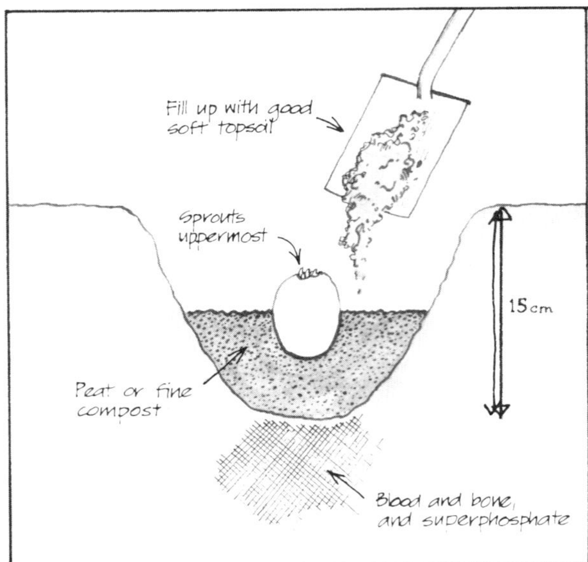

Earth up to prevent light reaching tubers

operation weeds between the rows and, if growth is rapid, no more weeding will be necessary.

Potatoes have only one critical period when water is very important and that is at flowering time. If rainfall is inadequate, a thorough soaking at that time will ensure that the process of tuber bulking gets under way. Too much water coupled with cool moist weather can favour the rapid spread of blight in susceptible varieties. You should therefore refrain from watering the foliage, especially in spring and early autumn, and protect the crop with fortnightly treatments of copper oxychloride spray. Some gardeners spray after each spell of rain. Aphids, which are responsible for spreading virus diseases, also need to be kept in check. Growing potatoes in a windy part of the garden will make it difficult for winged aphids to spread through the crop.

Harvesting

Start digging new potatoes when they are flowering and the lowest leaves begin to show signs of turning yellow. Get them out of the ground before they reach maturity or succumb to blight. Maincrop potatoes are ready when the tops begin to die off and collapse on the ground. "Organic" gardeners sometimes find that the tops stay green until the first frost knocks them back. If this is the case examine the tubers as a guide to maturity. They should be thick skinned and no longer able to be scraped. Try to arrange to lift them in a period of dry weather in mid autumn before the first frost arrives. Provided the tubers are mature, unbruised, and dry they will store well through the winter.

Choose a dark, frost-proof location, cool but not too dry. Large flat boxes placed on bricks in an earth-floored basement are ideal. Cover the tubers with dry sacks and inspect regularly, removing any rotting ones.

In the kitchen

The age of a potato will determine how it should be prepared and what cooking methods are most suitable. Freshly-dug early potatoes only require scrubbing, while stored or "old" potatoes should be scraped or peeled. Cut out any blemishes or eyes with a small sharp knife. Allow 500 g of potatoes to serve four.

The basic cooking methods of boiling, mashing, roasting and baking need no explanation. Our favourite potato variations add interest to this useful vegetable.

NEW POTATOES AND MINT BAKED IN FOIL

Serves 4

500 g small new potatoes
4 fresh mint leaves
½ tsp salt
freshly-ground black pepper
2 tb butter

Remove the skins from the potatoes. If recently dug the skin will come off with a scrubbing brush, otherwise scrape clean. Dry thoroughly. Lay them in the centre of a large piece of greased foil on a baking sheet. Place the mint leaves in and on the pile. Season and dot with butter. Seal the foil tightly. Bake at 200°C for 1 hour.

NEW POTATOES WITH LEMON AND GARLIC

Serves 5-6

750 g new potatoes
2 cloves garlic, finely chopped
grated rind of one lemon
1 tsp salt
freshly-ground black pepper
3 tb cooking oil
1 c milk

Scrape and slice the potatoes thinly. Grease an ovenproof dish. Layer the potatoes with the garlic, lemon rind, seasoning and oil. Add the milk. Bake uncovered at 200°C for 45-60 minutes until tender and golden-brown.

HELEN'S HEDGEHOG POTATOES

1 medium-sized "old" potato per serving
cooking oil
salt and pepper

Peel the potatoes. Using a sharp knife, make several parallel cuts about 1 cm apart down into the flesh. Cut almost to the base but be careful not to cut right through. Make another series of cuts at right angles to the first. Place the potatoes in a shallow ovenproof dish. Brush each one with oil and season well. Bake at 190°C for about 1 hour or until they are golden-brown and tender. The cuts widen with cooking giving the potato a spiky appearance, hence the name. Chopped rosemary, thyme or dried herbs may be sprinkled on before cooking.

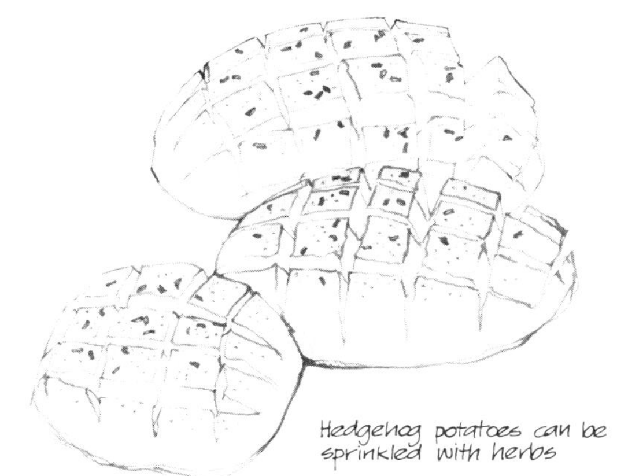
Hedgehog potatoes can be sprinkled with herbs

The next two recipes are for scalloped potatoes: the first an everyday version and the second a rich, creamy dish to serve for special occasions.

SCALLOPED POTATOES

Serves 6-8

An old favourite.

800 g old potatoes
2 small onions
2 tb flour
2 tb butter
1 tsp salt
freshly-ground black pepper
300 ml milk

Peel the potatoes and onions and slice thinly. Grease a deep covered ovenproof dish. A large dish is required as boiling over can be a problem. Place one-third of the potatoes in a layer at the bottom. Cover with half the onions, 1 tb of flour, ½ tsp of salt, a little pepper and 1 tb of the butter cut into small pieces. Add another layer of potatoes, keeping enough slices for the top. Cover with the remaining onions, flour, salt, pepper and butter. Place the remaining potato slices neatly over the top. Pour in the milk. Cover the dish and bake at 200°C for about 50 minutes until the potato slices are tender and the milk is absorbed. Remove the lid and bake a little longer to brown the top.

POTATOES AU GRATIN

Serves 8

1 kg medium-sized old or new potatoes
140 g grated cheese, tasty Cheddar or Gruyère
1½ tsp salt
freshly-ground black pepper
freshly-grated nutmeg
1 egg
300 ml cream

Scrape or peel the potatoes and slice thinly. Grease a deep ovenproof dish. Fill it with alternate layers of potatoes, cheese, salt, pepper and nutmeg. Reserve a little cheese for the topping. Beat the egg and cream together and pour over the potatoes. Finish with a good sprinkling of cheese. Bake at 180°C for 50-60 minutes. New potatoes will take a little longer. If the top browns before the potatoes are cooked, cover with a piece of foil.

YOGHURT OR SOUR CREAM DRESSING

½ c yoghurt or sour cream
1 tb lemon juice
½ tsp paprika
salt to taste

Combine the ingredients and mix well.

FRIED POTATOES OR CHIPS

This method provides crisp, golden chips without deep frying. The chips are cooked in a large frying pan with a lid by a combination of direct heat to brown the surfaces and steam to cook the interior.

Peel large old potatoes. Cut into very thin chip shapes (no thicker than 1 cm) or into 5 mm slices. Heat 2 tb of butter and 1 tb of cooking oil in a large frying pan with a tight fitting lid. Add the potatoes and season well with freshly-ground black pepper and salt (garlic salt is delicious). Cover and cook over moderate heat until they are browned on one side. Turn the potatoes over with a fish slice and continue cooking until most of the surfaces are browned and the potatoes are tender. You will need to turn them several times. If they are not crisp enough, cook for a few minutes longer without the lid. Drain on absorbent paper and serve immediately. Try cooking with a light sprinkling of finely-chopped rosemary or lemon thyme.

POTATO HERB FRITTERS

Serves 6

2 eggs
1 large rasher of bacon
1 shallot or small onion
2 tb mixed chopped herbs (parsley, rosemary, marjoram, tarragon, lemon thyme)
½ tsp salt
½ tsp garlic salt
freshly-ground black pepper
500 g old potatoes, peeled and grated
4 tb flour
cooking oil for frying

In a basin mix the eggs, finely-chopped bacon and shallot, herbs, salt, garlic salt and pepper. Add the potatoes and the flour. Mix thoroughly. Avoid allowing the mixture to stand before cooking. Fry spoonfuls of the mixture in hot cooking oil until they are browned on both sides. Drain on absorbent paper. Serve hot.

POTATO SALAD

Serves 6

Boil 750 g of new potatoes in their skins until they are just tender. Drain and, as soon as they are cool enough to handle, peel and cut into slices, quarters or cubes. While they are still warm, coat with 3 tb of French dressing and sprinkle with scissored chives or spring onions. Leave for several hours.

Just before serving add extra French dressing or the yoghurt or sour cream dressing on this page.

Other ingredients such as strips of green pepper, tomato wedges, diced celery, olives, strips or slices of salami and radishes may be added just before serving. Garnish with chopped parsley, scissored chives or paprika.

Pumpkins and winter squash

(Cucurbita maxima, Cucurbita moschata, Cucurbita pepo)

Varieties

These are grouped together because they grow over the summer months, are harvested in autumn when the fruits are mature and hard-skinned and they provide many tasty meals throughout the winter. The most common pumpkin types grown in New Zealand are Whangaparaoa Crown with a hard, grey skin, Triamble (a three-lobed type) with grey-green skin and the blue-grey Queensland Blue. These three keep well but their vigorous vines take up a lot of room in the vegetable garden.

Each plant needs a 2.5 x 2.5 m square of growing space but, if left unchecked, will ramble over all your other vegetables. If you have some waste ground or an old, weedy vegetable plot this will make an ideal pumpkin patch. Modern seed catalogues are listing more semi-bush pumpkin types, which occupy much less space. We have tried the Spirit F.1. Hybrid which has a 0.5 m spread.

Winter squash are not quite so hardy as the pumpkin and the larger types need at least five months frost-free to reach maturity. The large Hubbard squashes are oblong and pointed with warted green or golden skins. The smaller Buttercup squash is turban shaped while the popular Butternut is pear shaped with only a small seed cavity. These squashes are grown on rambling vines. The most successful bush squash has dark-green, acorn-shaped fruit up to 15 cm long and 13 cm across. Table Queen and Table King are good varieties of this type.

Leave 5cm of stalk
Note small seed cavity

Gold Nugget is an excellent bush squash producing small hard skinned fruits. The flesh is a bright orange and very dry

Cultivation

We have had good results raising seed in 7 cm diameter peat pots on a sunny window sill. Peat pots are ideal because they disintegrate in the ground when planted out and there is no disturbance to the roots. Fill the pots with seed-raising or potting mix and push two or three seeds end on into the soil. Keep them moist and warm (15-20°C) and germination will begin in as little as three days. At cooler temperatures it may take two to three weeks. When the first true leaves appear remove the weaker plants, generally those with spindly stems. Some plants may fail to produce true leaves so thinning out must be delayed until sufficient time has elapsed. Harden off the plants after two weeks by moving them outside under the eaves or into a mini-glasshouse. Do not plant the pots in the open ground until the weather is warm and all danger of frost is past.

Vine types can be grown on ridges or hills with 1.5 m spacing between plants in rows and 2.5 m between hills. Prepare the planting spot by digging in at least one bucket of compost or well-rotted farmyard manure. One cup of blood and bone and one of superphosphate can be sprinkled around the surface of the mound. In areas where the summer is very dry, extra watering can be allowed for by sinking a large tin (with holes punched in the sides and base) or an empty clay pot into the centre of the mound or beside each plant in the ridge. This decreases the danger of spreading mildew by hosing the leaves. As the fruit ripens it should be lifted clear of damp ground and supported on dry straw or pieces of wood. Mulching is commonly used in pumpkin and squash cultivation. Black plastic can be spread over the whole patch and the compost and peat pot inserted through holes cut in the plastic. A pine-needle, old hay or straw mulch also helps to retain moisture around the roots while keeping the humidity low around the leaves and fruit.

Pinching out the tips of leading shoots is sometimes practised to encourage laterals (the flower-bearing parts) but this is usually necessary only where the plant is making too much leaf growth. If extra-large fruit are required, thin the number of fruit set to one to three per plant. Occasionally hand pollination is needed in cool weather. This is done by rubbing a male flower with the petals removed into a female flower (which has a tiny pumpkin at its base).

Bush pumpkins and squash can also be grown on ridges or mounds. Try three to four plants on a 1 x 1 m mound.

Harvesting

You can usually tell when pumpkins and squash are mature by colour changes where the fruit touches the ground, slight shrivelling of the stem and the reduction of the number of leaves on the plant. In any case, harvesting should take place before the first frost and the fruit should be cut off leaving 5 cm of stem attached. Dry off the stem by leaving the fruit in a sunporch or on the window sill for a few days. Store the fruit in a warm dry place without too much light. Check regularly through the winter months for signs of rot.

In the kitchen

Pumpkins and squash can be put to many varied uses in the kitchen, for example in jam making, in soup, as a vegetable and in dessert pies and scones.

PUMPKIN SOUP

Serves 4-6

500 g peeled pumpkin or squash
1 medium-sized onion
1 tb butter
½ tsp freshly-grated nutmeg
salt and pepper to taste
600 ml chicken stock

Boil the peeled, chopped pumpkin and the sliced onion together in a minimum of water until tender. Put through a blender or fine sieve. Return to saucepan and add the butter, seasoning and stock. Reheat. The soup may be thickened with a little cornflour mixed with water. Serve sprinkled with chopped parsley.

Use a dry and brightly-coloured pumpkin or squash for the following vegetable recipes.

BAKED PUMPKIN WITH CREAM AND CINNAMON

Serves 4-6

500 g pumpkin, peeled and cut into 1 cm cubes
½ tsp salt
freshly-ground black pepper
3 dsp brown sugar
200 ml cream
1 tsp cinnamon

Place the pumpkin in a well-greased casserole. Sprinkle with salt, pepper and brown sugar. Pour the cream over the pumpkin and sprinkle with cinnamon. Cover and bake at 180°C for 1 hour until the pumpkin is tender.

The next recipe combines pumpkin with potatoes. Serve it as a colourful lunch or tea dish. It can also accompany meat for dinner. Cooking two vegetables together saves on fuel and washing up.

HELEN'S PUMPKIN AND POTATO CASSEROLE

Serves 6

500 g pumpkin, peeled and cut into 1 cm cubes
500 g potatoes, peeled and cut into 1 cm cubes
2 tb cooking oil
1 clove garlic
salt and pepper
pinch of chilli powder, or more to taste
2 c tomato purée

Pour the oil into a deep casserole. Tip gently so that the oil covers the sides. Layer the pumpkin and potato, add the finely-chopped garlic then the salt, pepper and chilli powder to taste. Pour in the tomato purée (this should come about half-way up the casserole). Cover and bake at 200°C for 45-60 minutes. When cooked, the pumpkin will have combined with the tomato purée and the potato cubes will be tender. Garnish with chopped parsley.

MASHED PUMPKIN FOR DESSERTS AND BAKED PRODUCTS

400 g of raw unpeeled pumpkin will make about a cup of cooked mashed pumpkin. There are two methods: boil the peeled and cut pumpkin in a little water until it is tender. Strain and mash. Or place unpeeled wedges in a baking dish skin side down and bake at 180°C until tender (about 30-45 minutes). Scoop out the pumpkin and mash it with a fork.

Pumpkin seems to have a natural affinity for spices. Traditional American pumpkin pie is a good example.

AMERICAN PUMPKIN PIE

Serves 6

Shortcrust pastry:

225 g self-raising flour
pinch salt
130 g butter

Sift the flour and salt into a bowl. Rub in the butter. Add sufficient water to make a stiff dough. Roll this out and line a 25 cm pie plate, overlapping the edge by 2 cm. Tuck the edge under and crimp the pie edge up to increase the height. Chill while preparing the filling.

Filling:

1 c mashed, cooked pumpkin
100 g brown sugar
pinch salt
1 tsp cinnamon
½ tsp ginger
freshly-grated nutmeg
2 small eggs
100 ml milk
100 ml cream

Mix the sugar, salt and spices together. Beat the eggs and stir in the milk, cream and mashed pumpkin. Add the sugar and spices. Stir to combine. Pour into the pie shell. Bake at 190°C for 45-50 minutes until the filling is set. Cool a little before serving with whipped cream.

GRANNY BROWNE'S PUMPKIN SCONES

These scones will be a beautiful orange colour if brightly-coloured pumpkin is used. Don't tell the family what is in them until they ask for more.

2 tb butter
½ c sugar
1 egg
1 c cold mashed pumpkin
3 c flour
3 tsp cream of tartar
1½ tsp baking soda
¼-½ c milk

Beat the butter and sugar. Add the egg and beat well. Add the mashed pumpkin. Sift the flour, cream of tartar and baking soda and add to the pumpkin mixture. Stir, adding sufficient milk to make a slightly softer-than-usual scone dough. Pat out to about 1.5 cm thick and cut into 12 to 16 pieces. Place on a cold, greased oven slide. Bake at 220°C for 10-15 minutes.

In jam making, pumpkins can reduce costs by extending expensive fruits. You cannot see or even taste the pumpkin in this apricot jam.

DRIED APRICOT AND PUMPKIN JAM

225 g dried apricots
700 ml water
450 g good-coloured pumpkin
8 tb lemon juice
1 kg sugar

Soak the dried apricots overnight in 500 ml of water. Next day peel the pumpkin and cut it up roughly into small pieces. Cook gently in the remainder of the water with the lemon juice until it is quite soft. Add the apricots with their water and cook about 10-15 minutes longer. Add the sugar, stirring until it is dissolved. Boil until setting point is reached (about 25 minutes). Pour into warm jars and seal with jam covers.

Freezing

As pumpkins and winter squash keep so well there is normally no value in freezing them. It is useful, however, to freeze small quantities of mashed, cooked pumpkin for using in desserts and baking.

Radishes

(Raphanus sativus)

Varieties

Many of the radish varieties available are quick-maturing, salad types. They range from round, red ones with names like Champion Globe, Stoplight and Cherry Belle to long, tapering radishes either white, as in Long White Icicle or red, as in Long Scarlet. In between are the two-toned red and white radishes: Sparkler is round and the popular French Breakfast is like an elongated turnip with a blunt end. These radishes mature in 28 to 42 days in early summer conditions. Champion Globe is worth trying in light soils and it is reputed to stand a little longer before becoming hot and stringy. Cherry Belle has the added virtue of resistance to pithiness.

One of the few winter radishes available is China Rose. It is sown in mid-to-late summer to stand in the garden over winter. It grows about 15 cm long, larger than the summer radishes and needs eight to nine weeks to reach maturity.

Cultivation and harvesting

Radishes thrive on rich soil which has been worked to a fine tilth over the top 10-15 cm. It must be capable of holding moisture so peat or sieved mature compost should be added. Sand should be worked into a heavy clay loam to increase its friability. The seed can be sown as soon as the ground warms up in spring but, unless the nights are cool (temperatures falling below 12-15°C), radishes tend to go to seed without making a "bulb".

Sow the seed directly into the garden with 2-5 cm between seeds and 10-20 cm between rows. The drills should be even and no deeper than 12 mm. Keep the radishes well watered and weeded. Once they dry out they become unpleasantly hot to taste.

Picking is usually spread over two weeks. Successional sowing of small quantities is best.

Winter radishes should be grown under similar conditions of soil and moisture. Make the drills 15-20 cm apart and thin the plants to 15-23 cm apart. They can be harvested right through the winter.

In the kitchen

Quick-maturing radishes: Pull the radishes just before they are needed. Wash well. Cut off the leaves and roots and place radishes on a plate with a small container of salt for dipping. Serve radishes this way as a crisp appetizer or snack.

Add whole, quartered or sliced radishes to salads to give colour, flavour and texture.

Use finely-chopped radishes as a topping for hot or chilled summer soups.

Winter radishes: Freshly-pulled winter radishes should be washed and peeled thinly. Slice, grate or cut into matchstick strips and add to salads or cook in casseroles.

Rhubarb

(Rheum rhaponticum)

Varieties

Rhubarb varieties are divided into early, main crop and ever-bearing types. If you are able to buy rhubarb crowns or raise the plants from seed you should choose the varieties to give a maximum cropping period from early winter to mid summer. Ever-bearing varieties are often most vigorous in winter but do not make the mistake of cutting the same plant throughout the year as this practice reduces vitality and future yield. Varieties that die down over winter are normally harvested when growth is at its peak in spring and early summer. These need to be left alone for the rest of the summer in order to store up energy in the crown for the next spring's leaves.

A good ever-bearing rhubarb is Topp's Winter while Giant Victoria and Oregon Giant are main crop varieties. Most people acquire rhubarb crowns from relatives and friends and their variety names are unknown. You might even inherit a genuine Early Albert or Hogan's Shillelagh in the garden of an older home.

Cultivation

Whatever the variety, rhubarb is only tender, crisp and juicy if well fed with bulky animal manure and compost. When planting out the crowns, dig a deep trench (75 cm) in a moist but well-drained part of the garden and fill it two-thirds full with old farmyard manure or mature compost. Top up with good soil so that the crown is just covered. If you are planting a winter-dormant variety leave the crown in a cool, shady place until the buds begin to appear on the crown. Then, using a sharp spade, divide the crown into sections each with one to two buds and plant the sections about 1 m apart with the buds just showing through the soil. If establishing an ever-bearing type, plant the sections as soon as possible after division, preferably in early winter. Never leave the crowns of this type exposed.

General maintenance of rhubarb clumps involves an annual dressing of farmyard manure in autumn and a cup of blood and bone in spring or summer after cropping is finished. Remove the flower heads before they open, trim off decaying leaves and control perennial weeds by careful weeding. Where dry summers are experienced rhubarb plants appreciate a mulch of straw, sawdust, or lawn clippings applied *before* the ground begins to dry out. Clumps should be divided when the stalk sbecome thin and weak.

Harvesting

If you can bear to wait, it is best not to start using your rhubarb until it has had a year to become well established or, in the case of plants grown from seed, two years. Harvesting the stalks too early may weaken the crown. In the second year start pulling but not too frequently. This danger can be avoided by having enough plants to adequately supply the family. If you want to freeze rhubarb for winter use or make jam, we suggest a minimum of six healthy plants for a family of four to six. To pull rhubarb stalks, twist carefully away at ground level. Never cut the stalks as this can lead to rotting of the crowns.

Cut off flower heads
Don't eat leaves: they are toxic
Twist leaves away from crown
Remove all dead leaves and stalks

In the kitchen

Young rhubarb stalks should be washed and sliced to the desired lengths. Older stalks should be peeled to remove coarse strings before slicing.

The first rhubarb of spring comes into its own when preserved stocks of other fruits are almost gone. Our families love stewed rhubarb with muesli for breakfast. Rhubarb stewed with thin slices of unpeeled orange and sweetened with honey is delicate and refreshing.

RHUBARB GINGERBREAD

Serves 8

A spicy pudding for cooler nights.

Cut 500 g of rhubarb into 5 mm slices and put them in the bottom of a buttered casserole. Add 100 g of sugar and place in the oven at 180°C while preparing the sponge. You can use frozen rhubarb in the same way, leaving it in the oven for 20-30 minutes until it is thawed and heated through.

Sponge:

115 g butter
55 g brown sugar
2 large tb treacle
1 egg
170 g flour
1 tsp ground ginger
1 tsp mixed ground spice
pinch of salt
½ tsp baking soda
2 tb hot milk

Cream the butter and sugar until fluffy, then beat in treacle. Add the lightly-beaten egg. Fold in the sifted flour, spices and salt. Dissolve the soda in hot milk and stir into the sponge mixture. Pour this over the hot rhubarb. Bake at 180°C for 30-40 minutes.

For a special occasion serve with whipped cream into which you have folded a little finely-chopped crystallised ginger.

ELSIE'S CREAMY RHUBARB TART

Serves 6-8

Pastry:

225 g flour
pinch of salt
½ tsp baking powder
115 g butter

Sift the flour, salt and baking powder into a bowl. Rub in the butter. Mix to a stiff dough with cold water. Roll out and line a 25 cm pie plate.

Filling:

1½ c finely-chopped rhubarb
¾ c sugar
2 tb flour
1 egg
1 tb butter

Mix the rhubarb with the sugar, flour and well-beaten egg. Pour the filling into the pie shell. Dot with butter. Bake at 200°C for about 35 minutes or until the filling is set.

NANCY'S RHUBARB AND YOGHURT FOOL

Serves 8

A refreshing, simple but glamorous dessert.

500 g prepared rhubarb
30 g butter
120 g castor sugar
1 carton plain yoghurt (200 g)
300 ml cream
30 g castor sugar
dark chocolate or crystallised ginger for garnishing

Cut the rhubarb into small pieces. Put into an ovenproof dish, cover and cook at 150°C for 45 minutes. Stir in the butter and 120 g of castor sugar. Purée in a blender or put through a fine sieve.

Beat the yoghurt and cream with 30 g of castor sugar until slightly thicker than the rhubarb purée. Mix all together gently. Pour into dessert glasses and chill. Decorate with grated chocolate or finely-chopped crystallised ginger.

The next two jam recipes use rhubarb to make other fruits go further.

BLACK CURRANT AND RHUBARB JAM

Our families like this version better than plain black currant jam.

700 g rhubarb, finely sliced
300 ml water
700 g black currants (stalks removed)
600 ml water
2 kg sugar (warmed in a slow oven for 20 minutes)

Cook the rhubarb to a pulp with 300 ml of water. Add the black currants and 600 ml of water. Boil for 20 minutes. Add the warmed sugar and stir until dissolved. Boil rapidly for about 15 minutes until setting point is reached. Pour into warm, dry jars and seal with jam covers.

RHUBARB AND RASPBERRY JAM

2 kg rhubarb, finely sliced
1.2 kg sugar
1 kg raspberries

Place the rhubarb in a bowl, sprinkle with sugar and leave overnight. Stir in the raspberries. Tip all into a preserving pan and bring slowly to the boil, stirring until the sugar dissolves. Boil until setting point is reached. Pour into warm, dry jars and seal with jam covers.

FRESH RHUBARB RELISH

Makes 1½ cups.

This relish can be eaten straight away with curries, pork or lamb or can be stored for up to two weeks in the refrigerator.

2½ c rhubarb, finely sliced
3 slices lemon
½ c water
¼ tsp salt
½ c sugar
¼ tsp cinnamon
freshly-grated nutmeg
¼ tsp ground ginger
¼ tsp ground cloves
½ tsp grated lemon rind
a little finely-chopped mint

Cook the rhubarb and lemon slices in the water and salt until soft. Add the sugar and stir until it is dissolved. Strain off any excess liquid. Remove and discard the lemon slices. Stir in the spices, rind and mint. Allow to cool.

Freezing

Rhubarb freezes very well and is quick to process. Choose young, tender stalks with few fibres. Cut into suitable lengths. Most books on freezing tell you to add 1 part of sugar to every 4-5 parts of rhubarb. We have found packing without sugar equally successful.

Salsify

(Tragopogon porrifolius)

Varieties

Salsify first appeared in cultivation in Italy early in the 16th century and was grown in English gardens by the 18th century. Few varieties are available. Mammoth Sandwich Island has a parsnip-like root which grows to about 5 cm in diameter and reaches 18-25 cm in length.

Cultivation

Like carrots and parsnips, salsify roots have a tendency to fork if they encounter bulky organic matter, clay lumps or stones in the soil. To counteract this you could prepare individual planting holes about 30 cm deep and 15-20 cm apart, fill them with a rich, sieved loam and plant three seeds per station, later removing the two weakest plants. Since the plants need 14 to 21 weeks to reach maturity, a spring sowing is usually made. The attractive plants need little further attention apart from occasional weeding and watering. Salsify plants are rather unusual in that they suffer from no major pests or diseases.

Harvesting

Dig the roots as required, taking care not to damage the skin. Salsify bleeds readily and the flesh discolours on exposure to air. Take care to avoid cutting or damaging the flesh.

In the kitchen

Scrub thoroughly and trim the root and stalk ends. Peel quickly and drop immediately into a basin of water containing a tablespoon of white vinegar or lemon juice. This reduces the rapid discoloration of the white roots. If they are too long to fit into a saucepan, slice them into convenient lengths. Allow 100 g for each serving.

Cook in boiling, salted water with a tablespoon of lemon juice until they can be pierced easily with a small, sharp knife. Drain well and cut into slices or chunks.

This delicately-flavoured vegetable is best served as simply as possible. Try the following ways:

Add butter and freshly-ground black pepper to the chopped vegetables.

Add sour cream, pepper and finely-chopped parsley or chives.

Serve with parsley sauce, béchamel sauce, cheese sauce or hollandaise sauce (see page 208).

Cover with French dressing and allow to cool. Sprinkle with chopped parsley or chives. You can also garnish with lemon slices before serving.

SALSIFY PIE

Serves 6

600 g prepared salsify
700 g potatoes
1 tb butter
salt and pepper to taste
milk to mix

Sauce:

2 tb butter
2 tb flour
1½ c milk
salt and pepper to taste
anchovy or seafood sauce to taste
2 tb chopped parsley
70 g grated Cheddar cheese

Cook salsify according to the method given above. Drain and place in a greased ovenproof dish.

Peel the potatoes and cook them in boiling, salted water until they are tender. Drain. Add the butter, salt and pepper and mash with a little milk to combine.

To prepare the sauce, melt the butter, add the flour and cook for 1 minute. Gradually pour in the milk, stirring constantly until the sauce thickens and boils. Add the seasoning and anchovy or seafood sauce to taste. Add the parsley.

Pour the sauce over the salsify. Top with mashed potatoes and sprinkle the surface with grated cheese. Bake at 200°C for 10-20 minutes until heated through and golden-brown.

Silverbeet

(Beta vulgaris var. ***cicla)***

Varieties

Silver Beet, Seakale Beet or Swiss Chard comes in many different varieties and sometimes plants with different names look identical in the garden. Basically there are four types of silver beet: one with light-green crumpled leaves (Lucullus), one with medium-dark-green smooth leaves and very broad ribs (Large Rib Dark Green, Medium Green), one with glossy, dark-green, slightly-crumpled leaves (Dark Green, Master Dark Green, Success Dark Green Curled, Broad Rib Fordhook) and one with crimson mid-ribs and veins with slightly-crumpled leaves (Rhubarb Chard, Red Stemmed). Newcomers to the field are a F.1 hybrid (Vintage Green) with smooth, dark-green leaves, and a very compact plant (Nu Green Semi-Dwarf). Rainbow Chard features a range of leaf and vein colours but unfortunately it is not available in all areas. This variety is both decorative and tasty. Most silver beets are ready for picking about 60 days after sowing.

In a class of its own is Perpetual Spinach Beet which has smooth pale-green leaves and slender stems. It will produce for up to 12 months from a spring sowing if it is kept well picked.

Cultivation

Recently-limed soil which is free draining and well manured is ideal for silver beet and spinach beet. The more organic matter in the bed, the nicer the flavour. It needs more nitrogen than its close relative, the beetroot, so a good fertilizer supplement would be dried blood or liquid manure. If a 5 cm-layer of poultry manure is dug in a few weeks before planting, no additional fertilizer should be needed.

Sowings are made in mid spring for summer cutting and in mid to late summer for late autumn, winter and spring supplies. Like beetroot, silver beet will bolt if it is exposed to a

a smooth leaf variety

Pave a small corner for a sturdy outdoor table
Plant annuals along vegetable borders for colour
A vegetable garden can be an attractive
setting for cooking and eating
Retaining wall built
of stone with fire
brick barbecue set in
Drainage holes
Plant aromatic herbs around barbecue
for sprinkling on to sizzling steaks and chops
Cobblestones on sand

These small trees are suitable for back gardens

Feijoa. Keep ground clear for harvesting fallen feijoas

Tamarillo

Crabapple. Ornamental and useful for making jelly

Lemon. The good cook needs a constant supply of lemons

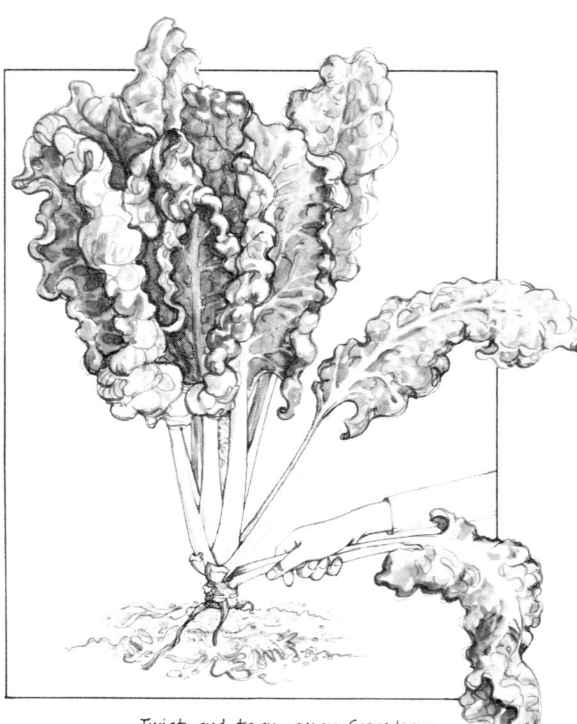

period of cold weather followed by warm temperatures (the biennial plant "thinks" that it has just been through winter and it is now time to flower and reproduce itself). The spring sowing is therefore best made under cloches in cold areas, or in boxes for planting out when the weather is settled.

a dark green crumpled leaf variety
Twist and tear away from base

Transplanting shock may also lead to bolting, but if the plants are moved when only 7-10 cm high, about 6 weeks after sowing, no ill effects should be noticed. The plants are spaced 30 cm apart in rows 45-60 cm apart. They appreciate a thorough watering in early summer followed by mulching. Very little further attention is required as the plants are unusually pest and disease free. Rust spots on leaves may appear after the plants have been producing for many weeks. Liquid manure or dried blood will give them a boost but you should give some thought to starting a new batch.

Harvesting

Just wander down the garden and pull off one or two leaves from each plant about half an hour before dinner. The leaves are pulled out at the base and twisted off like rhubarb.

In the kitchen

This useful vegetable is available all year round to provide the cook with a quickly-prepared and attractive green.

Wash the leaves and stalks thoroughly. Cut off the stalks and slice them into 1 cm lengths. Place the stalks in a large saucepan containing boiling, salted water, 1 cm deep. Cook until barely tender. Slice the leaves roughly and add to the saucepan. Cook and simmer until they are just tender but still a fresh green colour. Drain well and serve immediately with plenty of butter.

Butter-steaming is another good cooking method. Sauté the sliced stalks in butter with a little finely-chopped onion or garlic. Add the roughly-chopped leaves and cover the pan tightly. Cover over low heat until they are just tender. Season and serve immediately.

Freshly-grated nutmeg, a squeeze of lemon juice or a little finely-chopped rosemary are tasty additions. A smooth cheese sauce (see page 208) poured over freshly-cooked silver beet makes an attractive variation.

Very young silver beet leaves may be used with other greens in spring salads. Use a slightly sweetened French dressing.

SILVER BEET FRITTERS

Serves 6-8

Serve with meat dishes instead of potatoes and green vegetables.

400 g silver beet leaves (stalks removed — see below)
½ c flour
¼ tsp salt
¼ tsp sugar
¼ tsp finely-chopped rosemary
freshly-ground black pepper
1 egg
¾ c milk
oil for frying

Cook silver beet leaves in a little boiling, salted water until they are tender. Drain thoroughly. Chop finely and measure 1 c, firmly packed.

Sift the flour and salt into a bowl. Add the sugar, rosemary and pepper. Make a well in the centre. Combine the egg and milk. Pour in sufficient of this liquid to make a pouring batter. Beat until smooth. Add the measured silver beet and stir to mix. Heat a little oil in a large frying pan. Drop in spoonfuls of the batter and brown on both sides. Drain on absorbent paper and keep hot until all the fritters are cooked. Serve immediately.

Silver beet stalks (or ribs or chards as they are sometimes called) may be cooked and served without the leaves. They are delicious with tomato sauce or cheese sauce.

CREAM OF SILVER BEET SOUP

Serves 4-6

This produces an excellent creamy soup.

500 g silver beet
1 small onion, thinly sliced
1 medium-sized potato, diced finely
2 tb butter
800 ml chicken stock
salt and pepper to taste
3 tb sour cream
1 lemon or whipped cream for garnishing

Wash the silver beet thoroughly. Remove the stalks and slice. Melt the butter in a large saucepan, add the stalks, onion and potato. Cook gently with the lid on for 5-10 minutes until the potato is almost tender. Add the roughly-chopped leaves and cook for another minute. Add the stock and seasoning. Simmer for 5-10 minutes until the vegetables are tender. Put through a blender or fine sieve. Warm the sour cream in the saucepan. Gently pour in the soup, stirring well. Reheat without boiling. Serve garnished with a thin slice of lemon and/or a small teaspoon of whipped cream.

The sour cream gives the soup a desirable sharp flavour. If you haven't any sour cream, use top milk or fresh cream. Add about a tablespoon of lemon juice to obtain a similar sharpness.

Freezing

Silver beet freezes reasonably well. Blanch prepared stalks and leaves for 2 minutes. Cool and pack in meal-sized quantities in freezer bags. To cook, drop into a little boiling, salted water and heat until thawed and boiling point is regained. Drain and serve with a cheese or tomato sauce.

Spinach

(*Spinacia oleracea*)

Varieties

For many years gardeners chose between prickly-seeded spinach sown in late summer to early autumn for winter picking and round-seeded spinach sown in spring for early summer use. These standard types go under the names of Prickly Winter (also Dutch Queen) and Viking Round Summer (also Royal Denmark). Bloomsdale Long Standing is an improved summer spinach which is slower to bolt than the others. Unlike the other summer spinaches, its leaves are very crumpled, a feature which is more characteristic of the winter varieties.

Plant breeders are now concentrating on hybrid spinach varieties, which are very uniform in plant size and maturity, especially for the processed frozen-foods industry. One of these, Hybrid No.7, is available to home gardeners. This variety bolts early and should therefore be sown in early autumn (or winter in warm locations) so that it matures in cool weather. It matures earlier than the standard varieties and is resistant to downy mildew.

In warm regions spinach may be picked 40-45 days after sowing. In colder areas 63 days are allowed for a spring-sown crop and 77 days for a late summer-sown crop.

Cultivation

As for all leafy vegetables, the soil should be a rich loam, well drained and containing abundant organic matter to hold plenty of moisture. A summer crop may need partial shade by a row of beans or peas but winter spinach rows must be sunny and sheltered from hail and driving rain. Bolting is the major problem for summer spinach and it is often accelerated by overcrowding (spacing less than 30 cm apart) and a shortage of water. Sowing in a shallow compost-filled trench may help to prolong picking.

The seed is sown directly in the garden in drills 12-20 mm deep. Thin initially to 10 cm apart and, when the leaves begin to touch, thin again to 20-30 cm apart (the closer spacing for winter spinach). This time use the thinnings for a meal. The rows should be 30 cm apart.

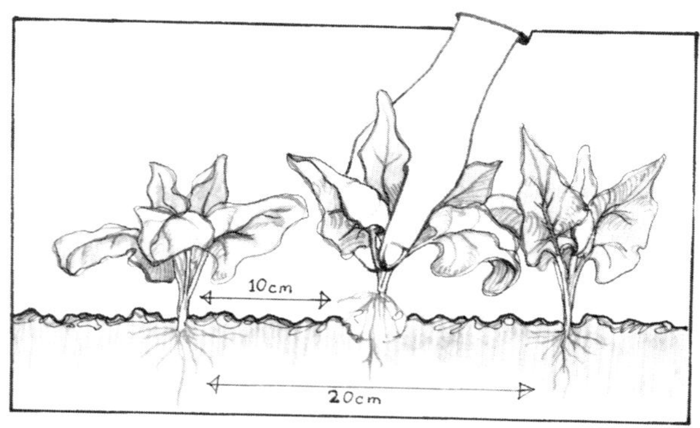

Initial thinning to 10 cm. When leaves touch harvest alternate plants

Hoe between the rows to suppress weeds and, in dry weather, give the plants regular overhead sprinkling.

Harvesting

Two harvesting strategies are applied to spinach. One is to pinch off a few leaves at a time from each plant, a method well suited for winter crops. The other is to grow a fast-maturing hybrid and harvest the whole row for freezing at one time. With this method the plants can be spaced 5-10 cm apart.

In the kitchen

Cut off the roots and stem bases from freshly-harvested spinach. Discard any yellowed leaves. Wash very thoroughly as any remaining grit will ruin the fine texture of the cooked spinach. Do not dry.

A kilogram of raw, prepared spinach will yield about 3 cups of cooked spinach, sufficient to serve four.

Place in a large saucepan without water. Cover tightly. Bring slowly to boiling point, shaking the pan frequently. Cook gently for 3-8 minutes until tender. Tip into a colander and press with a weighted plate. Leave for 2-3 minutes to drain.

To serve, melt 2 tb of butter in the saucepan. Add the drained spinach and season with salt, pepper and freshly-grated nutmeg. Reheat gently and serve immediately.

SWEET AND SOUR SPINACH

Serves 4

3 c cooked spinach
½ tsp salt
1 tsp sugar
1 tb lemon juice
2 tb butter
1 lemon for garnishing

Chop the spinach finely and add the salt, sugar and lemon juice. Melt the butter in a saucepan. Add the spinach mixture. Heat through, stirring continuously. Serve immediately as the fresh green colour is soon lost. Garnish with thin slices of lemon.

SPINACH SALAD

Serves 6

Raw spinach in a salad yields more servings than if it is cooked.

500 g prepared, raw spinach
100 g bacon

One or more of the following ingredients:

sliced mushrooms
cauliflower sprigs
cucumber, cubed
mild onion rings

Dressing:

2 tb lemon juice
4 tb salad oil
freshly-ground black pepper
freshly-grated nutmeg
½ tsp salt
¼ tsp sugar
1 tb finely-chopped parsley

2 hard-boiled eggs for garnishing

Dry the spinach thoroughly. Discard the stalks and any tough leaves. Tear into pieces and place in a salad bowl. Chop the bacon finely and fry until it is crisp. Drain off any fat. When the bacon is cool add it to the spinach. Add a selection of the other ingredients.

Mix the dressing ingredients together and pour over the salad. Toss gently. Garnish with quartered hard-boiled eggs.

SPINACH PANCAKES

Serves 6

Serve as a tasty lunch dish to make a little spinach go much further.

12 pancakes (see page 23)
250 g prepared raw spinach or ¾ c frozen spinach

Sauce:

4 tb butter
4 tb flour
½ tsp salt
freshly-ground black pepper
2 c milk
2 c grated tasty Cheddar cheese

Cook the spinach, drain and chop.

To prepare the sauce, melt the butter in a saucepan and add the flour, salt and pepper. Cook for 1 minute. Gradually pour in the milk and continue stirring until the sauce thickens and boils. Remove from the heat. Stir in 1½ c of the grated cheese.

Combine half the sauce with the spinach. Place a spoonful of the spinach mixture on each pancake and roll up. Place in a greased ovenproof dish. Pour the remaining sauce over the pancakes and sprinkle the surface with grated cheese. Bake at 180°C for 15-20 minutes until they are heated through and browned.

A delicious spinach soup may be made using the recipe on page 171 for Cream of Silver Beet Soup.

CREAMED SPINACH

Serves 4

3 c cooked spinach, chopped
30 g butter
salt and pepper to taste
freshly-grated nutmeg
¼ c cream, fresh or sour

Melt the butter in a saucepan, add the spinach and heat through. Add salt, pepper and nutmeg to taste. Stir in the cream. Reheat gently before serving.

Florentine dishes consist of a bed of freshly-cooked spinach topped with poached eggs or cooked fish. They are covered with mornay sauce, sprinkled with grated cheese and browned in the oven.

Freezing

Spinach is an especially useful vegetable to grow for freezing. A spring crop grows so quickly that it can be harvested before the ground is needed for a summer vegetable.

Blanch small quantities of prepared spinach for 2 minutes. Cool quickly and gently squeeze out excess moisture with the back of spoon. Chop and pack in recipe-sized portions in freezer bags.

Cook unthawed spinach in a little butter for about 7 minutes until it is heated through.

Spinach, New Zealand

(Tetragonia expansa)

Gardening books published in England and the United States are full of praise for the heat-resistant New Zealand spinach, but it was not commonly grown by New Zealand gardeners until the last decade. It is a succulent plant which spreads over an area of about one square metre. Although frost tender, it often re-establishes itself during the next spring and, if it is allowed to ramble up and through shrubs or hedges, it may not die down at all. As yet, it has not been taken in hand by plant breeders so there are no differing varieties.

Cultivation

New Zealand spinach should be grown on light, well-drained soils. Some books state that it does well in a hot, dry corner but our experience has shown that the plant should be watered regularly and grown in fertile ground for continual picking throughout the summer. The seed germinates slowly and it is advisable in short-season areas to start it in boxes or peat pots under glass. This enables the plants to grow away strongly from late spring. You could also soak the seed for 24 hours before sowing. Space the plants 45-60 cm apart and, as soon as they are 10-15 cm high, pinch out the tips to encourage side shoots. New Zealand spinach does not suffer from any pests or diseases.

Use only growing tips for cooking

Harvesting

Pinch out 7 cm-long growing tips as often as required through summer and autumn.

In the kitchen

Wash the freshly-harvested growing tips. Place in a large saucepan with 2 tb of water. Cover tightly and cook until tender. Tip into a colander to drain. Reheat gently with butter and season with salt, pepper and freshly-grated nutmeg.

For recipes, see the spinach section. The texture of New Zealand spinach is rather too coarse to use in salads. In cooked dishes it will substitute well.

Strawberries

*(**Fragaria** cultivars)*

Varieties

Whole books have been devoted to the subject of strawberries, and enthusiasts in France, Britain, and America have developed dozens of varieties. These fall into three main groups: summer strawberries which produce a main-crop in early to mid summer, alpine strawberries derived from the wild, autumn-fruiting European forms and ever-bearers which are probably the result of bud mutations in summer varieties. The ever-bearers are normally very large plants, carrying large fruit in flushes from early summer to late autumn. The so-called climbing strawberry belongs to this group.

In many areas home and commercial gardeners have concentrated on summer strawberries almost exclusively. This has not resulted in any increase in varieties, however, and often only one or two are available as plants for the new gardener. Red Gauntlet appears in the garden shops each year because it is a very heavy cropper, its fruit resists grey mould disease (botrytis) and its roots are resistant to red-core and verticillium wilt. However, it has a poor flavour when compared with some varieties grown in commercial plantations, such as Talisman and Cambridge Favourite.

Talisman is vigorous, compact and has berries of good colour and flavour. Royal Sovereign is grown in some areas and its tall, bright-green plants bear a medium to large crop of excellent flavour. Tioga is a fairly new variety which can be bought as rooted plants.

Some summer strawberries such as Talisman and Red Gauntlet may carry a small second crop in autumn, an extra bonus for the gardener who has a well-cared-for strawberry plantation.

Cultivation

If you are satisfied with Red Gauntlet you can start a new strawberry patch by buying the plants in early autumn. Otherwise, arrange with neighbours or friends in mid summer to let some runners from healthy plants root in small pots partly sunk into the ground. The pots should be filled to the top with a good loam or a mixture of equal quantities of peat, sand and rich compost. The first plant on the runner is the only one used for propagation. Any secondary plants are pinched out. If conditions are good, these plants can be detached from the parent and transplanted into their new bed in early autumn and allowed to bear fruit the next summer, provided they have made strong growth. They must be planted firmly with their roots just below the surface and the base of the crown at soil level.

The ideal soil for a strawberry patch is a medium to heavy loam which is well-drained

Let runners root in small pots set partially into ground

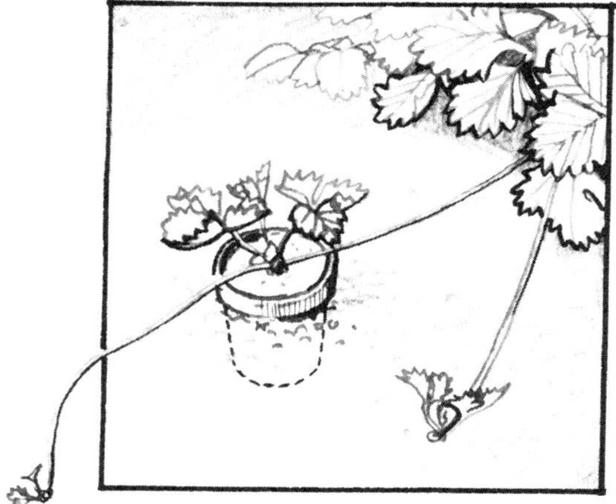

Pinch out secondary runners

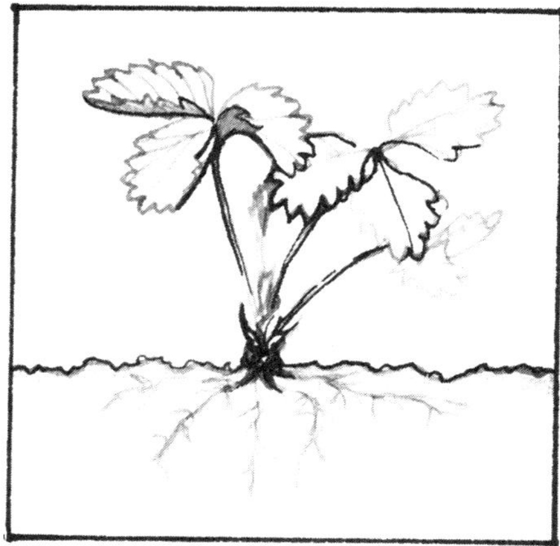

Make sure base of crown is at soil level

and open to full sunshine. Plenty of compost, decayed leaves or old animal manure should be worked into the bed a few weeks before early-autumn planting. Additional blood and bone, superphosphate and sulphate of potash applications can be made but there is a good case for dressing the beds with animal manure alone. It is felt that plants grown by this method are less prone to virus infection and produce heavier and better-tasting crops. Never use lime in a strawberry patch as the plant requires acid conditions.

The plants are usually set out about 30 cm apart in rows 45 cm apart. This allows for easy picking. If bird netting is to be used, make the beds 1.3 m wide containing four rows with closer spacing. As soon as the ground warms up in spring the bed is weeded and a mulch of pine needles or straw is placed around each plant. This is positioned so that the flowers appear above the mulch and the developing fruit lie on a dry bed. This prevents the berries being splashed with mud and succumbing to mould in wet weather.

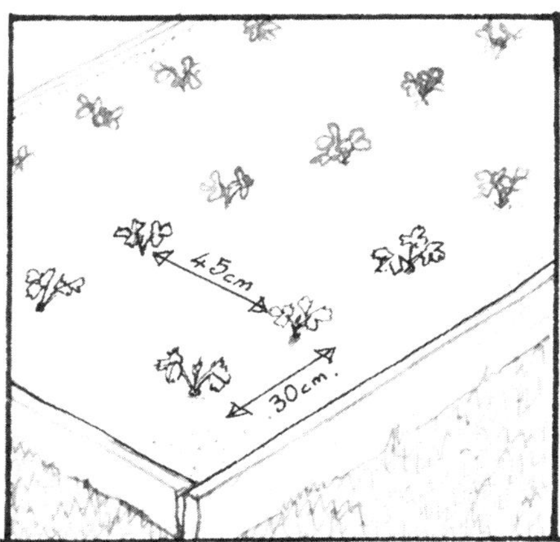

Spacing for strawberry bed

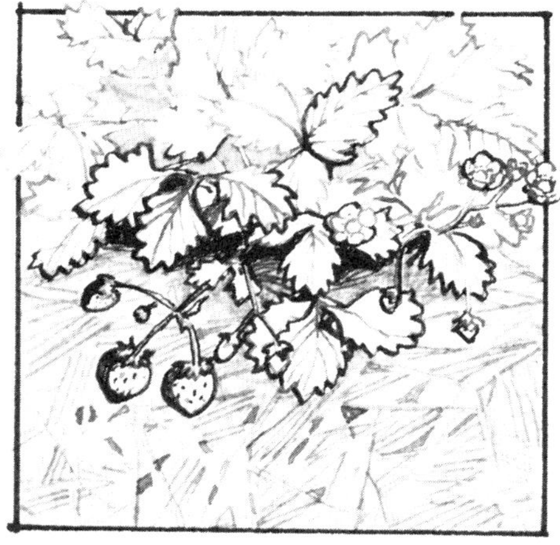

Mulch with pine needles or straw after soil warms up in spring

During the first fruiting season, runners are usually pinched out as soon as they appear. The following summer, however, one or two runners from each of the best plants should be rooted to supply replacement plants for a new bed. In some cold areas where spring planting is necessary, both flowers and runners should be pinched out during the first summer. These plants will crop heavily for two more years before they are replaced.

There is a growing trend to cultivate strawberries over black plastic. The ground must be very rich in compost and, on flat ground, the rows should be slightly mounded. This prevents the fruit from lying in small puddles which form in hollows on the plastic. The plants should be inserted in slits cut in the plastic. Extra slits may be needed in wide sheets to let rain through between the rows.

Strawberries are prone to several serious virus diseases which have been responsible for the loss of many old-favourite varieties. These viruses are spread by aphids and make their presence known by causing dwarfing of the plants, yellow edges on the leaves and distortion of both leaves and fruit. Occasionally dwarfing is the result of root rot or unsuitable soil conditions and the plant may recover. As a general rule, however, plants showing severe crinkling and yellow-edge are assumed to be infected by viruses and should be removed and burnt. Leaf spot is a fungus disease which can be treated successfully by spraying with a copper oxychloride solution and by picking off badly-affected leaves. Aphids sometimes appear on young leaves and on the fruit stems. Although they make little difference to the crop they spread virus diseases, so it is worth controlling them with a "safe" insecticide such as pyrethrum. Strawberry plants, like humans, may carry a virus disease without showing the symptoms. These may become a source of infection to susceptible plants through the agency of the aphid.

Harvesting

This pleasant job is best undertaken in dry weather if the strawberries are to be kept more than a day before eating or processing as jam. The combination of a slight bruise and dampness can lead to rapid decay of the fruit. As with tomato picking, detach the fruit with the hat-like calyx in position by pinching through the stem.

In the kitchen

Unless the strawberries are very dirty, avoid washing them. Wipe them gently with a damp cloth to remove any dust or grit. Remove the hulls (the calyx and the core beneath) with a blunt knife or with your fingers.

Many strawberry lovers would say that the only way to eat this fruit is with icing sugar and cream. We agree that they are superb served this way. You may, however, like to try them dipped in sour cream and brown sugar, with yoghurt or in the ways suggested in the following recipes.

STRAWBERRIES WITH PORT AND ORANGE JUICE

Serves 6

This is one of the simplest and most delightful ways of serving good, ripe strawberries when they are plentiful.

600 g prepared strawberries
2 tb castor sugar
2 tb orange juice
1 tb port wine (preferably the best quality)
200 ml cream, whipped and sweetened with 1 tsp vanilla sugar

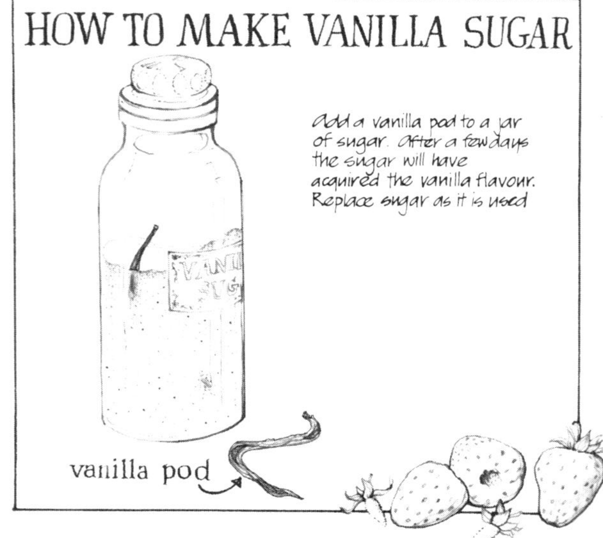

HOW TO MAKE VANILLA SUGAR
Add a vanilla pod to a jar of sugar. After a few days the sugar will have acquired the vanilla flavour. Replace sugar as it is used
vanilla pod

Sprinkle the castor sugar over the strawberries and mix thoroughly. Combine the orange juice and port wine and pour over the strawberries. Chill for 1 hour, turning the fruit two or three times. Serve in glasses with or without a topping of vanilla-flavoured cream. If the meal has been rich, the orange and port-flavoured strawberries are refreshing by themselves.

Variation: use an orange-flavoured liqueur instead of port.

STRAWBERRY YOGHURT TART

Biscuit crumb shell:

2 c crushed vanilla biscuits (225 g packet)
115 g butter, melted
¼ tsp grated nutmeg, optional
½ tsp cinnamon, optional

Combine the ingredients thoroughly. Press into a 20-25 cm diameter tin with a removable base, or use an aluminium-foil pie plate. Chill for 1 hour.

Filling:

20 prepared strawberries
2 tb honey
1 c plain yoghurt
225 g cream cheese
½ tsp vanilla

Slice each strawberry in half. Reserve eight halves for decoration. Cover the base of the shell with strawberries. Warm the honey and, when sufficiently liquid, pour over the strawberries. Whip the yoghurt, cream cheese and vanilla until it is thick and smooth. Spoon this over the strawberries. Chill thoroughly. Just before serving, decorate with the reserved strawberry halves.

STRAWBERRY DESSERT PANCAKES

Serves 6

12 pancakes (see page 23)
300 g prepared strawberries
1 tb castor sugar
1 tb orange juice
1 tsp port wine or orange-flavoured liqueur
2 tb melted butter
200 ml cream

Cut the strawberries into quarters, or smaller if they are very large. Sprinkle with castor sugar. Add the orange juice and port wine. Mix gently. Place about a tablespoonful of the strawberry mixture on each pancake. Roll up and place in a greased ovenproof dish. Pour the melted butter over the surface. Warm through in the oven at 180°C for about 10 minutes. Serve hot with whipped cream sweetened with a little vanilla sugar.

We have been so disappointed with the results of freezing and bottling strawberries that we no longer bother. Fortunately strawberry jam, especially the uncooked version, is delicious.

UNCOOKED STRAWBERRY JAM

The colour and fresh taste of this strawberry jam is superior to the cooked versions. The jam should be stored in a freezer.

600 g prepared strawberries
900 g castor sugar
half bottle of liquid pectin (115 ml) or equivalent made from pectin powder

Combine the strawberries and sugar in a bowl. Crush with a potato masher. Leave for 1 hour, stirring occasionally until the sugar has dissolved. Add the pectin and stir for 3 minutes. Pour into small, dry jars leaving 1.5 cm headspace. Cover with foil. Leave in the kitchen for 8 hours and then put into the refrigerator until they are jelled. This may take 24 hours. Store in a freezer until required.

STRAWBERRY AND GOOSEBERRY JAM

700 g prepared, green gooseberries
130 ml water
700 g prepared strawberries
1.4 kg sugar

Place the gooseberries and water in a preserving pan and simmer until tender. Add the strawberries and cook for 4 minutes. Add the sugar. Stir over a low heat until the sugar has dissolved. Boil rapidly until setting point is reached. Pour into clean, warm jars and seal with jam covers.

Swede turnips

(*Brassica napus* var. *napobrassica*)

Varieties

The name "swede" is linked with the theory that this vegetable originated in Sweden about 1781 as a hybrid between a turnip and some type of cabbage. Another theory is that it developed in mediaeval gardens where turnips and kale grew side by side and sometimes interbred. In the United States these vegetables are called rutabagas after their name in a Swedish dialect *rotabagge* (meaning "red bags"). The purple-topped varieties are available under a number of names including Champion Purple Top, Purple Top Garden and Superlative. Champion Purple Top withstands dry weather better than the others. It is unfortunate for swede-growers in some countries that the mildest of all varieties, White Perfection, is not offered by the seed merchants. It can be obtained in Australia and in the United States.

Cultivation

Swedes are described as hardier, milder and sweeter than ordinary turnips, but they are slower to reach maturity. In cold climates they may need as much as 20 to 26 weeks but, in milder areas, eight to 13 weeks are required according to variety. A late spring to early summer sowing is usually made in cool districts. Where it is milder, sowings can be delayed until late summer to early autumn. In both cases, harvesting takes place throughout the winter as swedes are far more tolerant of bad weather than turnips.

Sowings should be made directly in a well-worked, friable soil, which has been limed and fertilized for a previous crop such as peas or lettuces. A light dressing of superphosphate and old soot may be added at planting time. The drills should be about 2 cm deep and 40 cm apart. The young plants should be thinned to 22-30 cm apart and grown on steadily with careful attention being paid to watering in dry, hot weather. Evening hosing of the leaves is beneficial at this time to reproduce the cool, moist conditions which result in fine-quality roots. Mulching in late summer is also practised in mild areas, and this may prevent the development of powdery mildew.

Harvesting

Swedes are ready to eat once they reach the size of a tennis ball. It is often said that their flavour improves after a frost.

In the kitchen

Scrub with a vegetable brush and cut off the stringy stalk end. Peel thickly to remove the tough skin. Swedes may be sliced, diced, cut into chunks or strips, or grated. One medium-sized swede weighing about 1 kg will serve six.

To cook, place in boiling, salted water, cover

Swedes are bigger and sweeter than turnips but can be cooked in most of the same ways.

and simmer until tender. Drain.

Serve diced swedes with butter and pepper. If you like, add a squeeze of lemon juice and chopped parsley.

Swede purée is delicious. Mash a cooked and well drained swede with plenty of butter and pepper. To make a thicker and smoother purée, cook the swede with 1 medium-sized potato and put both through a blender with butter or cream and seasoning. Serve sprinkled with chopped parsley.

If the oven is hot, try baked swedes as a simply-cooked vegetable. Cut the swedes into 5 mm-thick sticks. Place in a small, greased casserole. Dot with 2 tb of butter and sprinkle with salt and pepper. Add 2 tb of water. Cover tightly and bake at 200°C for 30-40 minutes until tender.

GRATED SWEDES

Serves 4-6

3 c coarsely-grated swede (1 small swede)
2 tb water
2 tb butter
1 tb brown sugar
1 tsp soy sauce

Combine the ingredients in a heavy-based saucepan. Cover and cook gently, stirring frequently until they are tender-crisp (about 5 minutes).

FOIL-BAKED SWEDES WITH SWEET-SOUR SAUCE

Serves 6

1 kg swede
2 tb butter

Sauce:

2 tb butter
1 tb brown sugar
1 tb soy sauce
1 tb lemon juice
1 tsp Worcestershire sauce

Cut the peeled swede into 6 segments. Place each segment on a piece of foil, dot with butter and wrap tightly. Place the parcels in a baking dish and cook in the oven at 200°C for 1 hour or until they are tender.

To prepare the sauce, melt the butter in a small saucepan and add the remaining ingredients. Heat through.

Just before serving, unwrap the swede segments and cut into chunks. Pour a little of the sauce over each portion.

BAKED SWEDE AND POTATO

Serves 6

500 g swedes
500 g potatoes
1 tsp salt
freshly-ground black pepper
1 tsp dried marjoram or ½ tsp dried thyme
½ tsp sugar
¾ c beef stock

Peel the swedes and cut lengthwise into quarters. Slice finely. Peel the potatoes and slice finely. Layer the potatoes and swedes alternately in a greased casserole. Sprinkle each layer with salt, pepper, marjoram or thyme and sugar. Pour in the stock. Cover and bake at 200°C for 1 hour until tender.

For additional recipes see Turnips (page 202).

Sweetcorn

(*Zea mays* var. *saccharata*)

Varieties

Golden Bantam is one of the few old sweetcorn varieties still available. Although it is very sweet it produces only eight rows of corn. Hybrids now dominate the market because they are often earlier maturing, an advantage in cooler districts, and have more rows in each cob. They can be divided into early and maincrop types. Marcross Express and Yukon Hybrid are both listed as early. Golden Cross Bantam is one of the most popular maincrop corns. Each cob has about 12 rows and grows to 20 cm in length. Golden Grain Maincrop is much more prolific with 20 rows. Summit Hybrid and NK195 Hybrid produce long cobs (up to 24 cm) with 14-16 rows. In warm districts maincrop types are ready for picking in 85-90 days.

Cultivation

There are several fertilizer mixtures suitable for corn. These range from a 5 cm layer of poultry manure worked into the topsoil, supplemented with a tomato fertilizer or 1 c of blood and bone plus ½ c of superphosphate worked into each 3 m length of row. Whichever recipe you follow, start off with well-drained, medium to light soil in a very sunny position. It must be able to warm up quickly so that sowing can begin in mid to late spring. Germination is very uneven if the temperature is below 15°C.

Direct sowing can be made at a depth of 5 cm in short rows, in hills or in blocks. In row sowing, plant two seeds every 25-45 cm, later removing the weaker. The rows should be about 1 m apart. Never plant a single row as pollination will be very poor. Hills are usually spaced 1 m apart and six to seven seeds are sown on each. Thin to three to four plants when

Grow corn in blocks for good pollination

they reach 7 cm in height. For block sowing, mark out a grid with 30 cm intervals between the points and sow one to two seeds in each position. If your ground is slow to warm up, start the seeds in large peat pots under glass and then gradually harden them off before planting out in settled weather. Of course this method is only suitable for small quantities. In England and the United States cloches are often used.

Keep the plants weeded by hand or by very shallow hoeing and, if drought threatens, water the patch very thoroughly and mulch with straw. Earthing up is sometimes practised to hold the plants more firmly in windy areas. Tall varieties may need to be staked. Removal of the suckers is no longer considered to be of any benefit to the crop.

The corn cobs which start off as female flowers will not fill out unless they are pollinated by the male flowers or tassels which grow at the top of the plant. Wind and gravity carry the heavy pollen grains down on to the female flowers of the neighbouring plants. This is why a single row of corn is undesirable. In still weather some gardeners shake the plants gently each morning to ensure fertilization. In a few weeks the tassels wither and become darker and the silks also darken. It is not always wise to wait for these changes to be obvious before inspecting the cobs as, in hot weather, the stage when corn is sweet and tender may be missed. To check the cobs, the sheath should be peeled back carefully and a fingernail pushed into a seed. If watery fluid emerges the cob is immature, if milky fluid appears it is ready and if the seed centre is doughy it is past maturity.

Corn plants may be troubled by slugs or birds at the seedling stage. Tin collars or netting cages may provide a remedy. The corn earworm, a striped caterpillar, can be troublesome in areas where a lot of sweetcorn is grown. Various insecticides are recommended but a solution for organic gardeners is to cover the ears with a paper bag held on by a rubber band soon after the silks appear.

Harvesting

It was discovered many years ago that at a temperature of 26°C sweetcorn cobs lose half their sugar content (by conversion to starch) within 24 hours of picking. Obviously one should cook the cobs immediately after picking or store them in a refrigerator /if this is not possible.

In the Kitchen

"Corn on the cob" is undoubtedly the most popular way of serving home-grown corn. The secret of success lies in the cobs being freshly harvested and at the right stage of ripeness. The cook should have a saucepan of water coming to the boil before going into the garden to pick enough ripe cobs for the meal.

Strip off the husks, pull away the silks and trim the stalks to about 2 cm (enough to hold on to). Place the cobs in the boiling, UNSALTED water. Boil briskly for 5-8 minutes or until a kernel can be prised off fairly easily. Corn cobs which are not fresh will take longer to cook, about 15-20 minutes.

Serve with butter, salt and pepper or a savoury butter.

SAVOURY BUTTERS TO SERVE WITH CORN ON THE COB

Enough for 6 cobs

Seasoned Butter:

50 g butter
½ tsp salt
freshly-ground black pepper

Parsley Butter:

50 g seasoned butter
1 tb finely-chopped parsley

Chive Butter:

50 g seasoned butter
1 tb scissored chives

Mixed Herb Butter:

50 g seasoned butter
1 tb finely-chopped marjoram, parsley and tarragon or other combinations.

Cream the butter, seasoning and herbs. Chill. Roll into balls or cut into shapes.

BAKED CORN ON THE COB

Remove the husks and silks from freshly-harvested cobs. Place each cob on a piece of foil. Pour 1 tb of melted butter over the cobs. Wrap tightly and bake at 190°C for 20 minutes.

BARBECUED CORN ON THE COB

Prepare the corn as above. A little soy sauce may be added to the melted butter. Wrap each cob tightly and place it over a hot barbecue. Turn frequently. Cooking time will be about 15 minutes.

The family with a small vegetable garden is unlikely to tire of corn cooked in these ways. For those fortunate enough to have plenty of ground we have included the following recipes to help use any surplus.

CORN FRITTERS

Makes 12-14 fritters

These can be made with either fresh or frozen whole-kernel corn. If using fresh, cook the cobs first and then cut the kernels off with a sharp knife. Thaw frozen corn. You will need about 2 cobs to produce a cup of kernels.

⅔ c flour
1 tsp baking powder
1 tsp salt
2 eggs
¼ c milk
1 c whole-kernel corn
cooking oil

Sift the flour, baking powder and salt into a bowl. Beat the eggs lightly and mix with the milk. Make a well in the centre of the dry ingredients and gradually pour in the egg and milk. Beat until smooth. Add a little extra milk if necessary to obtain a thick pouring batter. Stir in the drained corn. Pour sufficient oil into a large frying pan to cover the base. When the oil is hot, drop in spoonfuls of batter in 1 tb lots. Brown on both sides. Drain the fritters on absorbent paper and keep them warm. Serve plain or sprinkled with paprika or castor sugar.

Corn fritters served with bacon or sausages make a satisfying lunch. We also serve them in place of potatoes with chops, steak or roast beef.

CREAMY CORN AND LETTUCE

Serves 6

2 c whole-kernel corn (cut from uncooked cobs with a sharp knife, or frozen whole kernels)
½ c finely-shredded lettuce
1 c soft breadcrumbs
2 eggs
½ tsp salt
¾ c milk
2 tb butter

Grease an ovenproof dish. Place half the corn, lettuce and breadcrumbs in the dish. (Reserve ½ c of breadcrumbs for the topping.) Add the remaining corn and lettuce. Beat the eggs and salt together and add the milk. Pour over the corn and lettuce. Top with the remaining breadcrumbs and dot with butter. Bake at 160°C for 40 minutes until set.

CORN CHOWDER

Serves 6

2 rashers of bacon
4 tb butter
2 small onions
4 tb flour
4½ c milk
1½ c cream-style corn (fresh or frozen, see page 185)
salt and pepper to taste

Chop the bacon finely and fry in a large saucepan until it is crisp. Add the butter and finely-chopped onion. Sauté until the onion is soft. Stir in the flour. Cook for a few minutes. Gradually add the milk, stirring until the sauce thickens and boils. Add the corn and seasoning. Reheat. Serve in pottery bowls.

CORN RELISH

A colourful relish to serve with hamburgers or steaks.

1 cucumber or 3 apple cucumbers, peeled
2 large onions, peeled
3 large tomatoes, skinned
1 green pepper, seeds removed
2 c whole-kernel corn (about 4 cobs)
½ c sugar

1 tb salt
freshly-ground black pepper
¾ c white vinegar
¼ tsp tumeric
½ tsp dry mustard

Put the cucumber, onions, tomatoes and pepper through a coarse mincer. Combine all the ingredients in a preserving pan. Bring slowly to the boil, stirring until the sugar dissolves. Simmer for 30-45 minutes until the corn is tender. Pour into hot, dry jars and seal.

Freezing

Corn freezes very well and is useful as a colourful addition to any meal.

Corn on the cob: speed with processing is important. Put a large saucepan of water on to boil. Gather and prepare the cobs. We like to cut large ones in half. Blanch for 5 minutes. Cool quickly and freeze. To cook, place unthawed cobs in a saucepan of cold water. Bring to the boil and simmer for 5 minutes.

Whole kernel corn: blanch the cobs for 5 minutes. Cool quickly. Using a sharp knife, cut off the kernels close to cob. These may be used in any recipe which needs whole-kernel corn. Freeze in small plastic containers.

Cream style corn: blanch the cobs for 5 minutes. Cool quickly. Using a sharp knife, cut off the kernels through their centres, leaving about half of each kernel on the cob. Scrape the cob with the back of the knife to remove the heart and juices. Freeze in small plastic containers.

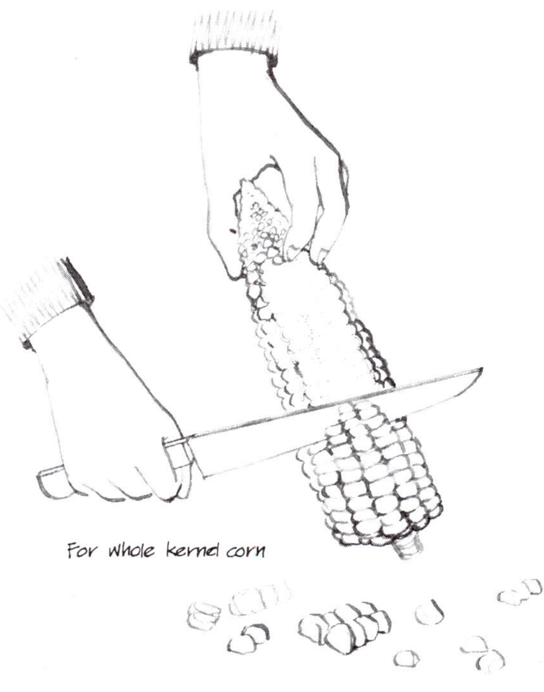

For whole kernel corn

For cream style corn

Sweet potatoes

(Ipomoea batatas)

Varieties

The sweet potatoes grown commercially in New Zealand today are not the Maori kumara, which was introduced by the Polynesian discoverers about a thousand years ago, but two varieties: Owairaka Red and Gisborne Red. Both of these varieties were developed from a strain brought into the country by whalers. Unlike the many ancient Maori varieties, modern sweet potatoes have a sprawling habit with long vines. Because of this the Maori called the new type *waina*.

The commercial red sweet potato was developed for uniformity of tuber size and other factors associated with mechanized agriculture. It does not have the flavour of some of the yellow-fleshed varieties. Some of these are grown in home gardens in warm areas and may be obtained through friends or neighbours. Natural mutations in skin and flesh colour and shape are quite common in sweet potatoes, and any interesting and unusual characteristics are worth perpetuating, provided that the plants have a normal yield and are not more prone to disease.

Cultivation

Sweet potatoes are tender plants of tropical origin. They need a five-month growing season when mean monthly temperatures exceed 17°C. Between 10°C and 17°C growth is slow and yields depressed. Below 10°C the plants soon die. A good indication of a region's suitability for sweet potato culture is the presence of outdoor tomatoes, cucumbers and sweet peppers in home gardens. The ideal soil is a sandy loam or volcanic-ash soil enriched with animal manure and compost. Heavy clay soils are quite unsuitable and they must be lightened by digging in large quantities of sand, gravel and compost.

Water requirements are not high and short periods of drought are tolerated towards the end of the growing season. Really heavy crops can only be achieved if rainfall (or watering) is regular, especially in the third to fifth month when the tubers are filling out rapidly. The soil should be well supplied with superphosphate, about half a cup for each metre of row.

The ancient method of propagation was to plant small, whole tubers in soil mounds in late spring. Nowadays large tubers are spaced out in a warm propagating bed (heated or in a glasshouse) in early spring and covered with fine, sandy soil. The soil temperature should be just above 21°C in the bed. A big tuber can produce up to 30 rooted sprouts which should be carefully pulled from the tuber five to eight weeks later when they have two to five leaves. They should be heeled in in a cold-frame or beneath a mini-glasshouse. It has been found that if the soil in the holding bed is full of fibre the plants make extra-vigorous root systems and eventually crop more heavily. Rooted plants can also be purchased from some nurseries.

As soon as the weather is settled and the nights warm, the plants can be transferred to the garden and set out on low mounds or ridges with 40 cm between plants and 60 cm between rows. They should be planted with the rooted section of the stem lying nearly horizontal in the soil but well covered. Water thoroughly at planting time. Regular weeding will be needed until the vines begin to cover the surface. After that, loosen the vines periodically to prevent them rooting, for these external roots promote further leaf growth rather than tuber bulking.

Harvesting

Some tubers can be dug for immediate use three-and-a-half to four months after planting, but those intended for storage and winter consumption should not be lifted until mid to late autumn. Choose a warm day (preferably before the first frost kills off the vines) and carefully cut the vines off just above soil level a few hours before digging commences. Slide a potato fork beneath the mound or ridge, loosen the soil and then pick out the tubers by hand. Do not throw them into boxes as the skins are easily bruised. If the weather stays settled small piles of harvested kumara can be left on a warm path for a week and covered with a thick sack. A combination of heat and high humidity helps the tubers heal any cuts or abrasions suffered during the harvest. If corky tissue does not form on damaged areas, organisms will enter and quickly reduce the tuber to a soft, putrid mass.

Curing is not really necessary if the tubers are fully mature and undamaged. Simply wrap each one in a single sheet of newspaper and place it in a broad box in an insulated shed or pantry where the temperature is about 13-15°C. Watch carefully for signs of rot and avoid handling them unnecessarily. Eat any scratched or bruised tubers as soon as possible.

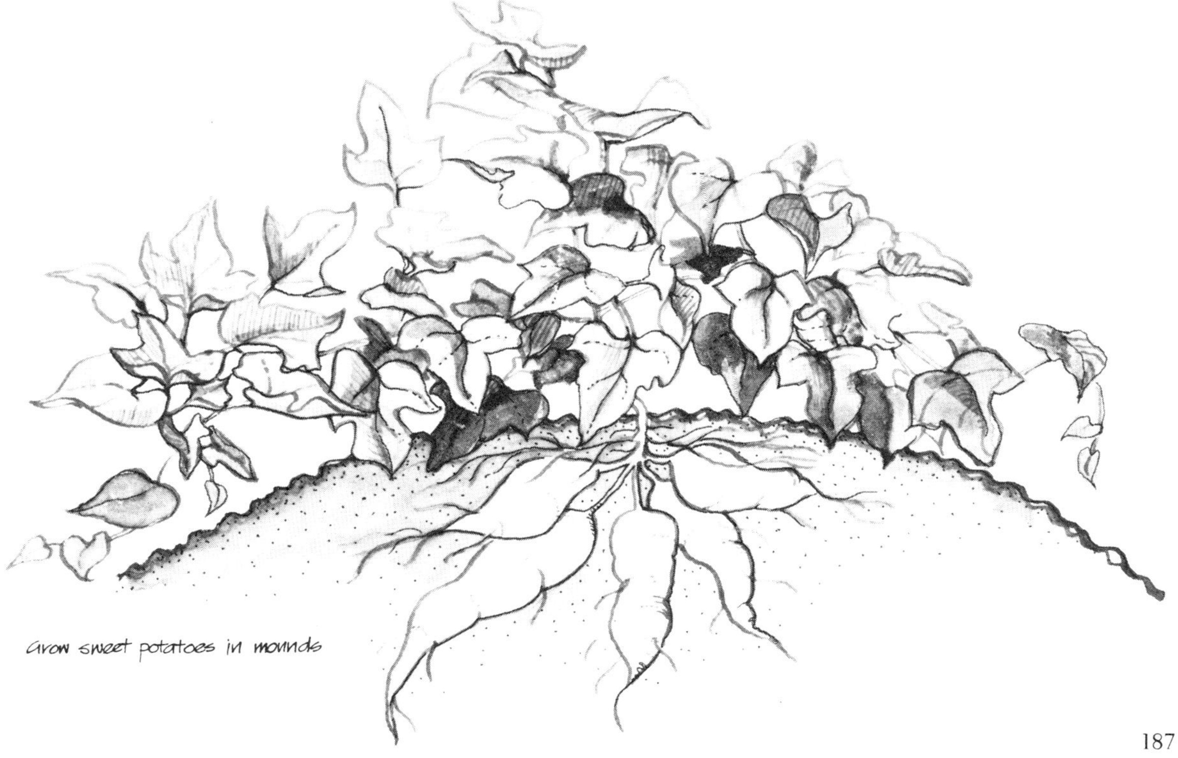
Grow sweet potatoes in mounds

In the kitchen

Scrub sweet potatoes with a vegetable brush and cut out any blemishes. Allow 100 g for each serving.

Sweet potatoes may be boiled, mashed, jacket baked or roasted like potatoes.

FOIL-BAKED SWEET POTATOES

Place each unpeeled sweet potato on a piece of foil. Brush with oil or melted butter. Wrap up tightly. Place the parcels in a shallow oven-proof dish. Bake at 200°C for 30-45 minutes until they are soft when squeezed. Season with salt and pepper. The moisture is retained in this method to produce a most succulent vegetable.

SCALLOPED SWEET POTATO AND APPLE

Serves 6

A good accompaniment to pork or sausages.

500 g sweet potatoes
1½ c thinly-sliced, peeled cooking apples
½ c brown sugar
4 tb butter
1 tsp salt

Peel the sweet potatoes. Cook in boiling, salted water until they are just tender. Drain. Dice into 1 cm cubes. Grease a casserole. Put in half the sweet potato and cover with half of the remaining ingredients in layers. Repeat. Cover with a lid. Bake at 180°C for 1 hour.

SCALLOPED SWEET POTATO AND TAMARILLO

Substitute skinned, sliced tamarillos for the apples in the recipe given above.

FRYPAN PORK AND SWEET POTATO

Serves 4

This is a "meal in a pan" recipe for cooks with little time.

1 tb butter
4 pork chops or 8 pork or beef sausages
4 medium-sized sweet potatoes
1 large onion
1 green pepper
1 tsp salt
freshly-ground black pepper
½ tsp chopped thyme
½ tsp chopped marjoram
2½ c diced tomatoes (fresh, frozen or bottled)

Melt the butter in a frying pan with a lid. Brown the chops or sausages. Tip off surplus fat. Peel the sweet potatoes and slice thinly. Arrange over the chops or sausages. Peel the onions and slice finely. Place on top of the sweet potatoes. Cut the pepper in half, remove

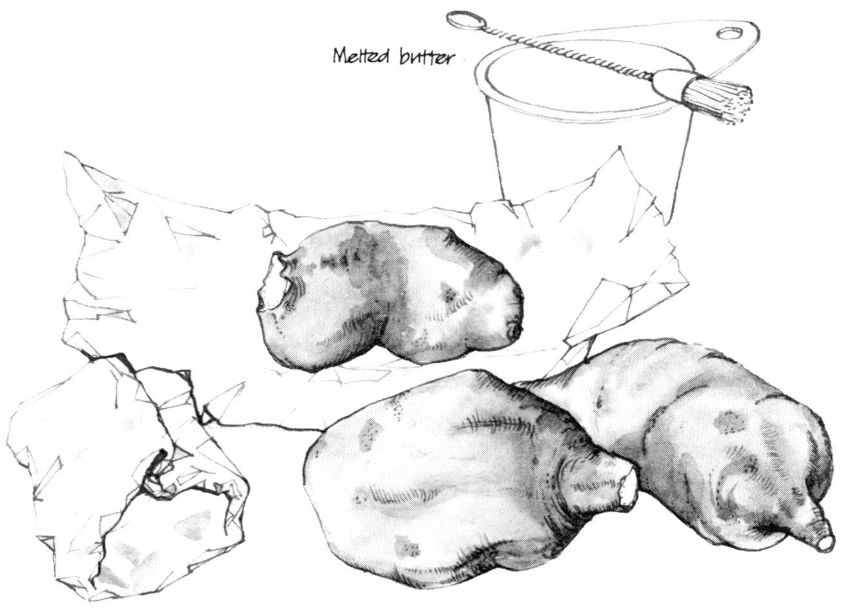

seeds and slice the flesh thinly. Add to the frying pan. Sprinkle with pepper and salt, thyme and marjoram. Top with the tomatoes. Cover the frying pan and cook over a low heat for about 1 hour until the chops and sweet potatoes are tender.

SWEET POTATO PIE

Serves 6

Like pumpkin, sweet potatoes can be used to make a dessert-pie filling. This recipe appeals to us because the sweet potato does not have to be cooked first, thus saving on the washing of saucepans.

Pastry:

225 g flour
½ tsp baking powder
pinch salt
115 g butter

Sift the flour, baking powder and salt into a bowl. Rub in the butter. Mix to a stiff dough with cold water. Roll out and line a 25 cm pie plate. Chill while preparing the filling.

Filling:

115 g brown sugar
55 g butter
1 egg
1½ c grated sweet potato (about 1 medium-sized sweet potato)
½ c cream
½ tsp ground ginger
grated rind of 1 orange
½ c thick sour cream (whip if not thick)
1 tsp raw sugar

Cream the butter and sugar. Add the egg and beat well. Grate the sweet potato and fold this into the butter and sugar. Add the cream, ginger and orange rind. Stir to combine thoroughly. Pour into the pie shell and bake at 180°C for 40-50 minutes until the filling is set. Spread the sour cream over the pie and sprinkle with raw sugar. Serve immediately.

SWEET POTATO SALAD

Serves 6

This unusual salad goes well with pork dishes. It can be made several hours ahead of serving time.

500 g sweet potatoes
2 oranges
half a small, mild onion or 4 spring onions
4 tb salad oil
1 tb cider vinegar
½ tsp salt
freshly-ground black pepper
1 tb finely-chopped parsley

Peel the sweet potatoes and cook in boiling, salted water until they are tender. Drain. Cut into 5 mm slices as soon as they are cool enough to handle. Peel the oranges, removing all the white pith. Cut horizontally into thin slices. Slice the half onion into thin slices and separate the rings or chop the spring onions including a little of the green part. Layer the sweet potatoes, oranges and onion in a salad bowl. Combine the oil, vinegar and seasoning. Pour over the salad. Allow to cool. Sprinkle with parsley just before serving.

Tamarillos

(Cyphomandra betacea)

Varieties

This subtropical evergreen or semi-evergreen shrub used to be known as the tree tomato. It grows rapidly to about 3-3.6 m high, but lives only eight to ten years.

The two main types are the yellow tamarillo and the red tamarillo. The yellow fruit has a milder flavour but the red fruit is more popular. New varieties are Red Chief and Solid Gold which have been selected for the quality of their fruit and their reliable cropping.

Cultivation

A very warm, frost-free position is required with light, well-drained soil. Tamarillos dislike wet feet as much as they dislike drought conditions. The large leaves, brittle stems and shallow roots call for maximum shelter from any winds plus the added security of a stout stake.

Tamarillos are easily grown from seed or from cuttings. Those grown from seeds produce tree-like shrubs with a straight main stem. Those grown from cuttings tend to develop into bush shrubs. Plant in spring in good soil allowing 1.5 m between the plants. Work in 2 cups of blood and bone into each hole and firm the topsoil around the roots. Feed with compost in early spring and mid summer.

Every year cut away dead, diseased and crowded growth. To ensure plenty of new fruiting wood, cut back the laterals once they have fruited. This ensures that the fruit does not grow at the ends of long, weak, spindly branches which may break. On bushier shrubs cut off the lower branches to stop the fruit touching the ground.

Harvesting

Because the fruit ripens over several months, harvesting starts in autumn and continues right through winter into the spring. Cut the fruits from the tree with the stalks attached. They can be stored for about four weeks in a cool place.

In the kitchen

To serve as fresh fruit, cut the tamarillo in half and provide a teaspoon to scoop out the flesh.

To remove the skin, pour boiling water over fruit and leave for 1 minute. Tip off the hot water. Impale the tamarillo on a fork and peel.

Tamarillos may be baked and served as a vegetable. Cut in half lengthwise, season and bake at 180°C for 15 minutes.

They combine well with sweet potatoes. Try the recipe on page 188 for Scalloped Sweet Potato and Tamarillo.

One or two peeled or chopped tamarillos make an interesting addition to winter stews.

Peeled and sliced tamarillos make a

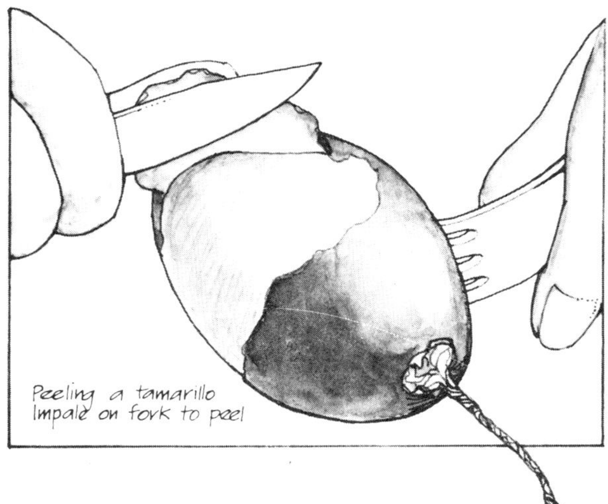
Peeling a tamarillo
Impale on fork to peel

delicious curry accompaniment.

To serve as a simple, uncooked dessert or breakfast fruit, slice peeled tamarillos into a bowl and sprinkle the layers with castor sugar (½ c of castor sugar to 500 g tamarillos). Leave in a cool place. After 8 hours they will have formed their own juice.

Two winter desserts combining tamarillos with kiwifruit are given on page 114.

TAMARILLO UPSIDE-DOWN CAKE

Serves 6

6 tamarillos
30 g butter
100 g brown sugar

50 g butter
100 g sugar
1 egg
1 tsp vanilla
170 g flour
2 tsp baking powder
¼ tsp salt
½ c milk

Peel and halve the tamarillos. Melt 30 g butter and mix with the brown sugar. Spread over the base of a greased ovenproof dish (20 cm square). Arrange the tamarillo halves evenly on top.

Cream 50 g butter and sugar. Beat in the egg and vanilla. Sift the flour, baking powder and salt. Fold into the creamed mixture alternately with the milk.

Spoon carefully over the tamarillos. Bake at 180°C for 30-40 minutes. Loosen the sides and invert on to a plate. Serve hot with cream.

TAMARILLO CRUMB PIE

Serves 6

Pastry:

225 g flour
½ tsp baking powder
pinch salt
115 g butter

Sift the flour, baking powder and salt into a bowl. Rub in the butter. Mix to a stiff dough with cold water. Roll out and line a 25 cm pie plate, overlapping the edge by 2 cm. Tuck the edge under and crimp. Chill while preparing the filling.

Filling:

400 g tamarillos
¾ c sugar
½ c flour
½ tsp cinnamon
80 g butter

Peel and slice the tamarillos. Mix the sugar, flour and cinnamon together. Rub in the butter. Sprinkle half the crumb mixture into the pie shell. Arrange the tamarillo slices evenly on top. Sprinkle the remaining crumbs over the surface. Bake at 190°C for 30-40 minutes until the pastry is golden and the fruit tender. Serve with cream.

FRYPAN PORK AND TAMARILLO

Serves 6

1 kg pork strips
2 cooking apples
6 tamarillos
2 small onions
3 tb brown sugar
½ tsp salt
¼ c water

Brown the pork strips in a large frying pan. Pour off any excess fat. Peel the apples, tamarillos and onions. Slice and place over the pork. Sprinkle with brown sugar and salt. Pour in the water. Cover the frying pan tightly and cook gently for 1-1½ hours until the pork is tender.

TAMARILLO CHUTNEY

An excellent-flavoured chutney with a good colour to serve with curries and cold pork.

1 kg tamarillos
300 g cooking apples
300 g onions
1½ tsp salt
½ tsp cayenne pepper
120 g raisins (chopped if large)
400 g brown sugar
300 ml vinegar
½ tsp whole allspice
¼ tsp peppercorns
¼ tsp whole cloves
2 dried chillies

Skin the tamarillos and chop finely. Peel, core and dice the apples. Peel and chop the onions. Combine the tamarillos, apples, onions, salt, cayenne, raisins, brown sugar and vinegar in a large saucepan. Tie the spices in a piece of muslin and add to the saucepan. Simmer gently for 1-1½ hours until thick. Pour into warm jars and seal.

Bottling

As for feijoas (see page 91).

Freezing

Peel and slice the tamarillos thickly or cut into halves. Layer with sugar (1 part sugar to 4 parts fruit). Tip into freezer bags.

Tomatoes

(Lycopersicon esculentum)

Varieties

Tomatoes are such a popular vegetable in many subtropical and temperate countries that plant breeders have devised hundreds of varieties to suit local demands and conditions. About 20 varieties are offered to home gardeners in our part of the world, only a small proportion of what the commercial grower can obtain.

These varieties can be divided conveniently into five main groups. Bush types like Dwarf New Yorker, Scoresby Dwarf and Roma sprawl over the ground and require no pruning or staking. The drier flesh of some of the dwarf varieties makes them ideal for sauce making. A notable tomato in this category was The Amateur Improved which bore fruit of excellent quality, equal to any glasshouse tomato. Unfortunately it is no longer offered by the seed merchants.

Tall-growing types require staking and pruning and include many of the popular long-established names such as Potentate, Moneymaker, Beefsteak, Grosse Lisse and Best of All. Russian Red is not as tall as these varieties but is more tolerant of cold conditions (not frost). Some seed merchants offer new tall-growing hybrids from time to time. These include Beefmaster F.1 Hybrid and Burpee's F. 1 Hybrid which are resistant to soil-borne wilt diseases. Burpee's F.1 Hybrid fruits have also been found to be fairly crack resistant.

Yellow tomatoes make up the third group and include the tall-growing Golden Jubilee and Golden Ponderosa. There is an increasing demand for these because of their low acidity (an important factor for families with young children who are prone to skin rashes).

Miniature or cherry tomatoes constitute a "novelty" group which may become more important as gardens become smaller and the number of flat-dwellers increase. With names like Patio Hybrid, Toy Boy F.1 Hybrid and Atom Bite Size they can be grown in pots, window boxes and hanging baskets. The fruits are small and sweet.

The fifth group, grafted tomatoes, have aroused great public interest in the last few years. A well-known, successful heavy-fruiting variety is grafted on to a plant with a vigorous and disease-resistant rooting system. The resulting plant has its top growth of the heavy fruiting variety supported by a double root system. The extra nourishment it obtains will sustain eight or more leaders and give an exceptionally heavy crop. Garden shops and nurseries supply planting and feeding instructions with these relatively expensive plants.

Cultivation

Tomatoes should be grown in soil rich in humus. This is best supplied by the addition of peat, finely-divided compost or very well-rotted animal manure. If possible incorporate compost and manure two to three months before planting. A base dressing of a tomato fertilizer (see page 8) is worked into the soil just before planting, about one-third to half a cup per square metre. After the first truss of fruit has reached grape size, a fortnightly side dressing of the same fertilizer can be applied starting with a teaspoonful per plant. The quantity should be later increased to a dessertspoonful.

Tomato plants are often purchased from a nursery, but it may be necessary to raise your own from seed if you wish to grow some of the less popular or newer varieties. Use "Jiffy" pots or peat pots filled with a sterilised, commercial seed-raising mix. Push two to three seeds into each pot, later removing the weaker seedlings. If temperatures are low, start the seedlings indoors and then transfer them to a cold-frame or glasshouse. Gradually harden them off. After eight to ten weeks they can be planted, pot and all, into their final positions, provided the soil is warm and all danger of frost is over. A mini-glasshouse or cloche may be used to warm the soil before planting and to protect the plants until they grow taller.

The date for outdoor planting varies considerably from district to district. We have found that nothing is gained by trying to advance the date because of a spell of warm spring weather, nor is it advisable to stick to the traditional date in a poor spring if the ground is still cold and wet. Mean temperatures above 15°C are essential for steady tomato growth.

Bush or dwarf varieties are planted out 60-90 cm apart. Allow them to sprawl over a straw mulch which will keep the fruit clean and dry. Tall varieties are grown 50-60 cm apart. Drive a stout stake, 2.5 m long, into the ground BEFORE planting the tomato about 15 cm away on the leeward side. The first tie should be made immediately. As the plant grows up pinch out all lateral growths as soon as they develop. They appear at the fork of the leaf

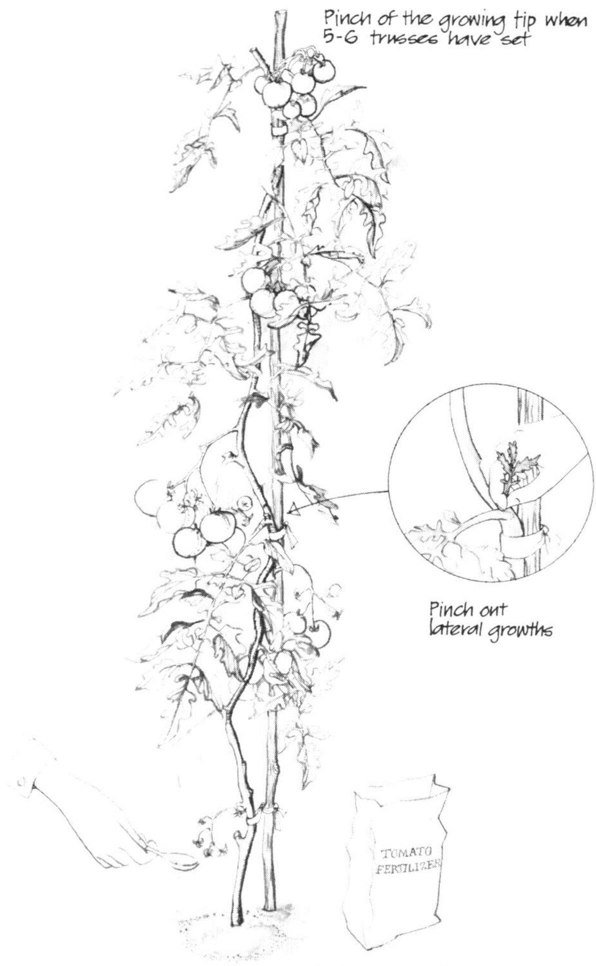
Pinch of the growing tip when 5-6 trusses have set
Pinch out lateral growths
TOMATO FERTILIZER
Side dress with 1-2 teasp of tomato fertilizer every two weeks after first truss has set

stem and the main stem. Tie the plants progressively every 20 cm of growth, allowing room for the main stem to thicken without being strangled. In cooler areas many gardeners pinch out the growing tip when five to six trusses of fruit have set.

Because tomatoes are prone to soil-borne diseases, they should not be planted in the same spot year after year unless the soil is sterilised or replaced. Fungus diseases can be kept at bay with regular applications of a copper oxychloride spray, especially in spring and early summer. Caterpillars may be troublesome in late summer to autumn. These are controlled with Derris Dust, carbaryl or they can be removed by hand. If serious tomato diseases are prevalent in your area you may need to use a commercial, all-purpose tomato spray, although you must be careful to follow the instructions on the packet.

Harvesting

One of the greatest delights for the home gardener who has not needed to spray his plants is picking the first ripe sun-warmed fruit, slicing it on to a piece of fresh bread and butter and then sampling that special flavour out in the garden. If spray has been used, however, the fruit must be washed before using. Tomatoes should be picked with the calyx attached to the fruit. This is done by pinching through the knee-like nodule about 1.5 cm above the calyx. Just before using, remove the calyx as you wash each tomato. This is a good way of keeping track of washed and unwashed batches of tomatoes.

In the kitchen

The size of this section indicates the popularity and versatility of tomatoes in cooking. As they are needed all year round we have included several preservation methods. We have not forgotten green tomatoes which tend to be wasted for want of suitable recipes. There are a number of wonderful uses for them.

To skin tomatoes — place them in a bowl. Cover with boiling water and leave for 12 seconds. Tip off the hot water and replace it with cold. The skins will then slip off easily. Where it is preferable we have specified skinned tomatoes.

TOMATO SALAD

Serves 6

One of the simplest and most refreshing ways of serving tomatoes.

6 large, well-ripened tomatoes (if picked after a day in the sun, the flavour is at its peak)
¾ tsp salt
freshly-ground black pepper
¼ tsp castor sugar
1 tb finely-chopped basil or chives
2 tsp wine vinegar or cider vinegar
2 tb salad oil

Discard a slice from the stem end of each tomato and remove any remaining core. Slice thinly with a very sharp knife. Arrange in a shallow serving dish. Season with salt, pepper and sugar. Sprinkle with herbs, vinegar and oil. Variation: add one very finely-sliced red-skinned onion to the layers of tomato slices in the dish.

TOMATOES STUFFED WITH COTTAGE CHEESE

Serves 4 or 6

Use small tomatoes for an attractive dinner-party first course or medium to large ones served on lettuce leaves for lunch. For both occasions serve with finely-sliced, buttered wholemeal bread.

4 medium-sized or 6 small, ripe tomatoes
salt
120 g cottage or cream cheese
salt and pepper to taste
1 tb finely-scissored chives
top milk
3 tb French dressing
1 tb mixed, finely-chopped herbs (basil, parsley, chives)

Skin the tomatoes. Cut a slice from the top of each one. Reserve the slices. Flick out the seeds with the handle of a small teaspoon. Remove the core of each tomato carefully with the bowl of the spoon or a small knife. Sprinkle a little salt into each one. Drain the tomatoes upside down.

If using cottage cheese, sieve it into a bowl. Cream cheese does not need sieving. Season well and add the chives. Add enough top milk to soften the cheese.

Over-fill the tomatoes with the cheese mixture. Replace the top slices on a slant and arrange the tomatoes on a serving plate. Combine the French dressing and herbs. Pour a teaspoonful over each tomato. Chill for 2 hours. Just before serving, add a further teaspoon of dressing.

NEAPOLITAN TOMATO SAUCE

This sauce is delightful when poured over spaghetti and topped with grated cheese. It is no trouble to prepare just a few minutes before serving. Use very ripe tomatoes to ensure a beautiful colour. Skin the tomatoes and chop the garlic ahead of time and assemble the other ingredients in readiness.

500 g ripe tomatoes, peeled and chopped
2 or 3 cloves garlic, finely chopped
salt and freshly-ground black pepper to taste
1 tb cooking oil
1 tsp chopped basil or parsley

Sauté the tomatoes, garlic and seasoning in oil for a few minutes. Do not allow the tomatoes to become pulpy as the fresh taste will be lost. Add basil or parsley and serve.

TOMATOES BAKED WITH HERBS

Serves 4

4 large tomatoes
1 tb finely-chopped onion
2 tb chopped basil
½ tsp celery seeds
4 tb dry breadcrumbs
2 tb grated Parmesan cheese
½ tsp salt
freshly-ground black pepper
2 tb butter

Cut the tomatoes in half horizontally and lay cut side up in a greased oven proof dish. Combine the onion, basil, celery seeds, breadcrumbs, cheese and seasoning. Spoon evenly on to the tomatoes. Dot with butter. Bake uncovered at 200°C for 15 minutes.

SCALLOPED GREEN TOMATOES AND CELERY

Serves 6-8

1 c chopped celery
1 medium-sized onion, chopped
2 tb butter
2 tb flour
1 tsp salt
2 tb sugar
½ tsp chopped dill leaves or fennel (optional)
freshly-ground black pepper
4 slices wholemeal bread, toasted and buttered
5 large, green tomatoes, chopped

Sauté the celery and onion in the butter until tender. Add the flour, salt, sugar, dill and pepper. Cut the buttered toast into small cubes. Add the tomatoes and three-quarters of the toast cubes to the celery mixture. Combine well and tip into a greased casserole dish. Cover and bake for 1 hour at 180°C. Remove the lid and cover the tomato mixture with the remaining toast cubes. Bake for a further 5 minutes until the topping is crisp.

CHINESE-STYLE BEEF AND TOMATOES

Serves 4-6

500 g rump steak

Marinade:

1 tsp salt
1 tsp sugar
2 tb soy sauce
2 tsp cornflour
1 tsp cooking oil

2 tb cooking oil
1½ c skinned, chopped tomatoes
1 c boiling water
2 tb cornflour
¼ c cold water

Cut the steak into 5 cm strips with the grain. Then cut into very thin slices across the grain. Place in a bowl with the marinade ingredients. Mix together thoroughly using a fork. Leave to marinate for 30 minutes.

Heat 2 tb of oil in a large frying pan until it is very hot. Add the beef mixture and stir-fry for 3 minutes. Put the meat back into the bowl. Add the tomatoes and boiling water to the frying pan. Cover and simmer for 3 minutes. Return the meat to the frying pan, cover and simmer for a further 3 minutes. Mix 2 tb of cornflour with ¼ c of water and stir into the frying pan. Simmer for 1 minute. Serve with rice.

TASTY TOMATO SOUP

Serves 4-6

It is not always easy to obtain a good flavour and colour with soup made from fresh tomatoes. Use really ripe tomatoes with this recipe to obtain a spicy and deep-coloured soup.

500 g ripe tomatoes
1 tb butter
1 small onion, finely sliced
1 dsp flour
½ tsp paprika
1 tb tomato concentrate (to improve colour)
800 ml chicken stock
salt and pepper to taste
bouquet garni
freshly-grated nutmeg
1 clove
1 tb sago
2 tb port wine

Wash the tomatoes, cut in half and scoop out the seeds using a finger or the handle of a teaspoon. Place the seeds in a small strainer and stir with a wooden spoon to obtain as much juice as possible. Discard the seeds. (If the seeds are left they tend to impart a slightly-bitter flavour when crushed in a blender or sieve.) Chop the tomato flesh roughly. Melt the butter in a heavy saucepan, add the onion and sauté gently until soft. Blend in the flour, paprika, tomato concentrate, tomatoes, juice, stock, seasoning, herbs and spices. Stir until boiling. Simmer for 30 minutes. Put through a blender or sieve. Return the soup to the saucepan, add the sago and simmer for 12 minutes or until the sago is cooked. Check the seasoning. Stir in the port wine.

PIZZA

In Italy "pizza" means pie. Pizzas were originally made from left-over pieces of yeast dough spread with locally-available toppings. These would usually include tomatoes, onions, slices of spicy sausage, grated cheese and herbs.

In many areas, scone-based pizzas have become popular but these lack the hearty, yeast flavour of a bread dough. This wholemeal yeast dough is well worth the extra few minutes' preparation.

Yeast dough: sufficient for 2 pizzas (approximately 25 cm). We make one to eat straight from the oven and one for the freezer to add variety to school lunches.

1 tsp honey
1 c warm water
1 tb dried yeast
2½ c wholemeal flour (or rye flour)
1 tsp salt
1 tb cooking oil

Combine the honey and the water at blood heat (should feel neither hot nor cold) in a large bowl. Sprinkle the yeast over the surface of the water and leave it in a warm place for 10 minutes. Add 2 cups of wholemeal flour together with the salt and oil. Beat well with a wooden spoon. Add sufficient extra flour to make a soft dough. Knead for 2 minutes. Divide the dough to suit your pizza tins. Pat and push each piece to fit a greased tin or pat out to form a circle on a greased oven slide. Leave in a warm place while preparing the topping.

Our favourite summer and autumn topping consists of:

4 medium-sized onions
2 tb cooking oil
500 g tomatoes
1 tb chopped basil
salt and pepper to taste
100 g salami
200 g tasty Cheddar cheese

These quantities will cover 2 pizzas.

Slice the onions finely and sauté in oil until soft. Slice the tomatoes. Cut the salami into thin strips and grate the cheese. Cover the pizza dough with the onions followed by a single layer of tomato slices. Sprinkle with basil and season well.

Arrange the salami strips evenly over the surface and cover with grated cheese. Bake at 230°C for about 10-20 minutes until the underside of the dough is golden-brown (lift the edge with a fish slice). Slide the hot pizzas on to a board and cut into wedges for serving.

In the winter we use preserved or frozen, chunky tomato purée and dried basil.

Bottled tomatoes

The tomatoes should be firm and a good colour. Almost fill a blanching basket with washed tomatoes. Plunge this into boiling water for 12 seconds and then into cold water. Remove the skins. If the tomatoes are large cut them into quarters, otherwise halves. Pack the tomatoes firmly into jars to within 2 cm from the top. A half-litre jar will hold 400 g of tomatoes. Add ½ tsp of salt to each half-litre jar and fill to within 2 cm of the rim with boiling water. Process by either of the following methods:

Water-bath method: cover the jars with seals and hand tighten the screw rings. Lower the jars on to a rack in a water-bath containing sufficient boiling water to cover the jars. Boil for 35 minutes. Remove and leave to cool.

Oven method: cover the jars lightly with a piece of foil and place in the oven at 140°C for 1 hour. Boil the seals for 3 minutes. Remove the jars from the oven one at a time. Overflow each jar with boiling water. Remove any seeds on or close to the jar rim and cover with a hot seal. Screw the ring on firmly.

Note: other vegetables, because of low natural-acid levels, are not safe for eating when bottled by these methods.

CHUNKY TOMATO PURÉE, FROZEN OR BOTTLED

This versatile mixture can be used in winter months for pizzas, for pouring over cooked spaghetti, as a base for winter soups or, if sieved, in recipes calling for tomato purée. The quantities given will fill 4 half-litre jars.

2 medium-sized onions
3 tb cooking oil
3 kg tomatoes
1 tb chopped basil
1 tb chopped marjoram
2 bay leaves
1 tsp celery seeds
1 tsp mustard seeds
1 tb salt
2 tb sugar

Peel and chop the onions. Heat the oil in a large saucepan and add the onions. Cook over low heat for 10 minutes. Skin the tomatoes, remove the cores and chop roughly. Add to the saucepan with the herbs and seasoning. Simmer the mixture for 10 minutes. Remove the bay leaves.

To freeze: cool the mixture and ladle it into convenient-sized plastic containers. We find yoghurt, cottage cheese or margarine containers are ideal. Label and freeze container.

To bottle: process in a water-bath for 15 minutes or in the oven for 30 minutes. See previous recipe for directions.

TOMATO SAUCE

Makes 4-5 litres

We have been making this excellent sauce recipe for several years. Sufficient must be made to last right through the year as our families much prefer it to commercial varieties.

6 kg ripe tomatoes
6 medium-sized onions
6 cloves garlic
25 g pickling spice
1 tsp celery seed
basil (a large stalk and leaves)
marjoram (a large stalk and leaves)
2 bay leaves
6 tb salt
6 c sugar
30 ml glacial acetic acid (buy from a chemist)

Chop the tomatoes roughly and place in a large preserving pan. Add the sliced onions and finely-chopped garlic. Bring slowly to the boil, stirring until there is sufficient liquid to prevent the tomatoes from sticking to the bottom of the pan. Tie the pickling spice and celery seed in a piece of muslin. Tie the stalks of the herbs together. Add the muslin bag and herbs to the boiling tomatoes. Boil uncovered for 1½ hours. Remove the muslin bag and herbs. Add the salt and sugar. Stir until dissolved.

Press the liquid through a mouli or coarse sieve. Discard the solids. Pour the sauce back into the preserving pan. Add the glacial acetic acid and bring back to the boil. Boil until the desired consistency is reached. This may take from 5-30 minutes depending on the variety of tomatoes used, the degree of ripeness and the season. The easiest way to be sure that the sauce is thick enough is to pour a teaspoonful on to a saucer and allow it to cool.

Heat clean jars in a slow oven. Pour the boiling sauce into the hot jars and seal immediately. We find 1 litre preserving jars convenient. They are easier to clean thoroughly and easier to seal than narrow-necked bottles. The sauce may be transferred to a favourite bottle for the table as required.

GREEN TOMATO MINCEMEAT

It is worthwhile making this mincemeat even if you have to sacrifice tomatoes which will ripen. It is not as rich as Christmas mincemeat but we prefer its fresh citrus flavour.

4 c coarsely-minced green tomatoes (about 5 large tomatoes)
4 c coarsely-minced, peeled and cored cooking apples (about 8 apples)
50 g shredded suet
1 c raisins
grated rind of 2 oranges
grated rind of 2 lemons
¼ c orange juice
2 tb lemon juice
¼ c cider vinegar
1½ c sugar
1 c brown sugar
1 tsp cinnamon
½ tsp salt
¼ tsp allspice
pinch ground cloves

Combine all the ingredients in a preserving pan. Bring to the boil, stirring continuously. Reduce the heat and simmer, stirring occasionally, until the mixture is thick. This will take about 1 hour. Cool. Pack in pie-sized portions (2 cups will fill a 20-25 cm pie) and freeze. To prepare pie: Thaw the mincemeat.

Pastry:

250 g flour
pinch salt
½ tsp baking powder
125 g butter

Sift the flour, salt and baking powder into a bowl. Rub in the butter. Mix to a stiff dough with cold water. Roll out to line a 20-25 cm pie plate. Keep the scraps and cut into strips to form a lattice topping.

Fill the pie with thawed mincemeat. Arrange the lattice. Bake at 200°C for 30-40 minutes. Serve with cream

UNCOOKED TOMATO AND CELERY RELISH

Celery gives this recipe much of its appeal. We therefore always plant some in early summer to be ready in time for the bulk of our tomato crops. It doesn't matter if the celery stalks are still small because, if they have grown quickly, the flavour will be excellent.

3 kg ripe tomatoes
800 g celery stalks
7 large onions
1 c salt
6 c sugar
2 c white vinegar
2 red or green peppers, finely diced
50 g mustard seeds

Put the tomatoes, celery and onions through a coarse mincer or chop them very finely. Stir in the salt. Tip into a jelly bag and drain overnight. Discard the liquid. Empty into a large bowl and add the remaining ingredients. Bottle and seal.

Drain salted tomatoes, celery and onion overnight

GREEN TOMATO CHUTNEY

1 kg green tomatoes
1 kg cooking apples
500 g onions
250 g raisins
500 g brown sugar
½ tsp ground ginger
1 tsp mixed spice
1 tb salt
600 ml vinegar

Quarter the tomatoes and remove the hard cores. Peel, quarter and core the apples. Peel the onions. Chop all these ingredients finely. Place in a preserving pan and add the remaining ingredients. Bring to the boil and then simmer uncovered for 1-2 hours until the chutney is thick and well cooked. Stir occasionally. Pour into clean, hot jars and seal.

Freezing

Frozen tomatoes collapse when thawed and are only suitable for adding to cooked dishes such as casseroles. Pack in freezer bags without blanching.

Turnips

(Brassica campestris* var. *rapifera)

Varieties

Quick-growing turnips were developed chiefly by French and Italian plant breeders and this is reflected in the names Milan White Top and Milan Purple Top. These varieties produce small, flattened globe-shaped roots with white flesh and a mild flavour. They are suitable for spring sowing and summer harvesting but do not hold well. White Stone (Snowball) also comes into this category. Its roots are round and white-skinned.

If turnips are required in late autumn and winter, sow the yellow-fleshed variety, Golden Ball, in mid to late summer. Once mature it will stand in the garden over winter if only light frosts are experienced. The white-fleshed hybrid, Just Right, is also suited to cool growing conditions.

Cultivation and harvesting

There is an old proverb, "turnips like a dry bed with a wet head". We are meant to interpret this as a friable well-drained loam coupled with moist growing conditions. Hot dry weather will lead to unpleasantly flavoured stringy roots but if the soil is made to hold moisture by the incorporation of plenty of compost, even mid summer sowings are successful. A general fertilizer may be used to supplement the compost. Lime the ground as you would for other brassicas.

Spring sowings are made 12 mm deep in drills 23-30 cm apart. Start thinning very early when the plants are only 2.5 cm high. Allow 10-15 cm between each plant. These turnips should be harvested at golf-ball size so they do not need to be spaced as far apart as winter types (20-25 cm). Some gardeners like to firm the soil in the row with a board to encourage swelling of the roots.

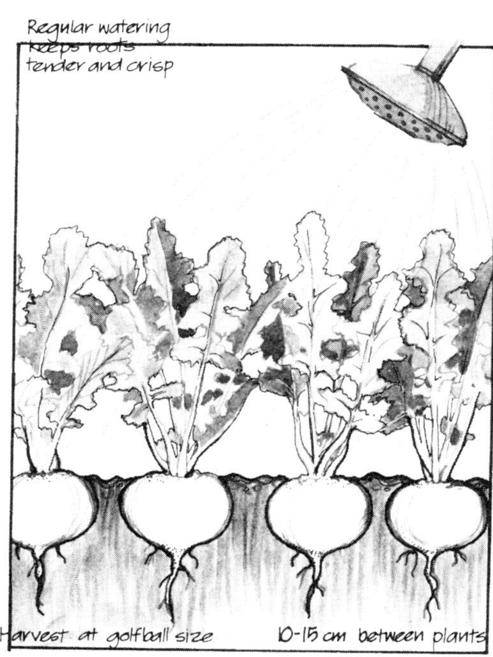
Regular watering
keeps roots
tender and crisp
Harvest at golfball size
10-15 cm between plants

Grow turnips quickly and without check. Regular watering, especially in the last three weeks before harvesting, keeps the roots tender and crisp.

Turnip tops can be used as a green vegetable. They are sown in autumn and left unthinned for harvesting like spinach in late winter to early spring. The varieties particularly suited for turnip top production are not available in some areas. An experimental meal consisting of the tops of both young and mature white turnips was not a success, and we do not recommend that you try them.

In the kitchen

Turnips are at their best when they are only 5 cm in diameter. Cut off the tops and the root. Wash and remove the tough skin with a vegetable peeler. Allow two to three small turnips for each serving.

Cook the turnips whole or quartered in boiling, salted water until they are tender. Drain. Serve with butter and pepper or freshly-grated nutmeg.

GLAZED TURNIPS

Serves 4

500 g small turnips (or swede turnip)
2 tb butter
1 tb brown sugar
½ c beef stock
freshly-ground black pepper

Cook the prepared turnips in boiling, salted water for 10 minutes. Drain in a colander. Melt the butter in the saucepan. Add the turnips, sugar, stock and pepper. Simmer gently until they are tender and most of the liquid has evaporated.

TURNIPS WITH CREAM SAUCE

Serves 4

500 g small turnips (or swede turnip)
130 ml sour cream
¼ c chicken stock
½ tsp sugar
¼ tsp salt
freshly-ground black pepper
1 tsp cornflour
2 tb cold water
1 tb finely-chopped parsley or chives

Place the prepared turnips in a saucepan with the cream, stock, sugar, salt and pepper. Simmer gently until tender. Remove the turnips and place in a serving dish. Keep them warm.

Thicken the sauce with the cornflour mixed with cold water. Bring to the boil, stirring constantly. Pour over the turnips and sprinkle with herbs.

Yams

(Oxalis tuberosa)

Varieties

Oxalis yams have been described as a minor tuber crop of the high Andes with little future. They were introduced to Europe by the Spanish and reached England in the 1830s where they were briefly popular. In countries like New Zealand with many inhabitants originally from the Pacific Islands, the name "yam" is a real source of confusion. This is because island yams are large and starchy and belong to the genus *Dioscorea*. An alternative Spanish name for the oxalis yam is oka, but this is seldom used in our part of the world.

Since yams are propagated vegetatively and are relatively new in many countries, no named varieties have appeared. But a look at yams in greengrocers' shops does show that some are a deep rose-pink and others a pinky-yellow. The latter are supposed to be less "acid". Attractive to look at with their shiny skins, they grow to about finger length and may be as thick as an egg. They have been increasing in popularity among home gardeners for the last two decades and their future in some areas looks good. Obtain tubers for propagation from friends, neighbours and greengrocers. As yet, commercially-grown oxalis yams are not treated with an anti-sprouting agent.

Cultivation

A warm location and well-drained, friable soil are important for successful yam growing. They do particularly well in a mulched, "no-dig" garden and can be fertilized with blood and bone and a little potash or wood ash. In mid to late spring when the danger of frost is minimal, set out the tubers 7.5 cm deep and 30-45 cm apart in rows 45-60 cm apart. After a few weeks' growth, earth them up as for potatoes or mulch with dry straw. They will need no further attention until harvest time as their foliage soon covers the ground and suppresses weeds.

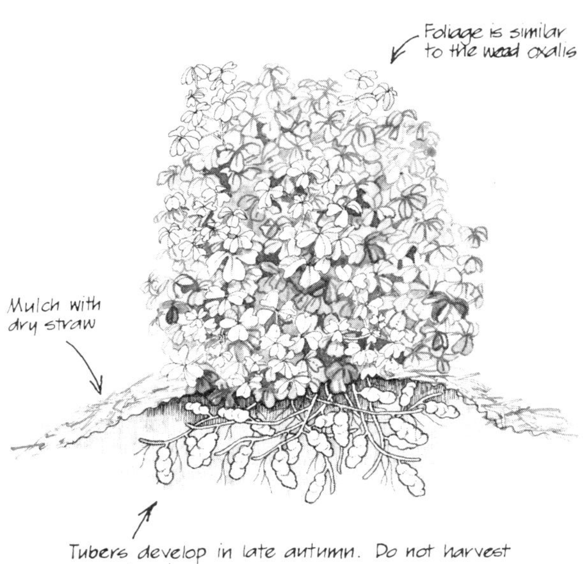
Foliage is similar to the weed oxalis
Mulch with dry straw
Tubers develop in late autumn. Do not harvest prematurely

Harvesting

Yams need a long growing season and are not normally harvested until after the first frost, when their foliage dies down. In frost-free areas the tops will stay green but growth will become very slow in early winter. Choose a period of settled weather and dig the plants with tops still attached. Leave in the sun on a porch or against a hedge for a few days until the tops have withered and then pack the tubers into boxes and store in a cool place. Set aside a box of the best tubers for replanting next spring.

In areas where the soil is well drained and frosts light, the tubers can be left in the ground and harvested as required through the winter. Be sure, however, to clean out the patch and re-fertilize before planting with high-quality tubers next spring. Otherwise the size and vigour of the yams may deteriorate. We have found it best to grow yams in a separate bed from other vegetables.

In Mexico, yams are exposed to the sun for several weeks until they are wrinkled and dry. In this state they are described as floury and sweet.

In the kitchen

The only preparation required is careful scrubbing and the removal of any bad blemishes. Allow 100 g for each serving.

Cut out any bad blemishes but do not skin

Yams may be cooked in boiling, salted water until tender but great care must be taken not to overcook them as they quickly become mushy. Serve with butter and freshly-ground black pepper.

We have found that baking and braising methods require less attention. Place prepared yams in a greased heavy-based casserole. Sprinkle with salt, pepper and 2-3 tb of melted butter or oil. Cover tightly and bake at 180°C for 45-60 minutes or cook gently over low heat, shaking the casserole frequently until the yams are tender.

ORANGE-BAKED YAMS

Serves 8

1 kg prepared yams
½ c brown sugar
¼ tsp ground ginger
freshly-grated nutmeg
½ tsp salt
grated rind and juice of 2 oranges
½ c water
4 tb butter

Place the yams in a greased roasting dish. Sprinkle with the brown sugar, ginger, nutmeg, salt and grated orange rind. Combine the orange juice and water and pour over the yams. Dot with butter. Bake uncovered at 180°C for 40-60 minutes, turning the yams several times.

SWEET AND SOUR YAMS

Serves 4-6

500 g prepared yams
2 tb butter
2 tb honey
1 tsp ground ginger
1 tb cider vinegar
½ tsp salt

Place the yams in a greased casserole. Combine the butter, honey, ginger, cider vinegar and salt in a small saucepan. Bring to the boil. Pour over the yams. Cover and bake at 190°C for 1 hour until tender

Mixed vegetable recipes

RATATOUILLE

In its place of origin, Provence, France, ratatouille is made from egg plants, peppers, tomatoes, onions and garlic. Many variations of the original dish have developed and, from our experience, all are delicious.

The ingredients may include several or all of the following: tomatoes, peppers, egg plants, onions, garlic, courgettes, green beans and herbs including bay, basil, parsley and thyme.

Serve ratatouille hot or cold (never chilled) as a delicious first course or as a colourful accompanying vegetable. Topped with poached eggs or garlic sausage, it can be served as the main dish of a light meal.

Use a large frying pan with a lid. Heat 2 tb of cooking oil and gently sauté 1 or 2 onions and a clove or two of garlic. Add skinned and roughly-chopped tomatoes. Cook until the vegetables begin to soften.

Other ingredients should be prepared and added as follows:

courgettes, sliced or cubed
egg plants, sliced or cubed
peppers, cut in half with the seeds removed and the flesh cut into strips
French beans, cut into 2.5 cm slices, blanched for 3 minutes and drained
1 or 2 bay leaves, a sprig of thyme, salt and pepper to taste.

Cook gently with the lid on until the vegetables are tender but not mushy. Serve sprinkled with scissored basil and/or parsley.

The proportion of ingredients is very flexible. Just use what you have to make a delicious, "home-grown" ratatouille.

Undercooked ratatouille may be successfully frozen. Thaw slowly at room temperature or heat gently in a saucepan.

VEGETABLE SANDWICHES

Use thinly-sliced, fresh wholemeal bread.

ASPARAGUS — cooked and mashed with salt and pepper
PEAS — cooked and mashed with chopped mint
CELERY — finely sliced with chopped, unpeeled apple and salad dressing
finely sliced with peanut butter
CUCUMBER — sliced with lettuce, salt and pepper
CARROT — grated with chopped raisins and salad dressing
grated with cheese and salad dressing
grated with yeast extract
CRESS — with yeast extract
BEAN SPROUTS — with yeast extract
with meat paste or liver spread
CABBAGE — as cole slaw
GREEN PEPPER — finely sliced with celery and salad dressing
MINT — chopped with raisins

CORN — cream style with lettuce and salt and pepper
LEEKS — young and very finely sliced with salt and pepper
TOMATO — sliced with cucumber, chives and grated cheese

MARGARET'S GAZPACHO

Serves 6
This uncooked Spanish soup is made using a blender.

1 clove garlic
6 medium-sized ripe tomatoes
1 large red-skinned onion, peeled
1 large green pepper
1 cucumber or 2 apple cucumbers, peeled
6 tb salad oil
4 tb lemon juice
salt to taste
a few grains of cayenne pepper
2 c tomato juice
120 g ham

Roughly chop the peeled garlic, 4 of the tomatoes, half the onion, half the green pepper with seeds removed and three-quarters of the cucumber. Place in a blender with the oil, lemon juice, seasoning and tomato juice. Blend until smooth. Chill for 2 hours.

Just before serving, dice the remaining tomatoes, onion, green pepper and cucumber. Place in a small bowl and season. Dice the ham and place in another small bowl. Check the seasoning and serve. The diced vegetables and ham may be added to each bowl at the table.

HAMBURGERS, RAW VEGETABLE PLATTER AND ACCOMPANIMENTS

This type of meal is very popular with children who will often enjoy raw vegetables but turn their noses up at the cooked versions. Preparation time is minimal and the results are attractive and highly nutritious. We use large, round hamburger buns, warmed through. No cutlery is needed.
Raw vegetables:

cauliflower sprigs
crisp lettuce leaves
slices of tomato
slices of cucumber
carrot sticks
radishes
cress
celery sticks
thin slices of mild onion
any other vegetable that your children like raw. Ours eat raw parsnip, kohlrabi, turnips, beans and cauliflower.

Provide 4-6 raw vegetables arranged attractively on a large platter.
Other accompaniments:

fresh or preserved beetroot pickle (see page 33) and 34)
mayonnaise — homemade (see page 209)
corn relish (see page 184)
pickled onions (see page 137)
pickled dill gherkins (see page 78)

Choose 3 or 4 accompaniments and serve them in small bowls.

Meat filling:
Serves 6

700 g mince
8 tb soft breadcrumbs
½ tsp chopped thyme
½ tsp salt
freshly-ground black pepper
1 egg
oil for frying

Combine all the ingredients thoroughly. Shape with wet hands into round patties about 1 cm thick and a little larger in diameter than the buns. Fry in a little oil for 3-4 minutes on each side.

Serving: the warm buns should be split and the hot, freshly-cooked meat patties put in the centre. The vegetables and accompaniments are added at the table as required.

A vegetable platter served with a cheese dip makes an attractive and simple dinner party starter.

CHINESE-STYLE VEGETABLES

This recipe is useful in early spring when only small quantities of vegetables are available.

Cut or slice finely any number or combination of vegetables:

cabbage
carrots, cut in matchsticks
onion
silver beet
broccoli
celery in diagonal slices
Chinese vegetables
beans
tomato quarters
bean sprouts
kohlrabi, cut into matchsticks

Heat 3 tb of cooking oil in a large, covered frying pan. When this is very hot, add the vegetables and stir-fry for 3 minutes until they wilt. Lower the heat and cook covered for a few minutes. The vegetables should remain slightly crisp. Mix 1 tsp of cornflour and 1 tsp of instant chicken stock together. Add ½ c of cold water and stir into the vegetables. Bring to the boil. Season with salt, pepper and a teaspoon of soy sauce. Serve immediately.

FAMILY FAVOURITE BEEF AND VEGETABLE STEW

Serves 6-8

A good recipe for cooks in a hurry. If you fill it with vegetables there will be no need to cook extras. Potatoes can be baked in the oven or added to the stew.

1 kg stewing steak

any or all of the following vegetables: onions, carrots, celery, turnips, swedes, leeks, tomatoes (fresh or frozen), celeriac, parsnips

1 tsp salt
1 tsp sugar
½ tsp curry powder
½ tsp cinnamon
2 tb flour
1 tsp dry mustard
½ tsp ground ginger
1 tb vinegar
1 tsp Worcestershire sauce
2 tb tomato sauce or concentrate
2 c water
2 bouquets garnis
parsley for garnishing

Cut the meat into 2 cm cubes and place in the casserole. Prepare the vegetables, cutting them into chunks larger than the meat cubes. Add to the casserole.

In a basin combine the salt, sugar, curry powder, cinnamon, flour, mustard, ground ginger, vinegar, Worcestershire sauce and tomato sauce. Mix to a paste. Add the water and stir until smooth. Pour over the meat and vegetables. Tuck a bouquet garni in at each end of the casserole. Cover and bake at 160°C for 3-4 hours.

Baked potatoes in their jackets should be put into the oven 2 hours before the stew is ready.

To cook potatoes with the casserole, cut them into halves or quarters depending on size and add to the casserole 1½ hours before the meal.

MINESTRONE

Serves 6

An Italian thick-vegetable soup.

3 tb dried haricot beans (soak overnight)
1.8 litres beef stock
2 medium-sized carrots, peeled
3 sticks of celery
3 small onions, peeled
2 leeks
2 cloves garlic
2 rashers bacon
3 tb cooking oil
1 tb tomato concentrate
bouquet garni
salt to taste
freshly-ground black pepper
2 c finely-shredded cabbage
2 tb grated Parmesan cheese or Pesto Sauce (see page 99)

Drain the haricot beans and cook in 600 ml of the stock for 30 minutes. Dice the carrots, celery and onions finely. Slice the leeks and chop the garlic finely. Cut the bacon into small, neat pieces. Sauté the carrots, celery, onions, leeks, garlic and bacon in the oil for 5 minutes. Add the remaining stock and seasoning. Add the beans and their stock. Simmer for 30 minutes. Chop the shredded cabbage crosswise so that pieces are no longer than 2 cm. Add to the soup. Simmer for 15 minutes. Serve in pottery bowls with a teaspoon of Parmesan cheese or pesto sauce.

Sauces

BÉCHAMEL SAUCE

1 c milk
a slice of onion
half a small carrot, chopped
6 peppercorns
1 bay leaf
1 clove

1 tb butter
1 tb flour
freshly-grated nutmeg
salt and pepper to taste
1 tb cream (optional)

Place the milk, onion, carrot, peppercorns, bay leaf and clove in a small saucepan. Cook gently for 5 minutes. without letting the milk boil. Strain the milk into a jug. Rinse the saucepan.

Melt the butter in the saucepan and add the flour. Cook gently for 1 minute. Gradually pour in the flavoured milk, stirring continuously until the sauce thickens and boils. Add a little nutmeg and check the seasoning. Stir in the cream.

MORNAY SAUCE

1 c béchamel sauce
4 tb grated cheese (half Gruyère and half Parmesan for a special occasion, otherwise Cheddar)
½ tsp prepared mustard (optional)

Make the béchamel sauce and remove from the heat. Stir in the cheese and mustard. Reheat gently without boiling.

PARSLEY SAUCE

2 tb butter
1½ tb flour
½ tsp salt
freshly-ground black pepper
1 c milk
3 tb chopped parsley

Melt the butter in a small saucepan. Add the flour, salt and pepper. Cook gently for 1 minute. Gradually add the milk, stirring constantly until the sauce thickens and boils. Add the chopped parsley just before serving.

CHEESE SAUCE

Follow the recipe for parsley sauce but mix in ½ cup of grated Cheddar cheese instead of the parsley. Reheat gently before serving.

HOLLANDAISE SAUCE

This is much easier to make than many people imagine. It is a creamy and delicate sauce, the perfect accompaniment to asparagus and other vegetables. We use two methods.

(A) BLENDER HOLLANDAISE

2 egg yolks
a few grains of cayenne pepper
¼ tsp salt
1½ tb lemon juice
115 g butter
2 tb cream

Place the egg yolks, cayenne, salt and lemon

juice in a blender. Switch on for 1 second only. Melt the butter until it bubbles. Turn the blender on and add butter in a slow, steady stream. Pour into a double boiler (or basin over a saucepan of water). Add the cream. Heat gently.

(B) TRADITIONAL HOLLANDAISE SAUCE

Use the same ingredients as for Blender Hollandaise.

Soften the butter. Add the egg yolks one at a time. Beat well with a wooden spoon. Stir in the lemon juice, salt and cayenne. Place in a double boiler and cook until the mixture thickens slightly. Add the cream.

Hollandaise sauce will keep warm for up to 1 hour over hot water. If it is too thick add a little more cream.

MAYONNAISE

Homemade mayonnaise is so much better than any commercial variety that it is well worthwhile making your own. It will keep for up to 2 weeks in a refrigerator.

QUICK AND EASY MAYONNAISE

Made with a blender.

1 egg
2 tb lemon juice or wine vinegar
1 tsp sugar
½ tsp dry mustard
½ tsp salt
freshly-ground black pepper
1 c salad oil

Place all the ingredients except the oil in a blender. Blend for a few seconds and then, with the blender still running, add the oil in a thin, steady stream. This makes a fairly thick mayonnaise which may be thinned with a little cream or top milk just before serving.

TRADITIONAL MAYONNAISE

2 egg yolks (at room temperature)
½ tsp salt
freshly-ground black pepper
½ tsp dry mustard
1 tsp lemon juice or wine vinegar
1 c salad oil (approximately)
extra lemon juice or wine vinegar to sharpen flavour

Beat the egg yolks, salt, pepper, mustard and lemon juice together in a clean bowl. Pour the oil into a measuring jug and start adding it to the egg mixture a drop at a time. Beat continuously. Gradually increase the addition of oil until you are pouring it in as a fine, steady trickle. Keep beating strongly. You will have added sufficient oil when the mayonnaise is shiny and thick enough to cut with a knife. Check the seasoning and add extra lemon juice to taste.

Should the mixture curdle, wash the beater or whisk and beat an extra egg yolk in another bowl. Gradually add the curdled mayonnaise, a teaspoonful at a time, while beating continuously.

FRENCH DRESSING

1 tb lemon juice or vinegar (wine, cider or herb)
3 tb salad oil
½ tsp salt
freshly-ground black pepper
pinch of sugar

Combine the ingredients in a small bowl and beat with a fork, or place in a jar with a lid and shake vigorously.

VINAIGRETTE DRESSING

Prepare French dressing and add 1 tb of a mixture of finely-chopped herbs (parsley, basil, tarragon, chervil, dill, savory and chives).

Books we have found useful

Kennelly, A.G. *The Home Vegetable Garden.* Bulletin 243, NZ Dept. of Agriculture, 1952.

Sunset Books. *Vegetable Gardening.* Lane, 1961.

Hamilton, R.G. *The Home Orchard.* NZ Government Printer, 1970.

Mossman, Keith. *The Kitchen Garden.* Sphere Books, 1972.

de Vaus, Norman. *Better Vegetable Growing for Australian Gardeners.* Landsdowne, 1973.

Loewenfeld, Claire. *Herb Gardening,* Faber and Faber, 1973.

Stevenson, Violet (contributor). *The Golden Hands Book of Growing for Cooking.* Paul Hamlyn, 1973.

Simons, Arthur J. *The New Vegetable Grower's Handbook.* Penguin Books, 1975.

Hurndell, L.C. *Culinary Herbs in New Zealand.* Crop Research Division, NZ Dept. of Scientific and Industrial Research, 1976.

Norwak, Mary and Mossman, Keith. *Growing, Freezing and Cooking.* Sphere Books, 1976.

Larkcom, Joy. *Vegetables from Small Gardens: A Guide to Intensive Cultivation.* Faber and Faber, 1976.

Beere, Geraldine and Bilton, Jan (Revised by Jill Brewis). *Freezing and Preserving.* Wilson and Horton, 1978.

Recipe index

Methods of preparation, cooking techniques and serving suggestions are to be found on the first page listed for each individual fruit or vegetable.